THE DECLINE AND FALL

OF THE

HEBREW KINGDOMS

AMS PRESS

NEW YORK

Ashur-bani-pal, King of Assyria

By permission of the Trustees of the British Museum

THE CLARENDON BIBLE

Under the general editorship of
THE BISHOPS OF NEWCASTLE AND OXFORD
AND CANON G. H. BOX

OLD TESTAMENT   VOL. III

THE DECLINE AND FALL

OF THE

HEBREW KINGDOMS

*Israel in the Eighth and Seventh
Centuries B.C.*

BY

T. H. ROBINSON
D.D.

OXFORD

AT THE CLARENDON PRESS

1926

Reprinted from the edition of 1926, Oxford
First AMS EDITION published 1971
Manufactured in the United States of America

International Standard Book Number: 0-404-05376-9

Library of Congress Catalog Number: 74-137284

AMS PRESS INC.
NEW YORK, N.Y. 10003

EDITORS' PREFACE

THE first volume of *The Clarendon Bible* series to be published was part of the New Testament, Canon A. W. F. Blunt's Commentary on *The Acts of the Apostles*. Since the publication of that work we have considered the question of the Old Testament, and its place in our series. The inclusion of the Old Testament literature raised a number of difficult and perplexing problems. In these circumstances the General Editors requested *the Society for Old Testament Study* to be good enough to prepare a scheme. This has been done by Canon G. H. Box, with the assistance of other members of the Society, and the scheme is as follows :

Six volumes are to be devoted to the Old Testament literature, five of which will be concerned with the literature proper, and one with the external history. They have been grouped according to the following plan :

  I. Introductory. The external environment of ancient and post-exilic Israel, and its influence upon the development of Israel's religion.

  II. From the Exodus to the Fall of Samaria.

  III. The Decline and Fall of the Hebrew Kingdoms (down to the Fall of Jerusalem 586 B.C.).

  IV. Exile and Restoration (down to the end of the Persian Period).

  V. The later post-exilic Jewish Church (from the beginning of the Greek Period to the second century B.C.).

  VI. Final volume. This will deal with the prehistoric materials, the significance of myth and legend ; the general view of the History given in the documents, &c.

a 2

In this series Vol. I will be a manual of history; Vols. II–V will deal with selected literature illustrating the period under review. In each book there will be a general introduction embracing about fifty pages, followed by a series of selected passages from the literature. *The text of these passages will not be printed*, but will be indicated in each case by reference to the R.V.; but notes and explanations will be given on the passages. And there will be extended special notes on important points. Selected bibliographies will be printed in each volume, and maps and illustrations will be a feature.

The treatment of the Old Testament literature thus differs from the plan adopted in the case of the New Testament. But the general principles underlying the treatment are the same. The main idea is to set the books in their historic environment and to give a general constructive view of the development of the religion, with the aid afforded by modern critical and archaeo-logical research. In particular, we desire to draw a clear line between what is historic and what is not strictly history; and for this reason the beginnings of Israel's history and religion are traced from the Exodus: the consideration of the material found in Genesis is postponed till the final volume. We hope and believe that the series of volumes on the Old Testament which is now launched will provide a real discipline and preparation for those on the New Testament.

In conclusion, we may repeat what has already been said in the Preface to the New Testament volumes, which sufficiently sets forth the general aim of the whole series, both of the Old and New Testament:

'The problem of the teaching of Holy Scripture at the present time presents many difficulties. There is a large and growing class of persons who feel bound to recognize that the progress of archaeological and critical studies has made it impossible for them to read, and still more to teach, it precisely in the old way. However strongly they may believe in inspiration, they cannot any longer set before their pupils, or take as the basis of their interpretation, the doctrine of the verbal inspiration of Holy

Scripture. It is with the object of meeting the requirements not only of the elder pupils in public schools, their teachers, students in training colleges, and others engaged in education, but also of the clergy and the growing class of the general public, which we believe, takes an interest in Biblical studies, that the present series is projected.

'The writers will be responsible each for his own contribution only, and their interpretation is based upon the belief that the books of the Bible require to be placed in their historical context, so that, as far as possible, we may recover the sense which they bore when written. Any application of them must rest upon this ground. It is not the writer's intention to set out the latest notions of radical scholars—English or foreign— or even to describe the exact position at which the discussion of the various problems has arrived. The aim of the series is rather to put forward a constructive view of the books and their teaching, taking into consideration and welcoming results as to which there is a large measure of agreement among scholars. It is hoped to include a volume on the principles and logic of historical criticism.'

HERBERT NEWCASTLE ⎫ *General*
THOMAS OXON. ⎬ *Editors.*
GEORGE H. BOX. ⎭

AUTHOR'S PREFACE

THE general purpose and scope of the series for which this volume has been prepared have been stated in the Editors' Preface, and it only remains for me to add a personal word. I have tried to carry out the wishes of the Editors, and to give a fair representation of the period covered. The work of selection of passages has not been easy. The eighth and seventh centuries are very rich in Hebrew literature, and the choice of passages for comment has been difficult. No doubt many readers will feel that there are numerous sections, especially from Deuteronomy and the Prophets, which ought to have been included, and some which might have been left out. I can only say that I have never trusted to my own views alone, but have done my best on this, as on all other subjects connected with the book, to get the advice of those best qualified to pronounce an opinion. At the same time, I have in each case been fully convinced myself of the desirability of the inclusion or exclusion of each passage that has been considered. The selection has been designed to present a general picture of the social, moral, and religious condition of Israel during the period, and much has been omitted which is of great interest, because it does not contribute sufficiently to this end. It is my hope especially that pupils in schools will be introduced to the work of the great Prophets, for their work and influence are of incalculable importance, not only for the history of Israel, but also for an appreciation of the place held by Islam and Christianity amongst the world's religions.

A certain amount—some may think a disproportionate amount —of space has been devoted to textual criticism. This has been done deliberately. As soon as serious study of the Old Testament is undertaken it should be realized that the Hebrew text on which our translations are based is in many places corrupt, unreliable, and even unintelligible. In this connexion it may be remarked that the Revisers' marginal readings are often superior to those in the text, especially where they are based on the Septuagint. Every effort has been made not to give too elaborate and extensive notes on the text. Where it is straight-forward and simple the comments have been reduced to a minimum, for it is the text itself on which stress should always be laid. It is in the later chapters of Jeremiah that this is per-haps more obvious than anywhere else, and if the treatment of the greatest of the Prophets appears to be scanty, I can only plead that the dramatic and fascinating story contained in Jer. 36-44 is in the main self-explanatory.

In the spelling of Assyrian and Babylonian names the *Cambridge Ancient History* has been the model, whilst Egyptian names have been written as in Professor J. F. Breasted's *History of the Ancient Egyptians*.

I regret that Dr. Welch's striking and important book *The Code of Deuteronomy* appeared too late to be considered in the writing of this volume. His treatment of the subject is thorough and attractive, but until it has been more fully developed on other sides than those of which he has yet been able to treat, it is impossible to pronounce a final judgement on the validity of his position. A similar remark applies to Dr. Moffatt's new translation, which should be available in every school where the Old Testament is seriously studied.

I have to acknowledge the help of many minds and hands in the preparation of the book. Useful suggestions have been made by schoolmasters and schoolmistresses, senior scholars and Sunday School teachers, and to them I would offer my grateful thanks. I owe a special debt of gratitude to several well-known scholars. Principal H. W. Robinson and Canon Box have been good enough to read the book in MS., and to make many useful criticisms and suggestions. Mr. Sidney Smith, of the British Museum, has given me such information as only an expert can on the history of Assyria and Babylonia, and has checked and corrected my translation from the Sennacherib cylinder on pp. 76–78. The maps I owe to the kindness and skill of my colleague, Dr. William Rees, and the Plan of Jerusalem to Professor R. E. Macalister. Miss E. W. Hippisley has been good enough to sanction the use of her Chronological Table. Further, the Clarendon Press has spared no pains to make the book as useful and attractive as possible in form.

Finally, I desire to express my personal hope that this and succeeding volumes in the series may do something to restore Biblical teaching to the place which it should hold in the school life of this country. The Old Testament has the reputation of being a difficult, and, in the main, a dull book. Yet hardly any of the old literatures of the world has so notable a body of enthusiastic students, and the difficulty has always been that of communicating their keenness to a public which in the nature of the case is dependent on the translations and interpretations of others. Needless to say I shall welcome constructive criticisms, especially from those who may have practical experience of the use of the book in schools. My only desire is to give the fullest introduction to the study of Scripture that is possible within the necessary limits of the series and the volume.

THEODORE H. ROBINSON.

CARDIFF, *December* 1924.

CONTENTS

Contents

LIST OF SELECTED PASSAGES

Contents xiii

The Book of Amos.

Contents

LIST OF ILLUSTRATIONS

List of Illustrations   xix

MAPS AND PLANS

PALESTINE
English Miles
0   10   20   30
Land over 1000ft.
"   "   3000ft.
Sidon
DAMASCUS
Tyre
Dan
Kadesh
PHOENICIA
Acco
SEA OF GALILEE
Ashtaroth-Karnaim
BASHAN
Mt. Carmel
Plain of Esdraelon
Lo-debar
Megiddo
Jiblean
GILEAD
Mahamaim
MEDITERRANEAN SEA
SAMARIA
Samaria
Tirzah
Ramoth Gilead
R. Jordan
Tappuach
Joppa
Gilgal
AGRICULTURE
PASTURING
Rabath-Ammon
Bethel
Ford
Michmash
Jericho
Mizpah
Geba
Gilgal
AMMON
JUDAH
JERUSALEM
Ford
Bethshemeth
Gath
Bethlehem
Nomads
Ashkelon
Tekoa
PHILISTINES
Moresheth-Gath
Lachish
Hebron
Gaza
DEAD SEA
Beersheba
MOAB
PASTURING
Nomads
Desert
NEGEB
Valley of Salt
EDOM
Desert
Nomads

INTRODUCTION

A. HISTORICAL BACKGROUND OF THE NEARER EAST IN THE EIGHTH AND SEVENTH CENTURIES B. C.

§ 1. *Assyria*

THROUGH the recorded history of mankind the centre of interest and advance in civilization has shifted gradually westward, and in the period which is immediately before us it had not yet reached the Mediterranean world as a whole. Two great powers, one Asiatic and one African, still stood facing one another at the opening of the eighth century, though the latter was obviously decadent, and its disappearance from the front rank of nations was only a question of time. On the other hand, the great Asiatic empire, that of Assyria, was just rising to the height of its power and the greatest limits of its extent. Its authority, largely maintained in earlier reigns by a series of military expeditions which were little more than plundering raids—at least since the time of Ashur-nasir-pal—was placed on a firm basis by the activity and statesmanship of Shalmaneser III, and after his death in 824 B. C. his successors, Shamshi-adad V (824–811) and Adad-nirari III (811–782), were able to extend their territories as far west as the Mediterranean, at the same time making good their hold on Babylon in the south and on the northern provinces. Shalmaneser IV (782–772), however, spent a large part of his reign in campaigns against Urartu in the north, being faced by an able prince named Argistis, who weakened the Assyrian position in the mountain territory under his rule and in his neighbourhood, though he did not succeed in winning complete freedom. There followed a troubled period for Assyria, revolts taking place in Hadrach and Damascus before the death of Shalmaneser, and risings occurring nearer home in the days of his successors.   The death of Ashur-nirari in 746 saw Assyria weaker than she had been for a century at least.

A change came with the accession of Tiglath-pileser III in 745.   This monarch does not seem to have belonged to the old royal house, but his character and achievements have justified later historians in placing him amongst the greatest kings who sat on the Assyrian throne.   In his first year he dealt with Babylon, and reduced to order its chaotic affairs.   The next few years were spent in campaigns in the north and west, the main object being the subjugation of Urartu and the opening of the old trade routes to the north-west.   The general planning of his campaigns shows Tiglath-pileser to have been a strategist of great ability, for his earlier efforts were directed at isolating the northern enemy.   With this object in view he invaded Syria and Philistia in several campaigns, and the west was secured to him by the fall of Damascus in 732.   Trouble in Babylon prevented him from completing his plans for the conquest of Urartu, but when he died in 727 the most difficult part of the task he had set himself was already accomplished.   He was succeeded by his son, Shalmaneser V, whose short reign (727-722) is chiefly remarkable for the final attack on Samaria.   The city, however, was not captured till after his death, and was the first conquest of his successor Sargon II.

In ability and energy Sargon was in no way behind Tiglath-pileser III.   He found it necessary at one time or another to fight on all four of his frontiers.   The first task, a fresh settlement of Babylonia, proved troublesome rather than difficult, and the greater part of his military activity was directed against Urartu and Palestine.   In both directions he was successful, and his operations secured the boundaries of the empire.   In Palestine, however, he came into contact with Egypt, whose intrigues were constantly stirring up fresh revolts in Philistia and Syria.   He met his death in 705, defending not only his own borders but in effect the whole civilized world under his sway, fighting against hordes of Cimmerians in the north.

Sargon's son and successor, Sennacherib, enjoyed a few years of peace before the intrigues of Babylonia and Egypt caused disaffection and revolt on opposite sides of his dominions.   The narrative in which he describes a series of campaigns in which he put down Marduk-appal-iddin (known to readers of the Bible as Merodach-baladan), and then turned to the west, is amongst the most familiar of Assyrian records. In the south he was faced by a coalition between the Babylonians and the Elamites, who conducted their actual campaign with considerable skill, only to find that they were out-manœuvred by a yet more able

Tiglath-pileser III receiving tribute.
By permission of the Trustees of the British Museum.

and energetic opponent. The revolt in Syria and Palestine was not independent of that in southern Mesopotamia, for Marduk-appal-iddin was the moving spirit there also. Most of the subordinate states threw off their allegiance to Sennacherib, destroying or putting to flight his representatives. One of these, Padi, king of Ekron, was handed over to Ḥezekiah of Jerusalem for safe keeping. In 701 Sennacherib, having put down the rebellion in Babylonia, led his troops westwards, and completely reduced the whole country. Judah, especially, was laid waste, forty-six walled towns being captured and over 200,000 of the population being deported. Though Jerusalem was not actually taken, Hezekiah was compelled to submit, and to become tributary once more to the Assyrian king.

Babylon was never content to remain under the yoke of a foreigner for any length of time, and in 689 Sennacherib was forced a second time to invade the country. This time he sacked the city of Babylon itself, and took for himself the title of king. He entrusted the government of the country to his son Esar-haddon, who, on the murder of his father in 681, succeeded after a year's fighting in securing the whole empire for himself. His reign, like those of his predecessors, was mainly one of conquest. Comparative peace in the east and south gave him an opportunity of advancing in the west, and in 674 he invaded Egypt, at the same time undertaking a siege of Tyre. Three years later the whole country acknowledged Assyrian supremacy, though the imperial hold on Upper Egypt was comparatively slight. Esar-haddon undertook a fresh campaign in 669, but died before he reached his objective, and this particular effort proved fruitless. He nevertheless had the glory of having added a new province to the empire, though its connexion with Assyria endured only for a short time. But this triumph was won at a heavy cost, for the great weakness of Esarhaddon's policy was the neglect of the northern frontier, where there were already signs of the massed racial movements which brought such calamity on western Asia fifty years later, and in the end contributed materially to the downfall of the Assyrian empire.

The reign of Ashur-bani-pal (669–626) was from some points of view the most brilliant in Assyrian history. Art, science, and literature reached a higher point than under any previous monarch, largely owing to the enlightenment and culture of the king himself. But at the same time the extreme limits of power attained by Esarhaddon were not maintained. Egypt revolted and was freshly subdued soon after the new king's accession, but recovered her independence in 658, as Assyria was occupied on her northern and southern borders. The Cimmerians were again active, and were seriously threatening Lydia, though it does not seem that any very important part in the struggle was taken by the Assyrians. On the other hand, a great revolt broke out in Babylonia in 652. Ashur-bani-pal's brother Shamash-shum-iddin held the throne of Babylon as a subordinate prince, and eventually succeeded in forming a coalition with the Elamites and the Arab tribes of the fertile crescent. In spite of an unusually strenuous resistance, Babylon was captured in 648, the Arabs were crushed by 638, and about the same time the kingdom of Elam was finally overthrown.

The last twelve or thirteen years of the reign of Ashur-bani-pal are a time of obscurity, for detailed records have not yet come to light. All that is certain is that they were years of calamity, and that the empire was thrown into confusion when the great king died. Civil war between rival claimants of the throne broke out in Assyria itself, and she was also faced with a coalition of the Babylonians with the Medes. She made a desperate resistance, but the forces arrayed against her were too strong for her, and slowly penned her within ever narrower limits. In 614 the allies took and sacked Ashur, the ancient capital of Assyria. Sin-shar-ishkun, the last king of Nineveh, made an attempt to secure the help of the Scythians, but, after engaging to fight for him, they betrayed him, and in 612 a combined army of Scythians, Babylonians, and Medes took and destroyed Nineveh itself. Fighting seems to have continued in an irregular fashion for some years, but the fall of Nineveh was the real end of the great Assyrian empire.

§ 2. *Babylonia*

Throughout the greater part of our period it is impossible to separate the history of Babylonia from that of Assyria. Southern Mesopotamia formed a part of the Assyrian dominions, though there were elements in the population and in the national feeling which tended to make this the most difficult and troublesome of all the subject states. In particular the nomadic tribes living round the head of the Persian Gulf (known as Kaldu = Chaldeans) were constantly entering the empire and infusing fresh strength into the peoples of the south. The Assyrian methods of dealing with Babylon varied. Sometimes a native prince was placed on the throne as a tributary, and when this was found to give too large an opportunity for rebellion, the king of Assyria himself assumed the title and functions of the king of Babylon, though he generally adopted another name in this capacity. This seems to have been the policy both of Tiglath-pileser III and of Ashur-bani-pal. One native prince, Marduk-appal-iddin, in particular made a strenuous resistance against the power of Sargon and his successors. Driven from his throne in 705 and compelled to take refuge in the southern marshes, he returned again during the reign of Sennacherib, and his revolt led to the complete destruction of Babylon in 689. Babylon was rebuilt by Esar-haddon, who took the title of king himself, and for a time secured peace in the south. On his death, however, the kingdom was divided between two of his sons, and one of the fiercest campaigns Ashur-bani-pal had to fight was against his own brother in Babylonia. On the death of Ashur-bani-pal the throne of Babylon was seized by Nebopolassar, a representative of the Chaldean element in Babylonia, and it seems likely that his accession marked the beginning of Babylonian independence. Details of his reign, however, are not available until the last decade, when we have the narrative of his association with the Medes and others in the war which finally broke the power of Assyria. The campaign was conducted by his warlike son, Nebuchadrezzar (Nabu-kudur-uṣṣur), but his work as a military leader was not finished even with the fall of Nineveh. A new attempt was made by the Egyptian king, Necho, to restore Assyria, and it was only after some years' fighting that Nebuchadrezzar won a final victory against him at Carchemish (605). Nebopolassar died in the following year, and Nebuchad-rezzar was left without a rival. It still remained to overthrow the minor states of the west, which had been subject to Assyria, but this proved a small matter for the power that had destroyed the empires of Assyria and Egypt. With the fall and sack of Jerusalem in 586 the work was done, and any subsequent revolts which took place were small affairs easily suppressed. Though no actual conquest of Egypt seems to have been carried out, Babylon was once more the mistress of the civilized world for a short but brilliant period.

Ruins of Ancient Babylon, 7th century B. C.

Inscribed brick of Nebuchadrezzar II, King of Babylon
By permission of the Trustees of the British Museum

§3. *Egypt*

The history of Egypt during the eighth and seventh centuries B. C. is somewhat obscure, except in so far as it is covered by Egyptian relations with other peoples. The 22nd Dynasty, which had occupied the throne since the days of Solomon, was drawing to a close, and its weakening power gave opportunity for a change not merely in the family but also in the race of the monarchs. For centuries Egyptian power had extended up the Nile into the interior of Africa, though the greater the distance from the centres of authority in the north, the more precarious was the Egyptian hold on the country. During the 22nd Dynasty there seems to have been a growing spirit of independence amongst the Ethiopians of the south, and a centre of civilized power was formed at Napata, not far below the fourth cataract of the Nile. As the power of Egypt (in the narrower sense) weakened, the Ethiopians grew stronger, and before the end of the eighth century, under Piankhi of Napata, they were able to undertake the enterprise of conquest in the north. The ruling king, Osorkon III, seems to have been too weak a character to meet Piankhi, but one of the Delta princes, Tefnakhte by name, resisted stubbornly. The first conquest was that of Hermopolis (Eshmunein), which capitulated after a three days' siege. This success was followed by the fall of Memphis, and Lower Egypt submitted to the conqueror.

Thus began the Ethiopian dominion, which lasted with short intervals down to the middle of the seventh century. One of the immediate successors of Piankhi was Shabaka, who is usually identified with the So of 2 Ki. 17[4], the Egyptian king to whom Hoshea appealed for help against Assyria. Amongst the results of that alliance was not merely the conquest of Samaria, but also the advance of Sargon as far as Gaza, which he captured in 720. This, for the time, put an end to Egyptian dominion in Palestine.

The greatest king of this dynasty seems to have been Taharka, son of Piankhi, the Biblical Tirhakah (2 Ki. 19[9]). He had not actually succeeded to the throne in 701, the year of Sennacherib's invasion of Judah, but was commander-in-chief under his uncle. His monuments claim extensive dominions in Syria

Shabaka.   From a relief in an Egyptian temple
Photograph by Mr. Percival Hart

and Palestine, but his authority there seems to have been merely nominal. It is clear that in 670 he was driven far to the south by the invasion of Esarhaddon, and though on the departure of the Assyrian armies he succeeded in recovering some of the lost ground, he never won back the actual delta. This remained an Assyrian province in name, though in practice it was divided into a large number of petty principalities, whose chiefs were either the heads of Assyrian garrisons, or natives who admitted the authority of Ashur-bani-pal.

It was from one of these local principalities that the resistance to the family of Piankhi sprang in the first instance. Tefnakhte seems to have died in or about 721, and his line continued to hold a prominent place in the delta. They had originally entered Egypt from the west, and belonged to a group of Libyan tribes who had given much trouble in early days to the kings of Egypt. They remained nominally subject to Assyria until the weakness of the latter and the invasions of the northern hordes broke the connexion between the two countries. At the same time the presence of the Scythians in southern Palestine, attested by Herodotus, prevented any movement northwards on the part of the Egyptians till after the capture of Ashdod by Psamtik. His son Necho, on reaching the throne, allied himself with Assyria, and, during the last struggles of that empire, did what he could to offer effective resistance to Babylon. Though his northern campaign in 608 came too late to help the Assyrians, it may have done something to postpone the final triumph of the Chaldeans. This was achieved in 605, when Nebuchadrezzar inflicted a decisive defeat on Necho at Carchemish, and crushed the last Egyptian hopes. Intrigues in Palestine still continued, but never bore practical fruit, save in the destruction of the Jewish state and the subjugation of the whole of Palestine to the Chaldeans. Once more, in 586, during the final siege of Jerusalem, a demonstration in force was made by Ha'abre' (called by the Greeks Apries), but this was abortive, and the Egyptian troops do not seem even to have risked a battle. Egypt had ceased to be one of the great military powers of the ancient world.

§4. *Israel and Judah in the Eighth and Seventh Centuries*

The key to the political history of western Asia is for many centuries the condition of Assyria. After the failure of Shalmaneser III to crush the power of Damascus and other southern states,[1] the western successes of Assyria seem to have been confined to the country north of Palestine, and though Shamshi-adad V and Adad-nirari III extended their empire to the shores of the Mediterranean, there seems to have been comparatively little interference with the south. The result was that such smaller states as Syria and Israel were left to quarrel amongst themselves. Of the two the former seem to have been the stronger, and through the reigns of Jehoahaz and Jehoash in Israel and Joash and Amaziah in Judah the Hebrew kingdoms suffered considerably from the incursions of their eastern neighbours. It seems that the latter occupied large districts to the east of the Jordan, and for the time both Bashan and Gilead were probably lost to Israel. It will be remembered that Ahab had met his death trying to recover Ramoth Gilead from the Syrians, and that seems to have been the last attempt of the kind made by any Israelite king for about a century. For the greater part of that time the war was waged on the soil of Israel to the west of the Jordan valley. No doubt the fortunes of the war fluctuated, for in 2 Ki. 13[5] we have a statement to the effect that Israel dwelt in their tents as aforetime, though the verses that immediately follow describe a condition of complete subjection to Damascus, in which Jehoahaz was allowed only a small guard in lieu of an army.

The weakness of the north, however, was not wholly shared by the south. It would seem that during the days of Israel's prosperity Judah was normally subordinate to her. The association of Jehoshaphat in the campaigns against Syria and Moab may not have been wholly voluntary. Whether this conjecture be correct or not, it is clear that the period of decline in Israel which followed the accession of Jehu was accompanied by some

---

[1] He was checked at the battle of Qarqar in 853 B.C. by a combined army whose largest contingents were supplied by Damascus and Israel.

sort of political revival in Judah. Amaziah (805–786) was strong enough to undertake an expedition against Edom, and the record implies the subjugation of the latter people. War followed between the two Hebrew kingdoms, provoked, according to 2 Ki. 14⁸⁻¹⁴, by the pride of Amaziah. Judah had been the weaker of the two since the days of Solomon, and it may well have seemed to the southern king that his rival was now so reduced in strength by the border wars with Syria and he himself so strengthened by his conquest of Edom that the two could at last meet on equal terms. If so, his calculations were at fault. Jehoash was a stronger man than either his grandfather or his father, and Amaziah's challenge brought humiliation on himself and on his country. Jehoash followed up a victory in the open field by entering Jerusalem and dismantling its fortifications to the north, thus laying the city more open to attacks from that quarter.

In other ways Jehoash showed himself a vigorous ruler, and it is worth noting that it was in his reign, many years before the effects of Assyrian pressure could be felt on Damascus, that the tide of the conflict between Israel and Syria began to turn. It seems likely that Israel had already achieved some success before the clash with Judah, for Jehoash could hardly have faced even Amaziah with the limited forces permitted to his father by Hazael. Be this as it may, it is clear that he was able to lead a successful revolt against Syria. The record of 2 Ki. 13²⁵ states that he defeated Benhadad, son of Hazael, in three pitched battles, and recovered the cities which had been lost. In all probability this refers to cities on the west of the Jordan, since territory to the east seems to have remained in the hands of Syria till the reign of Jeroboam II.

The reigns of Azariah of Judah and Jeroboam II of Israel cover the greater part of the first half of the eighth century, and form the most prosperous period of Hebrew history since the days of Solomon. Very little space is given to either reign in the Book of Kings—the two together are described in no more than thirteen verses—and in the case of Azariah the only event mentioned is his own sickness and the regency of his son which followed thereon. But the notice of Jeroboam, though very brief, is significant. 'He restored the border of Israel from the entry to Hamath to the sea of the Arabah' (2 Ki. 14[25a]). This is only half a verse, but it tells a great deal. Hamath lay in the far north, and even the territories claimed for Solomon had not extended far beyond it, though his dominions were said (1 Ki. 4[24]) to have reached the Euphrates at Tiphsah. Some light is thrown on the military successes of the period by a

View on the Euphrates near Keban Maden.

reference in Am. 6[13], which should probably be rendered, 'Which rejoice over Lo-debar, which say, Have we not taken Karnaim by our own strength?' The places named are on the east of Jordan, the former being mentioned in 2 Sam. 9[4, 5] as being in the territory of Machir (the eastern section of Manasseh), while the latter appears in 1 Macc. 5[23, 46], and may possibly be the same as the Ashtoreth-Karnaim mentioned in Gen. 14[5]. Other signs of prosperity are reflected in the prophecies both of Amos and Isaiah.

But the revival of the northern kingdom was but the upward

leap of an expiring flame, and there were men living in the days of Jeroboam who were to see Samaria destroyed and the greater part of the population carried away into a captivity where they perished as a nation. The decline began almost immediately after the death of Jeroboam. Its first symptom was political confusion. The kings followed one another rapidly. Jeroboam seems to have died in 741,[1] his son Zachariah was

A modern Assyrian.
Photograph by Mr. R. Gorbold.

murdered after a short reign by Shallum, and he in turn by Menahem. The new king does not seem to have lived more than two or three years, and his son and successor, Peka-hiah, was assassinated by Pekah. His reign, too, apparently lasted only a couple of years, and the story of the kingdom of Israel comes to an end with his successor Hoshea, who, however, enjoyed a reign of nine years.

All this meant not merely frequent changes in govern-ment and policy, but also growing weakness in the face of foreign enemies, at a time when there was need of the greatest strength.

Assyria was emerging from her domestic difficulties, and with the accession of Tiglath-pileser III in 746 was entering on the period of her greatest power. It would seem that some of the western states were aware of their danger, and an attempt was made to form a coalition which should play the same part as the Syrian confederacy had done a hundred years earlier under the leadership of Benhadad and Ahab. An alliance was

[1] See Note on Chronology of the Period.

Modern Damascus

*Photographed from the air by **Mr.** Alan Cobham*

formed whose leading members were Pekah of Israel and Rezin of Damascus. In Judah, Azariah and his son Jotham had both passed away, and the throne was occupied by Ahaz. The confederates tried to persuade him to join them, and on his refusal threatened to use force, planning to seize Jerusalem, and replace Ahaz by a Syrian nominee, Tabeel by name. Immediate and vigorous attempts were made to place Jerusalem in a state of defence. It is possible that the walls broken down by Jehoash had never been rebuilt, and one of the first acts of the government was to restore them, or at least repair them. So urgent was the danger felt to be that it seems that even houses were pulled down in order that their materials might be used for the walls. The student of Greek history will be reminded of the speed with which Athens built the Long Walls which connected her with the Piraeus. At the same time attention was paid to the water supply, which was always a difficulty in ancient Jerusalem till Hezekiah cut his aqueduct. Ahaz did not neglect diplomatic measures, but sent an embassy to Tiglath-pileser, offering homage to the Assyrian king if he would save him from the coalition.

This last step was his greatest mistake. It was entirely unnecessary, for Tiglath-pileser was not the man lightly to acquiesce in the formation of any anti-Assyrian league. We have no details of the invasion of Judah by Pekah and Rezin, if it ever took place, but in any case it was not pressed to extremes, for in a few month's the confederates were fully occupied with an Assyrian expedition, which proved fatal to them both. Damascus was taken and Rezin slain in 732, and in the same year Tiglath-pileser deported large sections of the Israelite population of the north and east, put Pekah to death and replaced him by Hoshea. By this time it would seem that Egypt was alarmed, and it was probably owing to her intrigues that Hoshea revolted. Shalmaneser V, who had succeeded Tiglath-pileser in 727, invaded Israel and laid siege to Samaria. The city resisted for three years, and it was only after the death of Shalmaneser in 722 that it fell to his successor Sargon. This completed the destruction of the northern kingdom as an independent political unit, though it was not till the next century that settlers were brought from various parts of the Assyrian empire to take the place of the deported Israelites, and the whole country was formally incorporated in the Assyrian empire, being ruled by a governor instead of by native princes.

Assyrian king on horseback.
Photograph by Giraudon.

Judah, however, survived as a vassal state. This may have been due in part to her geographical position. The great road running from the east and north to Egypt—the only channel of communication between Africa and Asia—passed through the territory of northern Israel. It was therefore essential for any power which aimed ultimately at subduing Egypt (as the

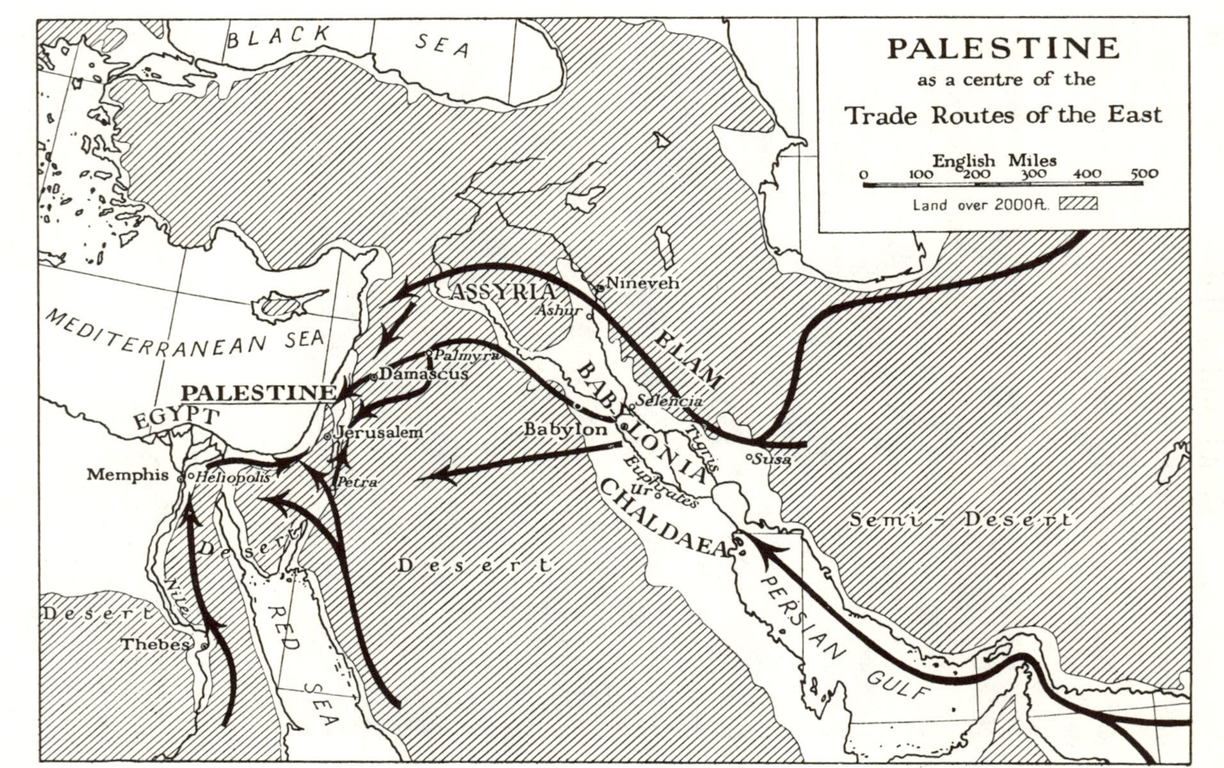

PALESTINE
as a centre of the
Trade Routes of the East
English Miles
0 100 200 300 400 500
Land over 2000ft.
BLACK SEA
MEDITERRANEAN SEA
ASSYRIA
Nineveh
Ashur
ELAM
Palmyra
Damascus
BABYLONIA
Selencia
Tigris
PALESTINE
EGYPT
Jerusalem
Babylon
Susa
Memphis
Heliopolis
Petra
Euphrates
Ur
CHALDAEA
Semi - Desert
Desert
Desert
Nile
RED SEA
Thebes
PERSIAN GULF

Assyrians seem to have done) to gain control of the country. But Jerusalem, and indeed practically the whole territory of Judah, lay to one side of the route, which crossed the plain of Esdraelon and ran down the coast region. No doubt a hostile garrison in the hills could have annoyed and perhaps seriously harassed an army on the march, but the importance of the position was far less than that of Samaria. The Assyrian kings could afford to leave Jerusalem alone or, on the march, to have sent a sufficient force to mask it, and it is a significant fact that when war did break out between Assyria and Judah, it was not necessary for more than a comparatively small detachment to move against the Judaean capital. But at the time there can be little doubt that the policy of Ahaz rather than the position of Jerusalem was responsible for the safety of Judah. After the fall of Damascus, Ahaz visited the captured city and did homage to Tiglath-pileser, to whom he had previously dispatched a large bribe. It appears that this submission had a religious as well as a political aspect. The record in 2 Ki. 16^{10-18} states that he saw in Damascus a kind of altar that was new to him, and that he sent orders to Jerusalem to have a similar one made for the Temple. On his return to the city he carried out a number of changes in the arrangements of the Temple, and it may be that these alterations in worship were due to the introduction of certain forms of Assyrian cult. The sacrifice of his son, recorded in 2 Ki. 16^3, may have been included amongst these rites, but such an offering was not often made except in dire extremity, and it seems more likely that this event is somewhat earlier. It may have been performed under the stress of invasion by the Syro-Ephraimite confederacy, and may be compared with a similar sacrifice offered up by Mesha when threatened by the joint armies of Israel and Judah (2 Ki. 3^{27}). At all events, throughout his reign it seems that Judah remained subject to Assyria without any attempt at revolt.

The accession of Hezekiah, son of Ahaz, may be placed in or about 725.[1] The slow progress of Assyria to the south continued, and with the fall of Ashkelon in 711 they reached a

---

[1] But see the Note on the Chronology of the Period.

point to which they had never penetrated before. This seems to have aroused the fears of Egypt to a still higher degree, and the death of Sargon was the signal for a widespread revolt. The nature of the Assyrian empire was such that it depended largely on the character of its king for its stability, and there were generally threats of revolt or actual rebellions in many parts of the empire on the accession of a new monarch. In that which broke out after the death of Sargon (705) the principal leader within the empire was Babylon, whose king, Merodach-baladan, was a life-long enemy of the dominant power, and did his best to throw off the yoke. It is probable that the embassy of Merodach-baladan to Hezekiah, recorded in 2 Ki. 20^{12-19}, had as its real object the stirring up of trouble in the west for Sennacherib. This, combined with the intrigues of Egypt, led to a general revolt whose story is familiar both from the famous record of Sennacherib and from the Old Testament. Detained by trouble in Mesopotamia, Sennacherib was not able to deal with his farthest vassals till 701, but in that year invaded 'the land of the Hittites and the land of the Amorites', in which latter Judah was included. The story of the invasion is told from both sides. Sennacherib claims to have captured forty-six fortified cities and innumerable smaller towns, and to have carried away over 200,000 prisoners. He besieged Hezekiah and laid an enormous tribute upon him. But he does not say that he captured Jerusalem, and it is probable that he preferred to achieve his ends by negotiation, since, even with the skill in siege operations which the Assyrians possessed, the actual capture of the city might have proved a long and difficult under-taking. The Biblical account is somewhat obscure, apparently owing to the presence of two separate narratives describing the same event. It is clear, however, that the attack on Jerusalem was not an expedition of sufficient importance to demand the presence either of Sennacherib in person or of the whole of his army. The besieging army is said to have suffered an appalling disaster, swift and terrible destruction falling upon them. It is interesting to note that Herodotus, who seems not to have heard of the existence of the kingdom of Judah, speaks of a battle with the Egyptians, in which the latter were successful owing to a plague of rats which attacked the Assyrian army and gnawed their bowstrings. A comparison of this narrative with that of 2 Ki. 19[35] has suggested to some readers that Sennacherib's army was attacked by bubonic plague. Be that as it may, it is clear that he was content with the submission of Hezekiah and the payment of tribute, feeling that it was unnecessary actually to destroy Jerusalem itself. The narrative in 2 Kings makes no mention of the ravaging of Judah, though there may be a reference to it in Is. 1[4-9].

The policy of submission to Assyria was continued throughout the reign of Manasseh, who succeeded his father in 696. He is condemned by the historian in stronger terms than any other king of Judah, possibly because his atrocities were nearer to the writer's own time and were therefore impressed more vividly on men's memories. His great crime was his apostasy, and, as in the case of Ahaz, this may have been due in part to Assyrian influence. Beyond a general account of his misdeeds the Book of Kings makes no reference to events in his reign, though 2 Chron. 33[11] speaks of his being carried captive to Babylon for a time. This may be a reminiscence of his attendance at a great *darbar* held by Esarhaddon in 677, at which twenty-two 'kings of the Hittites' did homage to the Assyrian king.

The reign of Manasseh's son, Amon, was cut short by assassination, possibly because it became clear that no improvement in the methods of government was to be expected from him. No important events have been recorded of the early years of his son and successor Josiah, though outside Israel great changes were taking place both in Mesopotamia and in Egypt. It will be remembered that in 705 Sargon had lost his life defending his empire against wild tribes from the north. Such peoples were for many centuries the greatest danger to which civilization was exposed, and from time to time they made more or less successful inroads into the south and west. The invasions of the Huns and the Tartars are those best known in European history. To the Greeks these miscellaneous hordes of northern savages were known as Scythians, and that is the name generally applied to them by modern historians of Assyria and Israel. The weakening of the Assyrian empire towards the end of the reign of Ashur-bani-pal made an invasion possible from the north, which, in turn, contributed to the downfall of Nineveh. It seems probable that in 626 bands of Scythians penetrated as far south as Palestine. Such an invasion is suggested by the language both of Zephaniah and of Jeremiah, though it has been held that the latter, at any rate, was not referring to them but to the Chaldeans, or that if he did refer to them it was merely a vague apprehension of possible calamity and not a description of actual events. Others find the 'Scythian' passages too vivid to be anything but references to actual events. It would seem that they swept with extraordinary rapidity from north to south. The open country was abandoned, the population took refuge in the fortified towns, and finally fled to Jerusalem. Even this appeared to some to be unsafe, and they sought an asylum still farther south. The enemy appeared before the walls of the city and attempted a surprise attack. It evidently failed completely, and such peoples had no machinery for the conduct of a siege. After the failure of the invasion—if it was a real invasion and not merely a raid by plundering bands—we hear no more of the Scythians in Judah. But the general effect of their movements was to weaken the Assyrian hold on the outlying provinces. Josiah was able to turn his attention to internal affairs, and it is not impossible that the comparative freedom from Assyrian interference which he now enjoyed gave an opportunity for the best-known work of his reign. The repair of the Temple, the discovery of the Law and reformation based upon it belong rather to the religious than to the political history of Judah; here it must be enough to note that these events probably had their political aspect. If we are right in supposing that the heathen elements in the cultus of the days of Ahaz and Manasseh were in part due to the Assyrian imperial worship, one of the signs of liberty would be the sweeping away of these features of the religious life of Israel. It will be remembered that a century later the attempt of Zerubbabel to rebuild the Temple after the return from the exile was interpreted as a political effort aimed at independence, and the same factor may have been present both in the work of Hezekiah and Josiah. The initial repairs of the Temple which led to the discovery of the

Law may have been part of a general attempt to strengthen Jerusalem against possible attacks, which were now to be feared, not only or even mainly from the Assyrians but also from the neighbouring tribes.

For thirteen years after the reformation Josiah seems to have enjoyed uninterrupted peace. In the meantime the combined

Egyptian infantry on the march.

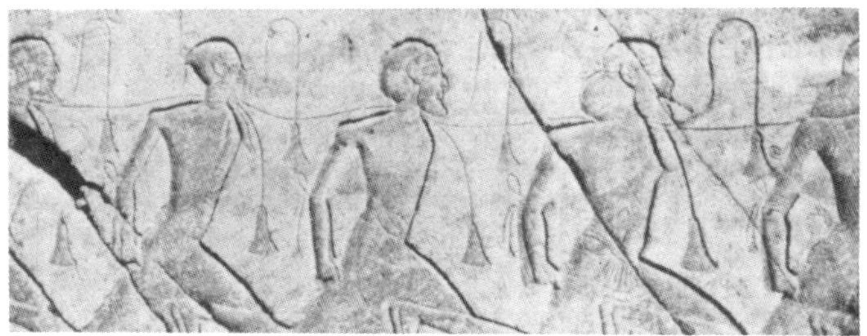

Semites made captive by the Egyptians.

armies of Babylon and Elam had destroyed Nineveh in 612, and the last remnants of the Assyrian power were struggling to escape their doom. It is quite possible that just as a century before Merodach-baladan had tried to secure the co-operation of Hezekiah, so now Nebopolassar had secured the help, or at least the benevolent neutrality, of Josiah. For when in 608 the young and vigorous king of Egypt, Necho, marched northwards to do what he could for the broken Assyrians, he first had to settle the affairs of Judah. Here the account is somewhat confused. Had we only the record in the Book of Kings, we should believe that the Egyptian king summoned Josiah to meet him at Megiddo and had him executed or assassinated there on the ground of his hostility to the Egyptians and their allies. In 2 Chron. 35$^{20-25}$, however, we have a circumstantial account of a battle in which Josiah was killed by Egyptian archers, and Herodotus mentions a great victory won in Syria by Necho, at a place whose name was 'Magdolus', i. e. Migdol. He is then stated to have captured the great city of 'Kadutis', which can hardly have been Jerusalem, and was much more probably Kadesh on the Orontes. Support for this conjecture appears from the fact that Riblah, where Necho met and imprisoned Jehoahaz, is in the same district as Kadesh, though the latter had largely lost the importance it possessed in the days of the great Hittite empire. In that case the battle of 'Magdolus' probably took place in the north—the name is not an uncommon one—and was not recorded in any contemporary account of the period which has yet come to light. Even the newly discovered Babylonian Chronicle, our most reliable source for the history of these years, mentions no battle fought by Necho in Syria. Herodotus no doubt derived his information from Egyptian sources, and it is to be regretted that we have no detailed narrative of this campaign from that point of view. In any case it seems that the tragedy of Megiddo was due to Josiah's support of the Babylonian cause, if he was not acting independently.

The dead king's policy seems to have been popular in Jerusalem, and the people, passing over the eldest son of Josiah, placed Jehoahaz on the throne. But Necho could not allow a representative of the pro-Babylonian party to retain power in his rear, and replaced the new king by his elder brother Eliakim, whose name he changed to Jehoiakim, perhaps as a concession to the religious feeling of Jerusalem. Jehoahaz was sent first to Riblah and then to Egypt, where he died a prisoner.

Of several of the last kings of Judah we have unusually clear character-sketches, particularly in the Book of Jeremiah. Josiah owed his popularity, it seems, less to his religious and political activities than to his democratic attitude and behaviour. He was one with his people, and did not keep his subjects at a distance. His government was marked by fairness in the administration of justice — always an important test of the character of an Oriental ruler. At the same time he was a man of strong personality, and the comparative mildness of his rule was in no way due to weakness. Jehoiakim was in almost every way a contrast to his father. He was the nominee of that foreign power which had destroyed the king whom the people loved and had deported the man whom they had chosen for their king. Either the knowledge of this unpopularity made him harsh and bitter, or these qualities made him unpopular. His theory of kingship was that of the typical eastern Sultan; his subjects were his slaves, and existed only to do his will. The same standard represented the only principle of justice which he knew. He tried to emulate the great monarchs of the world in his building operations, and the effect on a poor agricultural people was to reduce them to the position of serfs, labourers who received no pay for their services. His ecclesiastical policy was a reversion to the old days, and both the social and the religious instincts of the best elements in the people were against him. Yet he was a man of force and vigour, on the whole as faithful as circumstances would permit to the power that had placed him on the throne. It is worth noting that he alone of the last six kings of Judah died a natural death in the full enjoyment of his royal position.

The defeat of Necho at Carchemish put an end to any doubt there may have been as to the supremacy of Babylon. Probably Jehoiakim had to accept the position and recognize Nebuchadrezzar for the time as his overlord. But his leanings were always towards Egypt, to whose intrigues he lent a ready ear. In 597 he joined in a revolt of the Palestinian states, and a Babylonian army was sent into Palestine. Before it reached Jerusalem, however, Jehoiakim died, and was succeeded by his son Jehoiachin. The lad—he was only eighteen—found resistance impossible and wisely surrendered. He was carried away to Babylon, and with him were taken all the better elements in the population, only 'the poor of the land' being left behind. But another attempt was made by Nebuchadrezzar to preserve the forms of autonomy in Jerusalem, and he placed on the throne the youngest son of Josiah, changing his name from Mattaniah to Zedekiah.

Zedekiah, again, offered a striking contrast in temperament both to Josiah and to Jehoiakim. They had been alike in strength of personality if in nothing else ; Zedekiah, on the other hand, was conspicuously weak. He does not seem to have been a man of bad impulses, but he lived in times when the great need was for a consistent policy and a firm hand. Zedekiah had neither. He was helpless in the hands of the new nobility, and the most serious effect of the deportations of Nebuchadrezzar was the change they made in the court. Jeremiah expresses his view of the situation when he compares the old nobles to a basket of good figs and the new officials to a basket of figs so bad as to be utterly unfit for food, the very sight of which sickened men.[1] Selfish, shortsighted, and greedy, they kept their faces turned towards Egypt, and were wholly unable to read the signs of the political sky. A general revolt was planned in 592 by the Palestinian states, and it seems that Zedekiah was actually summoned to Babylon to give an account of himself. Four years later he definitely committed himself to rebellion, and the inevitable Babylonian army invaded Judah. The main purpose of the expedition seems to have been the reduction of northern Syria, and it was only a detachment that invested Jerusalem. The city resisted successfully for a time. A diversion was created by an Egyptian force which moved northwards, but after its retreat the siege was resumed. At length a breach was made in the walls, and the soldiery escaped, taking Zedekiah with them. Near the Jordan, however, they deserted him, and he fell into the hands of the Chaldeans. He was taken to Nebuchadrezzar at Riblah, his sons were killed before his face, and he himself was blinded and carried in chains to Babylon. The city was plundered, and both it and the Temple were laid in ruins. In so far as an organized community continued to exist, it maintained its short life under Gedaliah at Mizpah. But

---

[1] Ch. 24.

CAPTIVES BROUGHT BEFORE AN ASSYRIAN KING.   The first five figures are soldiers carrying the heads of their enemies.   Then follow two prisoners, and a third is just having his head cut off by another soldier.   Behind are women and children

Photograph by W. F. Mansell & Co.

his murder by Ishmael put an end to the last hope that any Judahite may have had, and the last remnants of the people fled to Egypt.

So ended the Hebrew monarchy. It had never been an extensive one, even if the limits assigned to the kingdom of Solomon were actually reached. It had come into being during a comparative lull in the age-long struggle between Egypt and the dominant Asiatic powers, but with the growth of Assyria its weaknesses had become more and more apparent. As a political entity Israel had lain between the upper and the lower millstone, with the inevitable result. Yet her greatness is not to be measured by her political fortunes. Her religion—a unique phenomenon in the faiths of the ancient world—gave her a power of resistance which enabled her to survive political annihilation. The exiles in Babylon did not, as those of other races did, forget their nationality, and when the opportunity came to re-establish themselves they were in a position to take it. It is true that the character of the new Judah was profoundly different from that of the old, but the historical sequence remained, and she continued to keep alive a strong sense of nationality based on her peculiar national faith. This has endured through the centuries. The time came when she gave birth to Christianity, and almost simultaneously suffered another political disaster from which there has yet been no recovery. Yet still her creed marks her out as separate from the Gentiles, and of all the nations who played their part on the stage of history in the eighth and seventh centuries B. C., she alone exists to-day.

B. SOCIAL AND ECONOMIC CONDITIONS IN ISRAEL

To a large extent the social and economic history of a people is conditioned by geographical circumstances. In so far as it does not depend on the character of the people themselves, it depends upon three factors: (*a*) the natural sources of the food supply; (*b*) the opportunities for manufacture; (*c*) the means of communication, both internal and external. In turn, these three factors influence the character of the people, which reacts again on them.

The land of the Hebrews falls into two large sections, separated from one another by the Jordan gorge. To the east the country is hilly and open, its contours being broken by torrent beds, down which the water rushes with great force and volume during the short rains, but which are dry and stony beds during the greater part of the year. Except in hollows and folds in the hills, or where a natural spring gives a fairly constant supply of water, the land is unsuitable for cultivation, though the presence of numerous wells makes it possible for a pastoral community to find sustenance for their flocks. The northern part of the country was renowned for its large cattle, and in the south lay Moab, a tolerably rich land for graziers. Gilead, which lay between, partook probably of the characteristics of both, though fertile arable spots are occasionally found.

To the west of the Jordan, the backbone of the country is a range of hills which forms a prolongation of the Lebanon mountains. This is broken in its northern portion by lower land which runs from the Sea of Galilee to the Mediterranean— the so-called Plain of Esdraelon. South of this lies the 'hill country of Judah', and the land becomes dryer as it goes southwards till it merges into the relatively desert land of Edom and the Sinai peninsula. The slope on the Jordan side is very steep, and is cut into sharp channels by winter torrent beds.[1] To the west the ground declines more gradually, and before the coastal plain is reached there is a series of low rolling foot-hills, known to the ancient Hebrews as the Shephelah. Here again there are numerous wadis, some of which form fairly extensive valleys, running well up into the hill country, and it is these routes that the caravan roads and railways have generally followed towards Jerusalem or other places in the mountains.   North and south of the Plain of Esdraelon there is a certain amount of arable land even in the hills, whilst the Shephelah and the maritime plain are very fertile, but south of Jerusalem cultivation becomes more and more difficult, till beyond Hebron it practically ceases.

The result is that the student of the history of Palestine has to deal with a country which offers great variations in the level and character of its civilization.   To the south and east the only possible forms of livelihood are those of the shepherd and the hunter, whilst in the centre and west, particularly in the Plain of Esdraelon, in the Shephelah, and in the maritime plain, agriculture flourishes.   The principal minerals are those found in the Dead Sea region, consisting of bitumen and deposits of various natural salts.   All metals have to be imported, none having been found in the country.

To this it should be added that its position between the Mediterranean and the Syrian desert necessarily makes Palestine (or a part of it) the great highway between Asia and Africa. There were caravan routes both to the east and to the west of the Jordan gorge (which is passable only in a few places), but the most important of these was one leading from Damascus across the valley near the Sea of Galilee and running through the Plain of Esdraelon to the maritime plain, where it pursued its way to Egypt.   This was, is, and apparently long will be, one of the world's great trade routes.

It may be safely assumed that before the conquest Israel was a nomadic people, and that even after taking possession of the land, those tribes which made their home in the east and south still continued to a large extent their ancient mode of life.   On

---

[1] The modern Arabic name for such a torrent is *wadi*.

the other hand, those which settled in the centre and to the west gradually, as they dispossessed or assimilated their predecessors, took to the operations of agriculture, and made good use of the fertility of the soil. There were, no doubt, parts of the country where these occupations were combined, and there seem to have been semi-nomads, whose areas of pasture

The Plain of Esdraelon.
Photograph by Fr. Vester & Co.

were limited, and who may have supplemented the produce of their flocks by some form of corn-growing. But amongst them we still have, evidently, that simpler form and organization of society which we associate more generally with pastoral than with agricultural races.

Pastoral tribes are much the same all the world over, and the opportunities for development are limited. The settled home, however, which agriculture demands, gives room for advance in many directions. Thus in the lowlands the social order developed from a tribal organization to one which consisted of small family groups each working and living on its own little section of the land. This means a system of small peasant farmers, a condition which breeds a sturdiness of character and a conservative outlook on life. The prevailing conditions are reflected in the legal codes of Israel, but perhaps the best picture is to be seen in the story of Naboth in the middle of the ninth century B.C. Here we have a typical small-holding—so small that Ahab wants to make a flower garden of it—and we see the tenacity with which the owner clung to his ancestral property. Further, the incident illustrates the respect with which even a Hebrew king like Ahab regarded the rights and the feelings connected with this ancestral property. It was left to his foreign wife to devise the plot by which the ground was seized for the Crown, and the narrative suggests that the king himself was no party to the proceedings, and was indeed ignorant of them, till Naboth was actually dead. Nevertheless Jezebel's action set a terrible precedent that was only too frequently followed during the next century.

The same reign seems to have witnessed the birth of a commercial system. The treaty made by Ahab with Benhadad after the Israelite victory at Aphek seems to imply some sort of commercial understanding between the two kingdoms which would be to the advantage of Israel. And the various references made by the prophets of a hundred years later leave no room for doubt that there was in their day a large amount of trade which passed through Samaritan territory if not through Samaria itself. No doubt such traffic was interrupted by the frequent border wars between the two peoples, but these seem for the most part to have consisted of plundering raids, and the merchants' caravans were not the worst sufferers. On the other hand this political unsettlement made the life of the cultivators difficult and uncertain. Even places so far from the border as Dothan were not safe, and throughout the greater part of the country there must have been for many years a great and wearing sense of insecurity. Inasmuch as the Syrians did not achieve any formal conquest, however, their sufferings served in some measure to maintain the morale of the peasantry, at least for war, and, with the end of the reign of Jehoahaz, Israel began to assert herself seriously against her rival. Jehoash seems to have cleared the country of these raiding bands, and so to have prepared the way for the striking successes achieved by Jeroboam II.

Between the days of Ahab and those of Jeroboam we have practically no evidence of the condition of the country, but in the middle of the eighth century the facts are fairly clear, and when the curtain is once more raised it is a very different picture that meets our eyes. During the preceding century a change had come over the whole country, both in city and in agricultural life. There had grown up in Samaria and elsewhere a class of wealthy persons who were engaged in commerce or in money-lending. Amongst them luxury had taken the place of comfort, and the best products of the known world were at their command. Isaiah speaks of the substitution of marble as a building material for stone, and of the planting of better-class trees instead of the inferior species which had been destroyed in war. Amos describes the extravagance of the furniture and the wasteful ostentation of the rich man's table. A change indeed from the days when Ahab himself went up and down the country trying to find fodder for his horses!

As so often, the increase of prosperity in one class was accompanied by a growing distress in others. The inequality in the distribution of wealth increased and the lower classes grew more and more wretched and miserable. The whole character of the social order underwent a change. The peasant farmers, perhaps tempted to extravagance by the increasing luxury of the great cities, or perhaps suffering heavy losses through the depredations of the Syrian marauding bands, would from time to time be compelled to borrow money. Oriental interest always appears to be enormous to the Western mind, and in addition there was, we may be sure, some kind of mortgage—usually on a man's land. Eventually this would fall into the hands of the city capitalist, who might retain the farmer, but as an employee, not as an independent worker. Amos complains bitterly of the rents that were demanded in such cases. Further financial distress would compel the man to mortgage his person and his family, and this time failure to meet his debts would result in slavery. Ownership of the soil was thus concentrated into the hands of a small group of men, and Isaiah fiercely denounces those who build up large properties for themselves. By 750 B. C. it would seem that from a system of small peasant proprietors the social organization had changed to one of large estates worked largely by serf labour.

It is not difficult to conjecture, from the hints occasionally dropped by the prophets, especially Amos, the means by which this change was brought about. One of the worst evils in Eastern life is the corruption of justice. A judge who is not venal is sufficiently rare to receive high praise, and it is not without reason that judicial impartiality is valued as highly as it is. It would seem that in cases where a mortgage was in question there had to be an appeal to a tribunal of some kind, and that the tribunal could generally be bribed. A claim for foreclosure on the person would be upheld by the local judge for a small fee, and Amos speaks passionately of the fact that it was possible to buy a man for a pair of shoes.

It is worthy of note that both Amos and Isaiah regard the women of the community as equally responsible with the men. They set the social standard (as so often), and made demands on their men which could be met only by fresh corruption and oppression. 'Cows of Bashan', Amos calls them, fat, luxurious, brainless animals, with no thought beyond the gratification of their sensuous desires. They were probably not worse than their men, but they were no better, and had to take their share of the blame for the rottenness beneath the fair surface, which made the social life of Israel a foul and deadly quagmire of iniquity. The 'upper' classes had aimed, perhaps without conscious deliberation or policy, at crushing and grinding down the 'lower orders'. Such a policy can have only one end—national and social ruin. If the attempt fails it will one day issue in a colossal upheaval, a social eruption such as that which befell France at the end of the eighteenth century or Russia in the first quarter of the twentieth. If it succeeds it results in a national emasculation which renders the people an easy prey to any attack from the outside—and foreign enemies were near to Israel in the eighth century B.C. It was no accident that she succumbed when she did. Her men had degenerated into a helpless mass of effeminate nobles and servile labourers, and so far from being able to repeat the successes of the preceding century, she fell swiftly before the Assyrian invader.

That Judah did not immediately share her fate was due to two causes. One was the geographical position of Jerusalem, which made her less dangerous to the armies of the greater nations at strife. The other was undoubtedly the fact that she was in some measure spared the social perils of her more powerful sister in the north. It is true that in the more fertile country of the Shephelah the corruption and oppression (as witnessed by Micah) were hardly less terrible than in the Plain of Esdraelon. But taken as a whole Judah was a less fruitful land than Israel, and included within her borders a larger proportion of the pastoral and semi-nomadic elements in the community. Whatever may have been the conditions in Jerusalem and in the western lands, Amos may be a fair type of the southern Judahite, strong, rugged, moral, and fearless, with little desire for luxurious ease and little respect for authority that was not backed by character. But gradually through the seventh century Judah too seems to have had her strength sapped by the same social poisons that had killed Israel, and in the days of Jeremiah Jerusalem was hardly better than Samaria had been in the time of Amos. So she, too, went her selfish way, and met her inevitable doom.

C. THE RELIGION OF ISRAEL IN THE EIGHTH AND SEVENTH CENTURIES

Few periods in the history of civilized man have been more fruitful in intellectual and spiritual development than the four centuries which closed with the death of Alexander the Great. In Persia, Zarathustra laid the foundations of a religion which has more closely approximated to the Christian spirit than any other. In China, Confucius set a standard of conduct and of character which were to remain the national ideal for nearly twenty-five centuries. In Greece, Solon and Thales were contemporaries of Jeremiah and Ezekiel, and Socrates and Plato of Ezra. In India, Siddharta, the Buddha, carried the pantheistic philosophy of the Aryan mind to its extreme logical borders, and discarded the gods as he knew them in order to make room for a genuine human righteousness. But nowhere was the spiritual upheaval more striking, or, in the long run, more enduring in its results, than in the obscure Palestinian 'buffer states' of Israel and Judah which lay politically between the hammer of the Mesopotamian world-powers and the anvil of Egypt. Nor was this primarily due to the religious genius of a single individual. We naturally think of an Amos, a Hosea, an Isaiah, a Habakkuk, or a Jeremiah, but just as in Greece the famous individuals succeeded because they were true representatives of all that ·was best in the Greek mind, so in Israel the teaching of the prophets ultimately won its way because it reflected and developed something that was inherent in the truest spiritual thinking of their people. If ever a nation was chosen and inspired as a whole to lead humanity to God, that nation was Israel, and it was the period now under review that proved the turning-point in the history of her soul.

The clue to the religious history of the period is to be found in the fact that Israel must be regarded not as one people but as two. The line of demarcation is not political, it is social and economic. For this purpose the division into two kingdoms is practically insignificant; Jerusalem and Samaria present the

From nomad life to settlement in Arabia
Photographs by Mr. R. Gorbold

same phenomena, and the Plain of Esdraelon which Amos saw offers the same problems as the Judaean Shephelah where Micah had his home.   The essential difference was between those Israelites whose life was still largely pastoral and those who had made their home in the arable portions of the land and had for some centuries settled down to a life of agriculture and commerce. The material conditions of the two sides of Israelite life have already been mentioned ; it remains to draw attention to the resultant contrast in religion.

The religion of a pastoral people nearly always exhibits a simplicity in externals which corresponds to the simplicity of their conditions of life.   There may be sacred spots, but within the tribe itself, as long as it maintains its wandering habits, there can be no true temple or other elaborate centre of worship. The belief in a vast number of spiritual beings, many of whom were associated with natural objects, no doubt leaves the nomad unlimited opportunities for the exercise of his religious instincts. He is surrounded by them.   To him every mountain and spring, every river and tree, every stone that he passes by the way, may be the home of some living power that he can worship.   At any moment a divine being may reveal himself in or from such an object, and the spot will be for ever sacred to the man and to his tribe.   But his daily life is not always lived within reach of such holy places.   He must wander far to find sustenance and water for his cattle, and any emblem of deity that he takes with him must be portable, whilst all that is used in ritual and worship must be of material that is easily obtainable even at a distance from the regions of the higher civilization.

Three of the sacred objects most revered in ancient Israel were traced back to the desert period.   These were the Bull, the Snake, and the Stones.   Had the priests of Bethel in the eighth century been asked why they worshipped their God in the form of a bull, they would probably have replied with a story which in some ways recalled that of Ex. 32.   But we may guess that they would have made Moses and not Aaron the author of the cult, and would have seen in the form which the molten gold assumed an expression of the will of their God, indicating the shape under which He would receive the adoration of His people.

A similar question addressed to the priests of the serpent shrine in Jerusalem would have been answered by a narrative not unlike that of Num. 21$^{4-9}$, whilst the history of the stones received at Sinai would be ample explanation of the sanctity of the Ark that contained them.   But all these things had passed from the

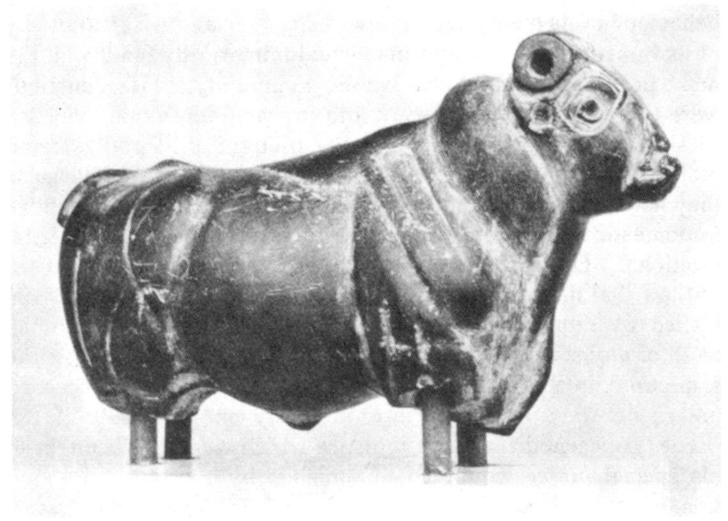

Stone figure of a sacred bull from Larsa.
Horns and legs of different material were inset. From back to front the material
is pierced, perhaps for the passage of a liquid intended to pour out of the
muzzle in a thin stream. Date about 2400–2200 B.C. (B. M. 116686.)

nomadic to the settled portions of the Israelite community, and could be visited and adored only by individual pilgrims to the great shrines.

Thus we are driven to think of the practical religion of the east and south of Israel as one which had virtually no outward material embodiments.   In these districts sacrifice was hardly practised, unless it were that of the Passover, and none of the earlier canonical prophets upholds the practice as a divine ordinance.   Their God was profoundly real to them, but it was inevitable that their maintenance of right relations with Him should depend far more upon their observance of certain rules of conduct than on any ritual. For the ancient Semitic mind always thought of its gods as being attached to particular tribes, and the general rule of 'one god one tribe' seems to have been fairly well observed amongst the neighbours of Israel. In some cases the deity was held to be the physical ancestor of the tribe, and in all he was vitally concerned with its fortunes and the behaviour of its members. He was stronger and wiser than any of its human elements, and his virtual immortality made him the most powerful force in the whole community. His functions were those of a leader in peace and in war (there is no evidence to show that a Semitic people ever thought of its god as being really defeated in battle; if his people failed it was because they had angered him and he had left them to their fate), a judge in domestic matters and an avenger of his tribe in their external relations. He was thus the special guardian of certain features of the tribal life. Disputes between different members had to be settled by him, and he might be invoked as a witness to the truth of any statement or to the good faith of a promise. At the same time, in these spheres of life he was not greatly concerned unless he were expressly introduced by one or other of the parties concerned. Acts of injustice which were not brought to his special notice would go unpunished by him, and falsehood was no sin unless it were committed under the oath. It is probable also that property disputes—which cannot be very extensive in a pastoral people where the institution of private property is confined to minor articles—did not affect him unless they were brought to him for settlement. In these circumstances only would cases of theft come before him. To these should be added a class of rules, very common and stringent amongst primitive peoples, which are usually summed up under the name *tabu*. Certain objects were associated with a god in a particular sense, and were therefore either withdrawn altogether from human use, or were hedged about with restrictions. For an ordinary man to touch one of these things might mean death, because the *tabu* was infectious and would envelop the offender as well as the original object. Articles under the *tabu* were not infrequently destroyed, whilst persons were put to death by the tribe as a whole to save it from dangerous contamination.

On the other hand, the god was vitally interested in matters which affected the blood of the tribe, for on that depended its very existence, and therefore his own standing. The most obvious of these were marriage laws and kindred subjects, and the law of blood-revenge. Sexual immorality and murder were crimes which must be punished by him, either directly or indirectly through the community as a whole. The general result was a fairly high moral standard, facilitated, no doubt, by the comparative simplicity of life in general, but making on the whole for social stability and personal good conduct.

Whilst on the pastoral plane the religion of Israel shared in all the characteristics which have been mentioned, yet it differed from all other religions in one fundamental respect. They were natural, and the relationship between the deity and the tribe had its roots in the very origin of the latter. With Israel this was not so. We can only speculate as to the pre-Mosaic religion of the different tribes of Israel, but we do know for certain that the genuine religion of the united people began on a definite historical occasion, and was brought about by a definite historical personage. The great work of Moses lay in the fact that he brought Israel to the sacred mountain, and there mediated for them a 'covenant' between them and the God who was henceforward to be the national deity. The name of this God was Jahveh,[1] and there is no reason to suppose that Israel in the days of Moses, or for centuries afterwards, had any further or higher conception of Jahveh than, for example, Moab had of their national god, Chemosh, or Ammon of Moloch.[2] But the relations between Israel and Jahveh were essentially unique, because of their historic origin. The religion of Israel was a partnership, voluntarily invited by Jahveh and deliberately accepted by Israel. It was no mere theoretical fancy to say that Jahveh had *chosen* Israel. That was, in fact, the truth that lay behind all their spiritual history and in the last resort made their progress possible. For the partnership was based on definite terms of agreement, and if either side departed from or broke those terms, the offended party was at liberty to terminate the relationship.

---

[1] This name should be pronounced *Yahwé*.
[2] The name was probably pronounced *Melech*.

Hence one of the permanent features of Jahveh was his faithfulness. If a breach arose, it would not be from His side, but from that of Israel. He would observe His side of the bargain; the only doubt was as to whether they would display similar fidelity. In the ordinary association of a god and a people, it was supposed that the god was dependent for most of what made his existence valuable on the fact that he had a people of his own. A god who for any reason had lost his tribe became a homeless and friendless spirit, supremely dangerous to any human being who might come under his power, but at the same time helpless and resourceless amongst his own class. The Jinn of Arab demonology are probably ancient gods of this type. But Jahveh had existed before the great Covenant, and had proved His power to be independent of Israel. He could therefore, at will, sever the connexion if the Covenant were broken, without serious injury to Himself, and though it is clear that such an end to the relationship might be interpreted as a confession of failure, yet the real failure would lie with the ruined people. Jahveh could make for Himself another nation, and in the end the world would know whose word should stand, His or Israel's.

Down to the Exile the pastoral section of the Israelite community seems to have continued to hold religious views and practices similar to those which have been briefly sketched. With the settled community of central and northern Palestine it was otherwise. They had entered on a life of agriculture, and to their minds it was more than doubtful whether a pastoral God was competent to meet the needs of their new life. In all matters which had affected Jahveh in the past, He was still revered, and, in particular, He remained the national God. But, as the testimony of Hosea shows, His ability to grow corn and wine and oil, the three typical products of the agricultural community, was seriously questioned. There were gods already in possession, the rather vague fertility spirits of the Canaanites, known under the generic name of Baals. If neglected they might become dangerous, and in any case it might be well to secure their help for the new mode of living with which Israel was experimenting. It seems almost certain that Israel took over the whole of the agricultural life, with its law, its religion, its language, its habits and customs, and even its mythology, from the Canaanites. When they realized at length from bitter experience that Jahveh would not tolerate such conduct (since He was a 'jealous' God), they compromised on a type of religion which is commonly called syncretism, and is by no means confined to Israel. This consists in the worship of one deity with the ritual and theology which really belong to another, the mixing of two religions, and the nominal adherence to the one with the practical maintenance of the other. The phenomenon is generally found where a conquering religion is superimposed on a native one without adequate spiritual guidance. Illustrations may be seen in some of the lower forms of Christianity and perhaps still more clearly in some extant phases of Northern Buddhism. To Israel Jahveh was now an agricultural God and must be worshipped as such. The result was an enormous expansion of ritual, much of which may have had its origin in sympathetic magic, being designed to help the God to do His work. Every township had its shrine, where the services proper to the old Baal of the place were now rendered to Jahveh. There were greater sanctuaries of national importance, whither the devout might go on pilgrimage. A system of animal and other sacrifice sprang up, and in extreme cases of danger or distress even human sacrifice might be offered. At the critical seasons of the agricultural year, the beginning of the ploughing, the beginning and the end of the corn harvest, special festivals were held. With the shrines were associated other practices, such as the giving of tithes and sacramental immoralities, which were probably supposed to play their part in assuring the fertility of the soil. Apart from iniquities which thus actually sprang up in connexion with the ritual, the new religious order tended to stress ceremonial and to obscure the moral elements in the older desert faith. It was not that these were wholly forgotten; nothing was taken away from the old religion in practice, but there was little or no attempt to adapt the principles underlying the earlier morality to the new conditions. Jahveh was still concerned where He had been concerned before, but men failed to extend the range of His ethical interests to a multitude of situations which had not and could not have arisen in the pastoral life. Land with all its problems, and commerce with all its intricacies, were factors in the new life which had little or no parallel in the old, and Israel did not see that Jahveh had something of profound importance to say on these subjects.

Such was the general religious situation at the beginning of the reign of Jeroboam II. In the middle of the ninth century a protest from the desert had been raised by Elijah, and the memory of his actions alike in the matter of the Tyrian Baal and in the treatment of Naboth by Jezebel doubtless remained. But in the main there was no real improvement, until the Israelite world was startled by the portent of the appearance at Bethel of another man from the half-desert of the south, the great preacher of righteousness, Amos. Further discussion of his message will be found in the section of this book devoted to him; it is enough here to note that his main stress was laid on the demand of Jahveh for social justice as far as the outward life was concerned, whilst he went deeper below the surface and insisted on right and direct personal relations between people and God. Israel must seek *Him* if she would live.

Amos is followed by Hosea, who, taught by his own terrible experience, laid yet greater stress on a personal attitude, and added to the picture of the moral character of Jahveh the concept of what is commonly rendered in our versions as 'mercy'. A nearer identification would be 'love', the highest and best attitude of a personal soul towards other persons, whether divine or human. In Isaiah we have the main outline completed by the transfusion of the idea of 'holiness' with a moral quality. To Isaiah a thing cannot be holy unless it is ethically good, and Jahveh's conception of ethical goodness is at least as high as that dictated by the conscience of His people.

Any improvement in the general situation that may have been due to the work of the great eighth-century prophets (and we have direct evidence of none, unless we make a doubtful exception of the destruction of the bronze serpent, and a partially successful attempt to abolish the local sanctuaries by Hezekiah) was temporary and evanescent, and the accession of Josiah in

639 found things much as they had been in the days of Jeroboam II and Ahaz. The reign of Manasseh, the successor of Hezekiah, had brought reaction. Possibly there were political factors in the situation, and some of the features of which complaint must be made were due to the imperial policy of Nineveh, to which power Manasseh was tributary, but all accounts and traditions agree in associating his government with one of the darkest periods of Judah's history. But when in 626 the death of Ashur-bani-pal and the storms of the Scythian inroads weakened the Assyrian power, it seems as though in Judah for a time the spring might show itself after the long winter. In 621 the discovery of a law book in the Temple, during the progress of repairs to the fabric, gave the impetus to a fresh attempt to translate the principles of the eighth-century prophets into practical life. The document on which the reforms of Josiah were based is generally identified with Deuteronomy or a part of that volume, and if the account of Josiah's proceedings given in 2 Kings 22 and 23 is historically trustworthy, the identification seems sound. The Temple itself was purged of all that was inconsistent with the moral demands of Jahveh as expressed by Amos, Hosea, and Isaiah, the local sanctuaries were abolished, and some, at least, of them were defiled beyond purification. If worship were concentrated in Jerusalem, as seems to have been the aim of the authors of Deuteronomy, it would be possible for the better influences in the government to keep it comparatively pure. Moreover, the humane tone which runs all through this most striking legal code was bound to have some effect on men's attitude towards God and their neighbours. Nevertheless, in the long run, even these gains proved to be evanescent, and the permanent effect of the discovery of Deuteronomy was of a quite different kind. It introduced into Israel the conception of a book religion. Hitherto Jahveh had made His will known only through men with whom He was in one way or another closely associated—prophets, priests, and others. Now His will was visible in written form, and could be known and read of all men. The result was a tendency to stereotype religion, but this effect was not felt for some centuries in any serious way, and for the time there was certainly a sense of stability and

durability. Mohammed saw the Jews as 'the People of the Book', and though by his time that book was greatly extended, it is to Deuteronomy that later Judaism in the first instance owed the peculiar character which justified this title.

The same period witnessed the activity of two others of the prophets whose work formed real landmarks in the spiritual history of the world. The first of these was Jeremiah, whose call to the prophetic ministry is usually dated five years before the discovery of Deuteronomy. In theology he had, it is true, little to add to the ideas already expressed by his predecessors of a century earlier, but he had nevertheless a profound influence on later generations. His was a peculiar situation. He has shown us his heart and allowed us to see his own struggles. His worst experiences were not battles against powers outside of himself, though these were not lacking; they were in their essence an inward conflict of the spirit. He found himself standing alone with his God, cut off very largely from any form of human companionship, and sometimes feeling a sense of desertion and rejection by his God which rent his very soul. Through these struggles he, first of all Israelites, developed a real personal religion, quite different from the national, tribal, or communal religion of his own and earlier days. The human unit of religion was to him no longer Israel but the Israelite, and out of his agony sprang that great richness of personal faith and individual relationship to God which has marked the sainthood of both Judaism and Christianity. At the same time his direct knowledge of the failure even of the Deuteronomic reform led him to emend the principles on which the old Covenant was based. It could not be a mere *thing*. Written with pen or stylus on papyrus or clay, it was still only a 'scrap of paper'. For permanent validity and for final efficiency it must be written on men's hearts, and so Jeremiah forecasted in one of his latest utterances that truth whose full meaning emerged only on the night when Jesus after He had supped, took the cup, saying, 'This cup is the new covenant in my blood'.

The doctrine of the righteousness of Jahveh inevitably led to questions regarding the government of the universe of men.

Babylonian tablet inscribed with the names, pronunciations, and meaning of cuneiform characters. This dictionary was a copy written in the tenth year of Artaxerxes, 442 B.C.

Habakkuk was the first to state to himself the problem as to why wickedness is allowed to oppress righteousness. Jeremiah followed him, it is true, but the first impulse seems to have been that of the 'minor' prophet. The answer which Habakkuk found—'the righteous shall live by his fidelity'—could not be accepted as final; the question was repeated, discussed, and re-discussed. Amongst other results it led to the composition of such Psalms as 37 and 73, and, greatest of all human literary works, the Book of Job. In the long run it led Israel to an appreciation of a genuine life after death, and though the conception arose late in Israel, and suffered much from materialistic imperfections, it held its own, and in combination with the Greek view of immortality found its expression in the Christian hope.

It is not without reason, then, that we speak of these two centuries as being the turning-point in the history of the soul of Israel. She began them, as far as central Palestine was concerned, on a fairly high level of civilization and with a position of comparative material prosperity. She ended them with the northern portion of her people destroyed as a political entity, and the south in turn on the verge of political extinction. But at the start she stood no higher in religion and ethics than any one of a score of contemporary peoples. In 600 B.C. religious ideals and aspirations such as no other people has ever developed or cherished had been set before her. She had been told that God was a God of principle, righteous, loving, and holy, and that He demanded in men a likeness to Himself. It is true that she had not as a people accepted these truths or seriously endeavoured to work them into the fabric of her national life. So the blow fell, and Jerusalem suffered the fate of Samaria. But when the 'warfare' was over, and a remnant returned to their own land, it was the nobler and more distinctive elements in her faith and life which were found to have survived. Under the influence of the picture of God drawn by the great prophets, she was able to advance to a full monotheism, and to find her way to a personal faith in a truly *living* God.

INTRODUCTIONS AND NOTES TO SELECTED PASSAGES

THE BOOK OF KINGS

INTRODUCTION

§ 1. *Date and Place of Compilation*

A SUPERFICIAL glance at the closing verses of 2 Kings makes it clear that the whole compilation could not have reached its present form till fairly late in the period of the Exile. For the last event recorded is the liberation of Jehoiachin and his elevation to royal favour by Evil-Merodach (in Babylonian, Amel-marduk) in the first year of his reign, i. e. in 561 B. C. It is further clear that the notice of this event is later than the death of Jehoiachin, for in 2 Ki. 25^{29,30}, the deposed king is mentioned as eating at the table of the Babylonian monarch all the days of his life. At the same time there is no mention or hint of the prospect of the return from captivity, so that we may safely say that the book had practically reached its present form somewhere between 561 and 538. The same narrative renders it almost certain that the final work was produced in Babylonia by one of the exiled scribes.

But there are indications elsewhere which seem to suggest that the compilation of the main portion of the book took place somewhat earlier than the Exile. There are hints in one or two places, such as 1 Ki. 8^8, 9^{21}, which imply that Judah, at any rate, was still in Palestine in the writer's time. At the same time the whole work seems to have thrown over it the atmosphere of the Book of the Law (i. e. Deuteronomy or a portion of it) on which the reformation of Josiah was based. These two facts place this main compilation in the short period between 621 and 585. Further, there is reason strongly to suspect that the compiler was aware of the death of Josiah and even of the deportation of Jehoiachin. This brings his work down to the reign of Zedekiah. In that case it may be inferred that the book was completed and revised by the exilic editor to whom we owe the record of Jehoiachin's release from prison.

§2. *The Compiler's Sources of Information*

It is obvious that the main compiler of the book had access to records which were far older than his own day. Three of these are expressly quoted (the two latter several times), and consist of the official annals or records of (*a*) Solomon, (*b*) the kings of Judah, (*c*) the kings of Israel. It was the custom at ancient courts to appoint an official called a 'mazkir' (= 'remembrancer'), whose duty it was to record the more important events of each reign so that they might be handed down to later generations and not be forgotten. In the case of Israel and Judah these records themselves have perished, but they were clearly in the hands of the compiler of the Books of Kings, for he makes frequent mention of them. It may be assumed that the events which they included were chiefly political conspiracies, wars, important building operations, treaties, and the usual material of ordinary 'secular' history.

There are, however, a certain number of narratives which cannot with any degree of probability be attributed to the official records of the royal courts. These are mainly of two kinds. In the first place there is from time to time detailed information about the Temple at Jerusalem which, it seems, would most probably be derived from the priestly records of that Temple. And there are others which are concerned with various prophets, and appear to have been taken either from biographies of individual prophets or from a collection of narratives dealing with them as a class. That there were such collections is suggested by phenomena which appear when we study closely the prophetic books themselves, as well as from the evidences afforded by the Books of Kings. The three prophets concerning whom most information has been preserved here are Elijah, Elisha, and Isaiah. There are notices of many others, but in no other case has so much material been employed by the compiler. There may also have been other sources of information on which he drew to a lesser extent than on those already mentioned.

§3. *The Compiler's Method*

A modern historian in setting about his task gathers together such material as he needs, and absorbs it into his own mind, reproducing as much of the substance of earlier records as he thinks necessary for his purpose, but, unless he indicates borrowed passages by inverted commas, always employs language of his own. Where he is quoting, and often where he is referring to his sources, he will add foot-notes telling the reader what are the authorities for the statements he makes. This was not the method adopted in ancient times. A writer used to take what he found in older documents and reproduce it to a large extent verbatim, without acknowledging his debt to any predecessor. If he had two or more accounts of an event he would either place them side by side or would interweave them with one another, selecting sentences and phrases from both to form his finished whole. This seems to have been the method of the compiler of the Books of Kings, though it is a good deal more obvious in the Books of Chronicles. In the reign of Josiah it is not impossible that he depends to some extent on his memory of events which had taken place during his own lifetime, but for the earlier material he necessarily had to rely on what others had written before him.

An Egyptian scribe,
5th Dynasty.

It is a comparatively simple task to write the history of a single state, but the compiler of the Books of Kings was concerned with two. He had a choice of methods. One would have been to have written the two histories separately; the other to attempt some regular sequence which would carry the story of both kingdoms along together. He chose the latter method, and taking the two kingdoms in turn kept the account as far as possible level. He starts with Jeroboam I of Israel, tells the whole story of his reign, and then turns to Judah, whose fortunes he follows till he has dealt with the last of the kings of Judah who came to the throne during Jeroboam's lifetime. He then turns to Israel again and carries on the history to the death of the last king whose reign was to any extent contemporary with that of the last king of Israel mentioned. This method enables him to pursue the two histories as parallels, and goes far to give the effect of the story of a single people.

The compiler is careful as far as possible to synchronize the reigns of the different kings by a kind of chronological cross-reference. At the beginning of each reign he states the year of the particular sovereign of the sister kingdom in which that reign began. The result is that he has a formula and a framework for his narrative, which runs somewhat as follows :

'In the *x*th year of A, son of B, king of Israel (or Judah), began C, son of D, to reign over Judah (or Israel), and he reigned *y* years'.[1] In the case of the kings of Judah he also adds the name of the king's mother. Then follows the narrative —in most cases a short one—of the events which he thinks worth recording, and the narrative closes with a notice of the king's death and burial, and the name of his successor.

§4. *The Compiler's Theological Position*

It is practically impossible to write history without having a definite point of view, which in some historians may be so emphasized as to amount to a prejudice. This is clearly the case with the compiler of the Books of Kings. It is a striking fact that we owe our knowledge of several important political events in the history of Israel and Judah not to him but to foreign sources. From the Books of Kings we should never have guessed at a combination of the forces of Ahab and Benhadad, still less of their fighting a great battle with the Assyrians and evidently checking their progress. If these events were recorded in his sources at all, the compiler of the Books of Kings clearly did not feel that they were necessary to his presentation of the history of the people, and still more that of the religion of the people. For he views all events from the standpoint of his own theological position, which is in large measure that of the great prophets, and more particularly that which found expression in the reformation which took place under Josiah in the year 621. It has been generally held that the literary basis for this reform —the Book of the Law discovered by Hilkiah in the Temple— was Deuteronomy or a part of Deuteronomy. This still seems to be the most probable account of the facts, but inasmuch as there has been growing up in recent years a feeling that Deuteronomy should be connected with Ezra rather than with Josiah, it would not be wise to be absolutely positive on the point. At the same time there can be no doubt that the spirit and outlook of the compiler are identical with those of Deuteronomy, and that he belongs to the same school of thought— whether earlier or later. To him the first demand of the true religion of Israel is the centralization of worship in Jerusalem. In addition to the historical notes already mentioned, his 'framework' for each king includes a religious judgement on his

---

[1] These synchronistic notes are clearly the work of the compiler, and are derived from the figures he read in the official records, or the summaries he used. For a discussion of these last see Note on Chronology of the Period.

character and actions, and his principal criterion is the extent to which he believed each monarch did or did not conform to the principles which find expression in Deuteronomy. Thus the establishment of a separate sanctuary at Bethel—or rather, the maintenance of an older sanctuary and its elevation to the same rank as that of Jerusalem—by Jeroboam I was a religious crime of the most serious kind, and every one of the northern kings is condemned because 'he walked in the ways of Jeroboam the son of Nebat who made Israel to sin'. Some, it is true, are guilty of yet worse offences, especially those who accepted and cultivated the worship of foreign deities, but the primary sin was the sanctuary at Bethel. In the case of the kings of Judah a certain number are commended as having done that which was right in the sight of Jahveh, and it is a noticeable fact that some of these are especially mentioned as having still permitted the local cults to be maintained—'howbeit the high places were not taken away'. The ground of approval in these cases seems to be that whilst the kings in question—Asa is a good illustration— permitted others to use the old sanctuaries, they themselves confined their religious exercises to Jerusalem. A particular standard of excellence in the eyes of the historian is attained by kings like Hezekiah and Josiah who endeavoured to make their subjects conform to their own rule.

It is necessary to take careful notice of the compiler's standpoint, because otherwise there will be apparent contradictions in the narrative. In 2 Ki. 14^{24}, for instance, Jeroboam II is condemned in the usual way, whilst in vv. 26, 27 he is regarded as a God-given deliverer, and described in terms similar to those used of the older Judges. Clearly these last two verses are written before the fall of Samaria, and probably before the death of Jeroboam, for the kingdom fell almost immediately into that confusion which preceded the end. The compiler has simply repeated them from his source, and has recorded his own judgement independently.

It is this standpoint of the compiler's which gives to the Books of Kings their value from the religious standpoint. There is much recorded in them that a more educated conscience would regard with dislike or even with horror; an obvious illustration is provided by the methods Jehu employed to root out Baalism. Clearly the compiler had no historical sympathy; he made little or no allowance for the views and feelings of the times concerning which he wrote. It may safely be said that a number, at any rate, of those whom he condemned were entirely unconscious of anything wrong in the acts or thoughts. We must avoid falling

A 'High Place' at Petra, showing the altar, a natural
rock hewn into shape

Photograph by Fr. Vester & Co.

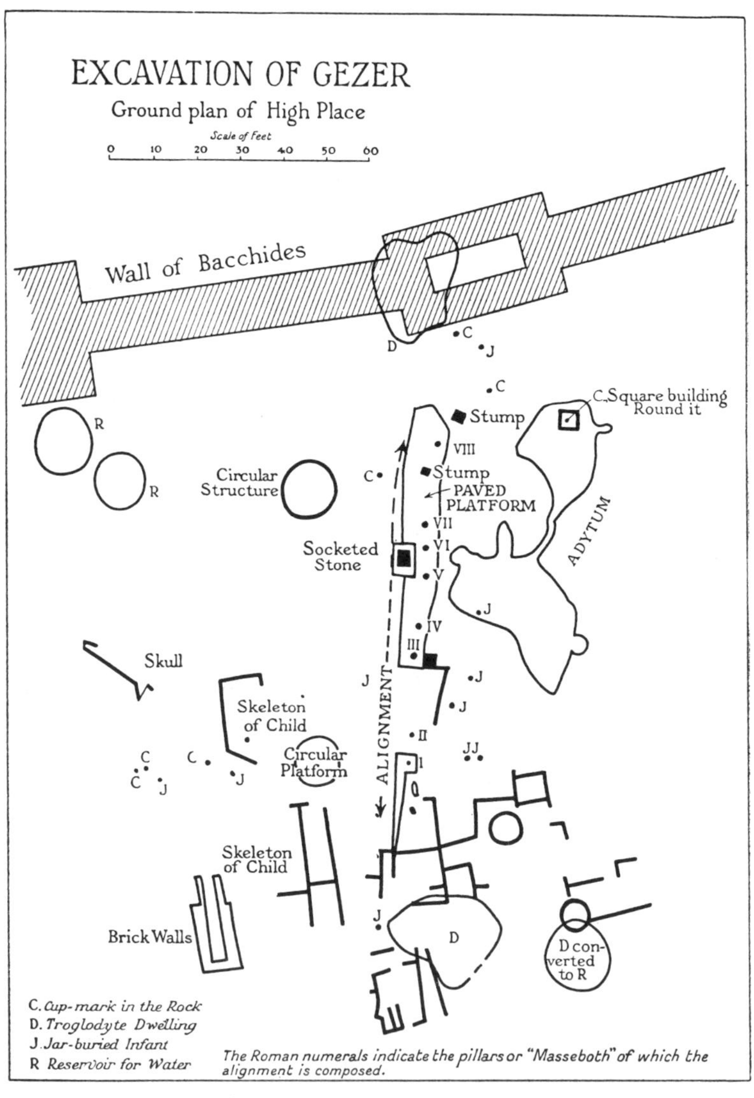

Reproduced by permission of the Palestine Exploration Funa

The ' alignment' in the ' High Place' excavated at Gezer.   It consists of a series of ' menhirs', and its position in the sanctuary can be seen in the plan on p 56.

Photograph by the Palestine Exploration Funa

into his error, and we must judge them in the light of their day and him in the light of his. Yet the fact that his views have been preserved for us is of inestimable value, for it helps us to see the more clearly the steady growth of that knowledge of God, that slow process of developing revelation to man which culminated in the life and death of Jesus.

NOTES ON 2 KINGS 14-25

14¹⁻²². *The Reign of Amaziah of Judah.*

The narrative begins with the usual formulas which have already been mentioned in the Introduction to the Books of Kings. The moral and religious judgement passed upon Amaziah is that he did that which was right, though with reservations. It would seem that for himself he refrained from using the local sanctuaries and was faithful to a comparatively pure form of cultus in Jerusalem. His error lay in permitting to others a licence which he did not exercise in person. The people still 'sacrificed and burnt incense in the high places'. The phraseology is that of the old sacrifice of communion, such as that which is mentioned in the first chapter of 1 Samuel. 'Sacrifice' denotes the slaughter of the animal, and it is to be noted that at this period the only occasion on which the Israelite was permitted to eat the flesh of one of his domestic animals was at such a sacrifice. 'Burning incense' is somewhat misleading to the modern ear. In all probability no 'incense' as we understand the term was used at all on these occasions, and the reference is to those portions of the victim that were burnt on the altar. As far as we can gather, the procedure at Israelite sanctuaries was somewhat as follows. The worshipper with his family came to the place, bringing their victim with them. The premises included not only the *debir*, or sanctuary proper, but courtyards and a certain number of rooms, probably arranged round an open space. The victim would be slain (probably by the worshipper) in an appointed place, the blood drained out of the body, the skin removed, the fat within the body taken away, and the rest of the carcass carried to one of the rooms for cooking. In this respect, as in one or two others, it is possible that the practice varied in different sanctuaries. As the flesh was being cut up and cooked the fat was burnt upon the altar. This was the share of the meal that was strictly appropriated to Jahveh, and being thus 'sublimated' by fire was supposed to be received by Him as 'a soothing savour unto Jahveh '.[1]   This done, the priest or his servant would go to the room in which the sacrificing family would now be gathered around the little stove on which a vessel containing the meat was cooking.   He would plunge a three-pronged fork into the vessel, and it was assumed that whatever clung to it was the portion assigned to him by Jahveh.   This he took away and ate at his leisure in his own quarters, probably inside an enclosure more sacred than that in which the worshippers' rooms were situated.   After his departure, when the food was ready, it would be served to all the members of the company gathered in the room by the head of the family, who thus had an opportunity of showing his affection to any of the circle to whom he might be especially attached by giving choice portions.   The company was not necessarily confined to a family, and we have references to occasions on which there was what we should call a municipal gathering.

Amaziah's abstention from such gatherings at the local sanctuaries was not his only virtue ; he also won the approval of the compiler by his treatment of his father's assassins.   That they themselves should be executed goes without saying, but the Oriental custom was to slay also the whole family of the criminals.   This Amaziah did not do, and his action is cited as an illustration of the principle laid down in Dt. 24[16].   There is little likelihood of his being acquainted with Deuteronomy itself, and this may be regarded as a further indication of the king's character.   His clemency was spontaneous, not enjoined on him by custom or law.

v. 7 records a victory of Amaziah over Edom in the ' valley of salt ', to the south of the Dead Sea.   This tribe had been more or less subject to Judah since the days of David, in the fashion of the age, that is to say, when Judah was strong enough she exercised authority over Edom, and at other times Edom was free to go her own way.   The occasional use of Ezion-geber (on the eastern arm of the Red Sea) by kings of Judah must have involved the subjection of Edom.   Jehoshaphat controlled the country, but in the confusion which followed the death of Ahaziah it is probable that the power of Judah was insufficient for her to maintain her hold, and a reconquest was necessary later.   The capture of Sela, the later Petra, must be held to involve the subjection of the whole country.

The narrative of the war between Israel and Judah described in vv. 8–14 is probably derived by the compiler, not from the annals of the kings of Judah, but from a northern source.   There is a tone of contempt

---

[1] For this name see p. 41.

in the way in which Amaziah is mentioned—shown especially in Jehoash's 'parable' (which must not be pressed too literally)—and the phrase 'which belongeth to Judah' in v. 11 is not likely to have occurred in the records of the Jerusalem court.   Further, Amaziah is said to have challenged Jehoash without any reason at all beyond his own desire to show his superiority.   It may well be, however, that in some sense Judah was subordinate to Israel, and that the challenge was an attempt to secure complete freedom.   Whatever the cause may have been, the issue was disastrous for Judah.   Amaziah was defeated at Beth-shemesh, situated on the edge of the Philistine plain.   He himself was taken prisoner and carried to Jerusalem.   The treasury and the Temple were plundered, and a section of the wall at the northeastern corner of the city was destroyed, so as to render it open to an army advancing from Israel.   This was the point where the natural defences of the city were weakest, and a wall was most necessary.

vv. 15-16 are practically identical with 13$^{12-13}$, and are clearly out of place in both connexions.   Their proper connexion is with the close of ch. 13, where the normal record of the reign of Jehoash ceases. They were introduced here probably in order to form an introduction to the compiler's note as to the length of time for which he believed Amaziah to have survived Jehoash.   This latter (v. 17) is probably not correct, and is the compiler's deduction from the figures which he had before him.[1]

The last few verses of this section describe the death of Amaziah, who fell through conspiracy as his father had done.   This happened several times in the history of the kingdom of Judah, and it is a noteworthy fact that it never involved a change in dynasty.   Whatever happened, southern Israel remained faithful to the house of David, and the compiler varies his formula in order to stress the fact of Azariah's popular election to the throne.   He also appends a note to the effect that Azariah was responsible for the recovery of Elath, the port on the eastern arm of the Red Sea near Ezion-Geber, whose place it seems to have taken in commercial importance.   As an important post Ezion-Geber is last mentioned in the days of Jehoshaphat. The compiler's reasons for placing this notice here instead of under the reign of Azariah are not clear.

14$^{23-28}$.   *The Reign of Jeroboam II of Israel.*

In accordance with his habit, the compiler now turns to a king of Israel whose reign, according to his chronological scheme, began

____

[1] See Note on Chronology of the Period.

before the death of Amaziah of Judah. This was Jeroboam II, whose accession marks the beginning of the last period of prosperity in the northern kingdom. The compiler explains this as the reward given to the house of Jehu for the extinction of the worship of the Tyrian Baal by that king, and quotes a certain Jonah, the son of Amittai, as having foretold the success of his family. The reference is to a narrative which has not been preserved by him in recording the reign of Jehu. It may be remarked here that the name of this prophet was used by the much later writer of the Book of Jonah in order to insist on the universal mission of Israel.

It will be noticed that we have here two judgements pronounced upon Jeroboam in the formula of introduction. One is favourable, and seems to have been taken from the annals of Israel, for it can hardly have been written after the death of Jeroboam. Here the king is described as a God-given deliverer, sent by Jahveh to rescue His people from the sufferings which had overwhelmed them. The language used of him recalls that applied to the Judges of the pre-monarchical period. The notice of him is brief, but it shows him to have been a successful warrior. His realms stretched before his death from Hamath in the far north to the Dead Sea ('the Sea of the Arabah '), and his conquests included Damascus and parts, at least, of Gilead. The 'recovery' of Damascus cannot mean more than the recognition by the Syrian king of the suzerainty of Israel.

15[1-7]. *The Reign of Azariah of Judah.*[1]

The popular election of Azariah to succeed his father Amaziah after the assassination of the latter has already been mentioned, together with a notice of his recovery of Elath on the Red Sea. The only event which the compiler records after the usual formal notice is the fact that in his later years he was afflicted with leprosy. The word rendered 'several' (Mg. 'lazar ') is quite uncertain. It seems to be connected with a root that ordinarily means freedom, but it is difficult to derive a suitable signification for the word here, and both the renderings in the R.V. are entirely conjectural.

During his illness his son Jotham became regent. The word 'judge' implies far more than the simple exercise of judicial functions. From

---

[1] It is only in the Books of Kings that this monarch is known by the name Azariah ; elsewhere he is always called Uzziah (except in 1 Chron. 8[12]), and various conjectures have been made as to the reason for the double name. It has been suggested, for instance, that, like Jehoiakim and Zedekiah, he assumed one or the other name on ascending the throne. In 2 Ki. 21[18] mention is made of a garden of Uzza, which may be an abbreviation of his name. But this is at best a mere possibility.

the point of view of the daily life of an Eastern community the settlement of disputes is one of the most important, if not the most important, duty of a ruler, and is taken as typical. But he who 'judged'
Israel must also have exercised practically all the functions of royalty,
including command of her armies in war. It is possible that Azariah
still had some control over the general policy of the people, but it may
be assumed that all the practical work which fell to a king was performed by Jotham during these years. The notice of Azariah's reign
closes with the usual formulas.

15⁸⁻¹². *The Reign of Zechariah of Israel.*

This notice contains little beyond the usual formulas and the statement that Zechariah fell by conspiracy. The Hebrew phrase represented by the phrase 'before the people' is obscure and unusual; it
can hardly mean 'in the presence of the people'. Probably the
words are due to textual corruption, and we should follow the LXX
in reading 'in Jibleam'. It is remarked that this reign, short as it
was, sufficed to fulfil the prophecy made to Jehu (mentioned in 10³⁰),
that four generations of his descendants should occupy the throne.
The four are of course Jehoahaz, Jehoash, Jeroboam, and Zechariah.

15¹³⁻¹⁶. *The Reign of Shallum of Israel.*

Except for the reign of Zimri, this is the shortest in the history of
Israel, and the only feature to be noted in it is the manner in which
it came to an end. It would seem that Menahem was in arms almost as
soon as Shallum, and was able to consolidate his power from his own
city of Tirzah. One other event in this rebellion is especially noted,
namely, the sack of a place which appears in the Hebrew text as
Tiphsah. But no such place is known from other sources, and it is
possible that this is a copyist's mistake for Tappuach, a town on the
borders of Ephraim and Manasseh. The cruelty ascribed to Menahem
is by no means abnormal in the East, and such acts have been perpetrated in modern as well as in ancient times.

15¹⁷⁻²². *The Reign of Menahem of Israel.*

The reign of Menahem possesses a sinister importance for the history of Israel, inasmuch as it saw the first dealings with an Assyrian
king that our Bibles record. We know from Assyrian records that
both Ahab and Jehu came into contact with Assyria, but in neither
case is the event recorded in the Books of Kings. Pul (Pulu) is an
alternative name for Tiglath-pileser III, assumed by him as king of
Babylon. This adoption of a separate name in relation to Babylon
was a sop to the national pride of that sensitive and rebellious people,

who were always amongst those most ready to rise against the power
of Assyria.   The exact reason stated for the payment of the tribute
is not clear.   The language used might imply that Tiglath-pileser
compelled him to pay it as the price of allowing Menahem to remain
on his throne, or it may mean that the latter approached the Assyrian
king near the beginning of his reign and offered this sum in return
for his support against possible rivals.   The latter view is reinforced
by the fact that when Menahem's son was murdered, the assassin

Typical weights.

(1) *A Babylonian duck weight, marked ' 8 '.* (2) *A mina weight,
inscribed by Nebuchadrezzar II, after the standard fixed by Dungi
about* 2300 B.C. (3) *An Assyrian lion weight, marked ' 5 '.*

Pekah, was clearly the head of an anti-Assyrian faction in Israel.   On
the other hand, the fact that the Assyrian army immediately withdrew, and the terms in which Tiglath-pileser himself refers to the
payment, strongly favour the former view.   The money was raised
by a poll-tax, placed on all men capable of bearing arms, amounting
to 50 shekels a head.   In weight of silver this would be roughly
equivalent to £5, but in purchasing power would be many times that
sum.   The words ' exacted . . . of ' represent a Hebrew phrase which
means literally ' brought out upon '.   Probably the text is corrupt, and
a very slight change would enable us to read ' demanded of '.

15^{23-26}. *The Reign of Pekahiah of Israel.*

Apart from the introductory and concluding formulas, the only reference is to the conspiracy by which Pekahiah lost his throne and his life. The phrase 'with Argob and Arieh' is very difficult to understand. The word rendered 'with' is more probably a preposition indicating the direct object of the verb, though this gives no meaning. Further, the word 'Arieh' means 'a lion', though of course it may have been the name of a place or of a person. 'Argob' is almost certainly a place name, indicating a district in Bashan, mentioned in Dt. 3^4, ^{13}, ^{14}, 1 Ki. 4^{13}, though it is not absolutely impossible that the word should have been used as the name of a person. It has been suggested that 'Arieh' (which has the article before it) is a corruption for 'Havvoth-jair' (see Dt. 3^{14}), and that the two names have been misplaced from v. 29, where they originally occurred in connexion with the places devastated by Tiglath-pileser.

It will be noticed that Pekah had connexions east of the Jordan, and this may explain his alliance with Damascus. It is even possible that it was in reliance on support from Damascus that he made his attempt on the throne.

15^{27-31}. *The Reign of Pekah of Israel.*

For the actual length of this reign see the Note on the Chronology of the Period. The reign is chiefly remembered as the time when the first captivity of Israel took place. Tiglath-pileser invaded northern Israel and carried off the inhabitants of all the district north of the Plain of Esdraelon. Ijon and Abel-beth-maacah have been identified with places lying in the hills to the north of the Lake of Huleh (the ancient Waters of Merom), Janoah seems to have lain farther west, on the slope of the mountains towards Tyre, whilst Kadesh and Hazor are in the neighbourhood of Lake Huleh. The mention of Gilead in this connexion is a little strange, and some have thought that the name was accidentally included in the text through its resemblance to 'Galilee'. In that case the names Argob and Arieh, now in v. 25, will originally have been a marginal note on the word Gilead here, added after the latter was inserted in the text. But whether the operations of Tiglath-pileser on this occasion included the districts east of the Jordan or not, it is clear that the population and territory of Israel were considerably reduced.

The narrative states that Pekah in turn met his death at the hands of an assassin, Hoshea by name. Tiglath-pileser himself claims to have put Pekah to death and to have placed Hoshea on his throne.

There is no real discrepancy between the two narratives, since Tig-lath-pileser's statement may mean no more than that he supported Hoshea in his revolt and confirmed him on the throne when it had been carried out.

The synchronistic note at the end of v. 30 is absent from some MSS. of the LXX, and may be the later addition of a careless scribe. It disagrees both with v. 33, which gives the reign of Jotham as lasting sixteen years only, and also with 17^1, which identifies the date of Hoshea's accession with the twelfth year of Ahaz. Whilst we must not rely too much on the detailed figures that have come down to us in our Hebrew Bibles, it is clear that the compiler can hardly have been responsible for so obvious a contradiction.

15^{32-38}. *The Reign of Jotham of Judah.*

The relation of Jotham's rule to that of his father has already been mentioned in connexion with the reign of Azariah, and a reference to the dating of the two kings will be found in the Note on the Chrono-logy of the Period. Two events are recorded in this reign. The first of these seems to have been taken from the royal annals, and is the building of an ' upper ' gate to the Temple. This seems to have been on the north side of the precincts, for there is no earlier reference to a gate in that direction, whilst such a gate is mentioned by Jeremiah (20^2).

The other notice appears to have been due to the compiler him-self, who states that it was in the reign of Jotham that the coalition of Rezin and Pekah began to threaten Judah. The necessary revision of the dates makes it unlikely that this was accurate as far as Pekah was concerned, for it seems probable that Jeroboam II was still on the throne when Jotham died. But it is not impossible that Rezin was already intriguing to form his anti-Assyrian alliance, and was trying to force Judah to join him.

16. *The Reign of Ahaz of Judah.*

16^{1-14}. *Introductory formula, with expansions.* On a series of kings of Judah, Joash, Amaziah, Azariah, and Jotham, the compiler passes a general approval. Ahaz, however, is condemned in unqualified terms. The reason is given in vv. 3, 4, which state that he followed the religious policy of the northern kingdom (i.e. apparently, that he worshipped a golden calf), and also the fact that he offered up his own son in sacrifice. It must be remembered that the compiler's judge-ments are based on a law which was unknown till the reign of Josiah, and what to him was an ' abomination ' may have been regarded as the highest act of piety in earlier days (cf. Mi. 6[7] where the prophet seems to think of human sacrifice as being no worse than animal sacrifice, though it is equally futile as a means of atoning for sin) The deity to whom Ahaz offered his son is not mentioned, and we are left to believe that this gift was made to Jahveh Himself. The story of the sacrifice of his son by Mesha king of Moab (3[27]) shows that the practice might still be carried out in times of extreme need, or when the ordinary rites proved ineffectual. The analogy of the same narrative suggests that such a need would most likely arise when a king was actually besieged by his enemies, and in danger of destruction. It is therefore not impossible that the event here recorded took place during the Syro-Ephraimite war, and was the means adopted by Ahaz for keeping off his enemies. It is perhaps worth noting that no account of any protest or condemnation of this action on the part of Isaiah has come down to us, though he must have been alive and working as a prophet at the time. Another of the religious crimes of Ahaz was that he not merely, like his immediate predecessors, failed to prohibit his subjects worshipping at the local sanctuaries, but that he himself took part in this worship— evidently in the eyes of the compiler a far more heinous offence.

16[5-9]. *The Syro-Ephraimite war.* Further details of the war are given in Is. 7[1-6]. From this passage it appears that the design of the confederates was to dethrone Ahaz and to set an Aramean named Ben Tabeal (Ben Tabeel?) in his place, thus securing the support of Judah against Tiglath-pileser. From both narratives it appears that the danger was for a time very serious, though both state that the actual assault on Jerusalem was a failure. But the conflict resulted in a real loss of territory to Judah, especially in the south. The account is somewhat confused, but it seems clear that in v. 6 the marginal reading 'Edomites' is correct instead of 'Aramaeans', i.e. 'Syrians'. The mistake is an easy one in Hebrew, being due to the similarity between the two letters ד and ר (D and R). But if that is so, then it seems also likely that 'the king of Syria' and 'to Syria' earlier in the same verse are mistakes for 'the king of Edom' and 'to Edom', and that the name of Rezin was only inserted in the text after the false reading had arisen. The weakness of Ahaz owing to the invasion would give the Edomites an opportunity of asserting their independence and recovering their seaport. But whether it was Syria or Edom who benefited, it is clear that the southern portion of his dominions, including his opening for the eastern and southern trade, was lost to the king of Judah.

vv. 7–9 describe the first direct contact between Judah and Assyria. In his anxiety and even despair, Ahaz sent tribute to Tiglath-pileser, with the request that he would come to the rescue of Jerusalem. This was an unnecessary step, since it is probable that the Syro-Ephraimite alliance was aimed in the first instance at resisting further Assyrian encroachment in the west, and the Assyrian king

A human sacrifice. A jar excavated at Gezer which was found to contain infant's bones.

Photograph by the Palestine Exploration Fund

must necessarily regard the alliance as a challenge. But as described by the historian of Judah the action of Ahaz was directly responsible for the invasion of Syria. It is curious that no notice is taken in this narrative of the attack on Samaria, and it has been suggested that the mention of the invasion is simply due to the desire of the compiler to give an historical setting for the changes which Ahaz introduced into the Temple ritual. This may be a part of the explanation, but it is also true that the captivity of Galilee has already been described in 15²⁹, and the compiler may have thought it unnecessary to repeat the information.

The site of Kir is not certainly known. A country or people of this name is mentioned in Is. 22⁶ in terms which suggest that it lay to the east of Mesopotamia, and it may have been this district which is intended. Amos mentions it as the original home of the Syrians (9⁷), and indicates it as the locality to which they will ultimately be carried away captive (1⁵). It is possible that the name was originally absent from the text of Kings and was introduced later from the text of Amos, for the LXX seems to have omitted the word here.

vv. 10-18 are devoted to ecclesiastical matters, which are described in some detail. Probably the preceding verses were taken from the royal annals and this narrative from the Temple documents which were in the hands of the compiler. Not merely did Ahaz pay a heavy tribute, but he was also compelled to meet Tiglath-pileser and offer homage to him in person at Damascus. Whilst there he saw an altar of a type which was new to him, and sent detailed specifications to Uriah the priest (also mentioned in Is. 8²) with instructions to have a similar one prepared by the time the king returned. The natural suggestion of the passage is that this was an altar dedicated to one of the gods of Damascus. But this is not necessarily the only or the correct deduction. Syria was now being reorganized as an Assyrian province, and there is reason to believe that in these circumstances one of the indications of the sovereignty of Assyria was the introduction of her own cult into the conquered land. It may well have been an altar of the god Ashur, erected after the subjugation of Damascus, which Ahaz saw and had copied, and it is not impossible that the worship of this god was actually introduced into Jerusalem. The principal difficulty in the way of this suggestion seems to be that Ahaz and his successors certainly offered sacrifice to Jahveh on the new altar, and neither Ashur nor Jahveh is likely to have been thought of as willing to share an altar with another deity.

The old altar was probably constructed by Solomon, though the record has not been preserved in the Book of Kings. 2 Chron. 4¹, however, describes such an altar, and the writer seems to be relying on some ancient and trustworthy source. The new altar was apparently of stone, if the verb 'build' has its usual meaning. Moreover, stress seems to be laid on the fact that the old altar was of bronze, whilst the material of the new one is not mentioned. It would appear, also, that the new was much larger than the old. The latter was removed from its position in front of the main Temple building, and placed on the north side. All sacrifices, whether those of the king or of his subjects, were in future offered on the new altar, the old one being reserved for purposes of divination.

This was not all. Ahaz was now tributary to Assyria, and this meant probably a large annual payment. Ordinary resources were insufficient to meet the demand, and further inroads had to be made. upon the Temple treasures. Such gold as there had been was already gone, but there were in the Temple great vessels of bronze which might serve the purpose. The chief of these were the great 'sea' and the ten lavers, constructed by Solomon. (Cf. 1 Ki. 7²³ ³⁹.) Whilst the articles themselves were indispensable for the service of the Temple, the bases on which they stood were very costly, and could be spared. Accordingly Ahaz removed the bases or wheeled stands on which the lavers were supported, and took the sea down from the oxen on which it had stood, placing it on a stone pavement. It may be remarked that the mention of the 'borders' in v. 17 is probably due to accidental insertion, for the Hebrew phrase represented by 'the borders of the bases' cannot be construed in that (or in any other) sense. Though it is not stated, it may be assumed from the last clause in v. 18 that the bronze was used in payment of the tribute. The first part of v. 18 is quite obscure. That there were some structural alterations made in the neighbourhood of the Temple and the royal palace may be taken for granted, but what exactly they were it is no longer possible for us to determine. The notice of the reign of Ahaz closes with the usual formula.

17. *The Reign of Hoshea of Israel and the Captivity of the North.*

vv. 1–6. *The historical narrative.* As has already been remarked (p. 20), the Assyrian empire was held together largely by the personality of its king, and the accession of a new monarch was commonly the signal for a revolt. So it would seem to have happened on the death of Tiglath-pileser in 727. Egypt was growing nervous about the possible advance of Assyria to her territories, and it was to her interest to stir up as much trouble as possible for the eastern power. The So (called by the Assyrians Sib'e) mentioned in v. 4 is either to be identified with Shabaka, or with a vassal king under Piankhi.

It is possible that the narratives in vv. 3–4 and 5–6 are derived from different sources. Shalmaneser V made only one campaign against Israel, but it is possible that he captured and imprisoned Hoshea early in its course, then undertaking that siege of Samaria which was not completed till after his death. Even so it is not easy to see how or why the city resisted for three years after the capture of its king, but the only alternative seems to be to substitute the figure twelve for nine in the reign of Hoshea. It seems certain that Tiglath-pileser placed him on the throne in 734, and that Samaria was taken in 722. The narrative of the fall of the city is told with customary brevity. It was captured and the inhabitants of Samaria were deported to various places in and beyond Mesopotamia, where they were ultimately absorbed into the general population.

vv. 7–23. *Theological explanation of the fate of Samaria.* It would seem that the larger part of this passage is due to the work of the exilic editor (see Introduction to the Books of Kings), but vv. 21–3, which attribute the calamities of Israel to the sins of Jeroboam I, seem to be due to the main compiler, who, as we have seen, is to be dated shortly before the captivity of Jerusalem. To him the sin was a double one, consisting on its political side in revolt from the legitimate dynasty, the house of David, and on its religious side (though the usual detail is not given here) in the establishment and worship of the golden bull at Bethel and Dan.

The exilic editor has a somewhat different, and indeed a broader outlook. To him all history is the result of a divine plan, with which the wills of men may conflict, but only to their own ultimate ruin. It is true that he has not that fully developed theory of a universal mission of Israel to the world whose best expression in the Old Testament is to be found in the Book of Jonah, but he does think of Jahveh as designing Israel to be His own peculiar people. They are to be distinct from all the nations of the world as Jahveh is distinct from all the gods. To this end He had rescued them from their Egyptian slavery, and had driven out their predecessors in the promised land. Yet instead of gratefully consecrating themselves to Him, they had followed the Canaanites in their abominable worship. The first feature of this apostasy was the breach of the Deuteronomic law of the single sanctuary. Every spot, whether it were the great fortified city or only a lonely watch tower, had its own shrine, with its sacred stone (E.V. 'pillar') and wooden post (R.V. 'Asherim'), where the local sacrifices were regularly offered. But they went further than this, and indulged in various forms of foreign worship, such as the cult of the stars and different forms of divination. They had had their warnings. Prophets had been sent to them from time to time—both Israel and Judah were involved, and indeed some of the sins were those of later Judah rather than of Israel—but men had taken no notice of them. The association between Jahveh and His people had been ratified by a solemn covenant, and of that they were reminded, but to no purpose. And at last the patience of Jahveh was exhausted, and He could no longer endure their iniquity; there was only one thing to be done with them, and that was done. They were carried away, and as a nation ceased to exist.[1]

A ' Maṣṣebah' or sacred stone pillar.

vv. 24–41. *The re-settlement of Canaan and the religious position of the colonists.* This section is clearly composite, and its various elements seem originally to have been entirely independent of one another. It is impossible to assign any of them with confidence to one or other of the familiar sources employed by the compiler. The first may have come from the annals of Judah, though that does not

---

[1] We ought, however, to guard against an impression that the land was completely depopulated. Probably the great mass of the country people remained, and other settlers were imported. There is evidence of a campaign of Sargon against Israel later than 722, and the great deportations do not seem to have taken place till the time of Ashur-bani-pal, in the middle of the seventh century.

appear very likely, whilst other historical statements have been drawn from sources which we can no longer in any way identify.

Of these different narratives, the first, in vv. 24-8, describes the importation of colonists from various places. Cuthah seems to have been situated in the north of Babylonia, to the north-east of the city of Babylon. The site of Avva is entirely unknown, but Hamath is possibly the well-known city in northern Syria and Sepharvaim may be either a place in the same district or a corrupt form of the name of the city of Sippar, near Babylon on the east bank of the Euphrates. It appears that the settlement was not made for nearly eighty years after the fall of Samaria, for these deportations were not likely to have taken place except after a revolt in the cities from which the settlers were taken. Ez. 4$^{8-10}$ speaks of Ashur-bani-pal ('Asnapper') as the king who was responsible for this step, and the most likely point in his reign was after the suppression of the great rebellion in which Babylon took a leading part in 648. By this time, the country, having been sparsely inhabited for several generations, would be largely overrun by wild beasts, so that the plague of lions is easily understood. But it was interpreted by the colonists as being due to the anger of Jahveh, the God of the land, who would insist on having proper worship paid to Him. Some such idea of the jealousy of a local deity may well, in earlier ages, have been to some extent responsible for the readiness with which Israel adopted the worship of the gods whom they found in Canaan at the Conquest. With this explanation of their troubles in mind, they sought to discover the 'manner'—a wide term, covering all that we understand by religious practices—of the God of the land, and Hebrew priests were brought for them from Assyria, to teach them how Jahveh should be worshipped. This is clearly an attempt to explain the origin of the Samaritan community.

A second narrative with the same object is contained in vv. 29-41. As it stands, this includes a theological section resembling vv. 7-20 in tone and language, but probably later still in composition, inasmuch as it refers to a written law, and not merely to the will of Jahveh communicated by prophets. It is hardly suitable to its present position, for it deals, not with the sins of the new settlers, but with those of the Israelites whose place they had taken. This section extends from the middle of v. 34 ('they fear not the Lord . . .') to v. 40, and seems to have been slightly adapted at the beginning, and possibly the end, to its present position.

Omitting these verses, it will be seen that the countries mentioned

are identical with those of v. 24, except that the name Cuthah is spelt
Cuth. But most of the gods are as yet unknown from other sources.
The only one whose name has appeared on any known inscription is
Nergal, the god of Cuth, who was widely revered in Babylonia, as
appears from the frequency with which his name is used in men's
names. Succoth Benoth has been connected with a name of the
goddess Belit or Ishtar, but Babylonians might be expected to
worship Marduk. No references to any of the others have yet
been noted. For their cult and ritual the new-comers used the old
sanctuaries which had been left by the Samaritans, and employed by
them in the worship of Jahveh. There is a contemptuous note in
the mention of 'priests from among themselves', which is clearly
a reference to the priests of the later Samaritan worship. This was
regarded by later orthodox Jews as entirely illegitimate, and the
writer evidently desired to emphasize the irregularity of their position.
At the same time he has to admit that they did adopt the worship of
Jahveh, though he insists that they combined with it a maintenance
of their former religion, without attempting to explain how they came
to combine the two. The whole of the narrative of vv. 29-41 seems
to be later than that of vv. 24-8, on which it may possibly be based,
and to date from a time when deep hostility was felt by strict Jews
of Jerusalem and Judea towards the Samaritan race and religion.

18-20. *The Reign of Hezekiah of Judah.*

The greater part of this section appears again in Is. 36-9. The
opening verses (1-12 and the section vv. 14-16) in 2 Ki. 18 do not
appear in Isaiah, which, however, includes a Psalm of Hezekiah
(38^{9-20}) which is not found in the Book of Kings. The similarities
between the two are so close elsewhere as to make it practically
impossible that they should be independent of one another, and in
particular there are notices common to the two which seem to be
due to the compiler of the Book of Kings. This and other features
render it extremely probable that the final editor of the Book of
Isaiah included this matter from the Book of Kings. The original
source whence the compiler of Kings drew it can hardly have been
either the royal annals or the Temple records, and was probably
a collection of narratives about Isaiah similar to those which gathered
round the name of Elijah and Elisha. Such collections seem to have
been not uncommon; there was certainly one which dealt with
Jeremiah, though no portion of it was utilized by the compiler of
Kings. The three principal subjects mentioned are (*a*) the invasion

of Sennacherib, (*b*) Hezekiah's sickness, (*c*) the embassy of Merodach-baladan. It is probable that these are no longer in their original chronological order, for there is reason to suspect that the embassy of Merodach-baladan was connected with the western revolt which led to the invasion of Sennacherib.

18[1–8]. The introductory formula is longer for Hezekiah than for any other king, because the historian feels it necessary to explain the reasons why so favourable a judgement was passed upon him. The theological outlook of the compiler is well illustrated by the events which he singles out for special mention. Hezekiah undertook a complete religious reform, anticipating in some ways that carried through by Josiah a century later. The first step, and in the eyes of the compiler the most important one, was the abolition of the local sanctuaries and the concentration of worship in Jerusalem. The failure to do this is mentioned in several cases as being the one religious blot in the career of several kings who otherwise win approval. A more interesting detail is the destruction of the bronze serpent, whose origin was ascribed to Moses. This seems to have been an ancient object of reverence, and was probably associated with Jahveh Himself. The narrative referred to is to be found in Num. 21[4 ff], where it is worth noting that the species of serpent mentioned as being represented by this bronze figure was that known as the 'saraph'. This, it will be remembered, is the name given by Isaiah to the attendants of Jahveh whom he saw in his great vision in the Temple. The word 'saraph', however, is not applied to it in the present passage, the more general term 'serpent' being employed. All things considered, it would seem that no objection was felt, till the time of Hezekiah, to the worship of this emblem of Jahveh, and it is interesting to find that we have no record of any protest made by Isaiah against its use. As has been suggested elsewhere, whilst there is no reason to doubt Hezekiah's religious honesty or his genuine zeal for purity in ritual, it is at the same time possible that there was a political element in the reform, and that it was in some way connected with his attempt to throw off the yoke of Assyria.

The religious theory of the compiler's time, based on the prophetic doctrine that sin is always punished and righteousness always rewarded in this life, demanded that Hezekiah should receive the appropriate blessing for his conduct. Accordingly the compiler commits himself to the statement that Hezekiah was successful in all his undertakings. Two instances are quoted, one being the rebellion against Assyria, and the other a victorious war against the

Serpent worship
The Goddess Uatchet worshipped under the form of a serpent
By permission of Sir Wallis Budge and Messrs. Methuen

Philistines. It is possible that there is some connexion between
the two. We know that Hezekiah was one of the leaders of the revolt
against Assyria, and that one feature of that revolt was the removal
by force of all the Assyrian governors and vassal kings from the
Philistine cities. It is quite likely that it was an expedition undertaken in this connexion that is alluded to in v. 8. The 'success' of
both these undertakings must be held to be very doubtful. Certainly
Hezekiah escaped with his life and his crown from the Assyrian
invasion, but his country was terribly desolated and he himself, after
suffering a severe siege, wascom pelled to pay an enormous tribute.

18$^{1-12}$ repeat shortly the story of the fall of Samaria. They add
nothing to what has already been said on the subject, except to give
a couple of synchronistic notes. Allusion has already been made to
difficulties which arise on these points, and a discussion of the whole
question will be found in the separate Note on the Chronology of the
Period.

18^{13}**–19**^{35}. *Sennacherib and Judah.* There is a famous inscription of
Sennacherib, describing the events of the first eight years of his
reign. He came to the throne on the sudden death of Sargon in 705,
and his first expedition (against Babylon) was undertaken in the
year 703. He describes this and the expedition of his second year
(703–702) against the Aramaean tribes east of the Tigris and peoples
in the Median hills, and then continues :

'*In my third expedition I went to the country of the Hittites. Luli,
king of Sidon, was cast down by fear of my royal brilliance, and fled
afar into the midst of the sea and died. The greater Sidon, the lesser Sidon,
Bit-zitti, Zarephath, Mahaliba, Ushu, Aksib, Akko, his strong fortified
cities, where were also pasture and water, his fortified towns the terror of
the arms of Asshur overthrew, and he cast himself at my feet. Tuba'lu
I placed on his royal throne, and tribute, yearly tribute, gifts to my majesty,
I imposed upon him for the fourth time. All the kings of the Amorites
brought rich presents, great gifts, before me, and kissed my feet. And
Zidkah, king of Ashkelon, who had not submitted to my yoke, the gods of
his father's house, himself, his wife, his sons, his daughters, his brothers,
I carried away and brought to the country of Asshur. Sarru-ludari,
son of Rukibti, its former king, I set over the men of Ashkelon, and gifts
of tribute, my royal presents, I laid upon him, and he bore my yoke. In the
course of my expedition, Beth-dagan, Joppa, Banaibarka, Azuru, Zidkah's
cities, which did not hasten to fall at my feet, I besieged, took and utterly
despoiled. The governors, princes and men of Ekron, who had thrown*

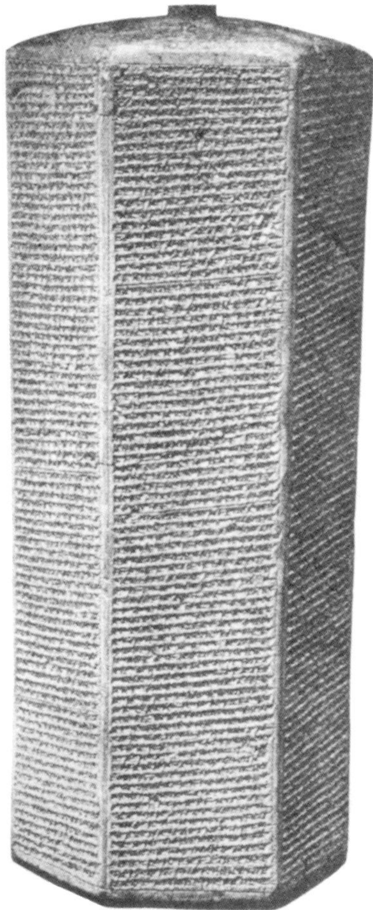

*The cylinder recording the early campaigns of
Sennacherib from which the passage
quoted on pp. 76–8 is taken*

Padi, their king and the sworn ally of the land of Assyria, into chains of iron and handed him over to Hezekiah of Judah . . . their heart was afraid. They called on the kings of Egypt, the bowmen, chariots and horses of the country of Ethiopia, forces without number, and they went to their help. In the district of Eltekeh they set themselves in array against me. . . . The charioteers and the sons of the king of Egypt, together with the charioteers of the king of Ethiopia, my hands captured alive in the battle. Eltekeh and Tamnâ I took and utterly destroyed. To Ekron I drew near, and the governors and princes who had committed sin I slew, and their corpses I lifted up and bound upon stakes. The children of the place who had committed iniquity I counted as spoil. The rest of them who had not committed sin and wrong, whose guilt was not proved, I ordered to be released. Padi their king I took from the midst of Jerusalem, and set him on his royal throne, and my royal tribute I imposed upon him. And Hezekiah of Judah, who had not bowed beneath my yoke, 46 of his strong cities and numberless small towns in their neighbourhood I besieged and took. 200,150 men, many children, male and female, horses, beasts of burden, sheep, camels, cattle and flocks without number I took from them and accounted as spoil. Himself I shut up in Jerusalem, his royal city, like a caged bird ; strong forts against him I built. His towns which I had spoiled I took from his country and gave them to Mitinti, king of Ashdod, Padi, king of Ekron, and Sil-Bel, king of Gaza, and made his country small. To the former tribute gifts, my royal presents, I added tribute, ana laid it upon him. As for Hezekiah himself, the fear of my royal armies cast him down. . . . I had brought after me to Nineveh, my royal city, 30 talents of gold, 800 talents of silver, . . . beds of ivory, thrones, stools of ivory, elephants' skins and teeth, ebony . . . . to pay tribute and to do obeisance he dispatched his messengers.'

This is a consistent narrative, and, allowing for the somewhat bombastic royal Assyrian style, may be taken as fairly representing the course of events in 701 from the point of view of Sennacherib. In the Book of Kings, on the other hand, we have three separate narratives, of which the two latter are of some length and have a certain number of phrases in common. They are difficult to harmonize alike with one another and with the Assyrian record, if they all refer to the same series of events. But it is possible that the last has in view a different expedition, said to have been undertaken against Egypt in the year 690, of which very few details survive on the Assyrian side, perhaps owing to the fact that it ended in disaster.

18[12-16] form the first of the three, and this narrative seems to have been taken from the annals of Judah. The date in v. 13 is hardly

ASSYRIANS BESIEGING A CITY

Photograph by Giraudon from the bas-relief in the British Museum

correct. Sennacherib came to the throne in 705, seventeen years
after the fall of Samaria. This last event took place, according to
v. 10, in the sixth year of Hezekiah's reign, which would place the
accession of Sennacherib in the twenty-third year and the expedition to Palestine in the twenty-seventh.[1] The narrative states that
Hezekiah made his submission before Jerusalem was attacked while
Sennacherib was at Lachish, in the district in which Ashkelon stood.
This is quite consistent with Sennacherib's account, which makes
Ashkelon his principal objective. He does not say that he took
Jerusalem, and the language which he uses suggests that Hezekiah
offered to surrender before he was actually attacked. The two
accounts agree in one small detail ; the tribute offered by Hezekiah
included a sum of eighty talents of gold. Part of the money was pro-
cured by stripping the doors of the Temple. It may be worth noting the
three stages in the spoliation of the Temple. Joash had handed over
to Hazael, king of Damascus, the votive offerings in the Temple (12^{19}),
Ahaz had surrendered some of the furniture of the outer court, and
now Hezekiah removed a portion of the treasure of the sacred building
itself.

18^{17}–19^8 form the second narrative. This possibly refers to the
same events as those which are briefly described in vv. 14–16.
Sennacherib sent a detachment from Lachish, apparently less to
undertake a siege of Jerusalem than to try to frighten Hezekiah into
submission. He placed in command of it Rabshakeh, and the text
of Kings adds Tartan and Rabsaris. All three are official titles, the
Rabshakeh being a high military official, the Tartan the commander-
in-chief, and the Rabsaris the chief of the eunuchs. Though all are
mentioned in the text of v. 17, it is only the first who takes any
prominent part in the proceedings, and it is at least possible that the
other two names have been inserted in the text by a learned scribe
who was familiar with the Assyrian court and its officials. In the
same way the words 'and they went up and came to Jerusalem' are
absent from Isaiah and several ancient authorities for Kings, and are
probably due to accidental repetition of words already in the text.
Probably, then, the verse should run : 'And the king of Assyria sent
Rabshakeh from Lachish to King Hezekiah with a great army to
Jerusalem. And he went up and came and stood . . .' The 'upper
pool' is generally identified with a pool known as the *Birket Mamilla*
less than a quarter of a mile from the ancient wall of the city. There

---

[1] For further discussion of the details see the Note on Chronology of the Period.

THE POOL OF HEZEKIAH

Photograph by Fr. Vester & Co.

he was met by a group of officials, Eliakim, governor of the palace—practically the Prime Minister or Grand Vizier, Shebna, the chief royal secretary, and Joah, the Recorder. The two former are mentioned in Is. 22$^{15-25}$, a passage in which the prophet denounces Shebna, who was a foreigner, and at that time held the office assigned to Eliakim in the present passage, and foretells that he will be succeeded by Eliakim. The connexion between the two is difficult to establish, but on the face of it Shebna would seem to have been degraded to a lower office before the Assyrian invasion. At the same time it is not clear that a dismissed minister in an Oriental monarchy would be likely to secure any post at all after his removal from office. Isaiah does not seem to have regarded him as a man of the best character, and denounced him for the extravagance of the tomb which he had prepared for himself and for his ostentatious use of chariots.

Through these three men the Rabshakeh sent Hezekiah a message. It is an attempt to make Hezekiah realize the weakness of his position. He has no adequate military resources of his own—Rabshakeh is ready to make a wager on that point; he cannot trust Egypt, for Egypt is unreliable and dangerous to her own allies (this, as the history of Judah showed, was only too true); he cannot place his confidence in Jahveh, for he has destroyed Jahveh's sanctuaries throughout the land. Indeed the Assyrians have come at Jahveh's call to avenge the insult done to Him by the centralization of worship in Jerusalem. Such claims were not uncommon on the part of conquerors, and nearly two hundred years later when Cyrus took Babylon he asserted that he came as the champion of the city's gods.

The Rabshakeh spoke in Hebrew—'Jewish' as they called it—which every one on the walls would understand. The envoys begged him to speak in Aramaic, the common language of diplomacy and commerce for centuries, from Mesopotamia to the Sudan, as extant letters and inscriptions show. It had taken the place of the Babylonian tongue which was used for this purpose in the days of Abraham, and was in turn supplanted by Greek after the conquests of Alexander. This led the Assyrian to make an appeal to the people at large, exhorting them to desert, and warning them of the privations of a siege. Again he insists that there is no hope to be derived from their religion, for no other gods have yet been able to save their respective peoples. Of the illustrations quoted, Hamath had fallen in 720, Arpad (not far from the modern Aleppo) in 743-740. Sepharvaim (if the identification with Sippara be correct) had been repeatedly taken by Assyrian armies. Hena and Ivva are quite unknown, unless the latter is to be identified with the Avva of $17^{25,\ 31}$, and even so we are completely ignorant of its position. Inasmuch as it is unlikely that even the Rabshakeh would have suggested that the gods of these places could have been interested in Samaria, it looks as though some words had fallen out near the end of v. 34, and the LXX may be right in reading 'where are the gods of Samaria' immediately before 'have they delivered Samaria out of my hand?'

This speech met with no response, Hezekiah's orders on this point being fully obeyed, and the messengers returned to the king. On hearing what had passed, he, with every sign of mourning, had recourse to Isaiah. This is characteristic of these narratives of the prophets, which often place the inspired man in a position of respect and authority. The coming of Jehoahaz to Elisha during the siege of Samaria by the Assyrians (ch. 6^{32}–7^2) and Zedekiah's consultation of Jeremiah (Jer. $37^{17\ ff.}$, $38^{14\ ff.}$) are other illustrations of the same tendency. The prophet's reply is that there is nothing to be afraid of, for Sennacherib will be compelled to return to Assyria by a 'rumour'. The use of the word 'spirit' in this connexion suggests that what Sennacherib is to hear is some direct intimation from Jahveh, not a message conveyed by men. It is idle to guess at its purport. The prophecy that he should die by violence was indeed fulfilled, but not till twenty years after the date to which the prophecy is assigned. By the time that Rabshakeh reached him he had left Lachish and gone to Libnah. The site of this latter town has not been identified with certainty, but from a reference in Jos. 15^{42} it was clearly somewhere in the Judaean Shephelah, and apparently not far from Mareshah, the home of Micah. Neither this town nor Lachish is mentioned by Sennacherib ; possibly both were amongst the forty-six cities of Judah which he destroyed.

The remainder of ch. 19 is occupied with a second account of an invasion of Judah. It differs from the first account in several respects. In the first place, the invasion is stated to be due not to rebellion on the part of Hezekiah, but to a northward movement of Tirhakah, king of Ethiopia. In the second place, instead of a force supporting officials who carried a verbal message, a letter is sent. (It would seem that the first words of v. 10 are due to the compiler.) Apparently the narrative has been somewhat shortened at the beginning, for it is not likely that it opened as abruptly as v. 9 does. It is thus extremely difficult to identify the two expeditions, especially when it is realized that the earliest date at which it is possible to place the accession of

Tirhakah to the Egyptian thronc is 693. Consequently, it is better to assume a second invasion of Sennacherib, between the years 690 and 681. Perhaps, however, the name of Tirhakah has been introduced by accident into the text, and the Egyptian king in question was really Shabaka. In that case it would be possible for us to assume that the two expeditions were really the same, and that the two descriptions come from different sources.[1] Assyrian references to the last years of Sennacherib appear to be incomplete.

The substance of Sennacherib's letter is similar to the argument used by the Rabshakeh in his address to the people of Jerusalem; other gods had not been able to protect their cities, how should the God of Israel? It is quite probable that the list of places mentioned is due to the compiler. All four are in the upper basin of the Euphrates, though the last is somewhat difficult to identify exactly, as it seems to have been the habitat of a semi-nomadic tribe. All had been included in the Assyrian empire from the tenth century onwards, except that it was found necessary to reconquer the 'children of Eden' in the ninth century. The other places mentioned in v. 13 were conquered by Sennacherib himself, and appear also in 18^{34}.

It will be noted that in this narrative the king does not send to Isaiah, but prays over the letter in the Temple. The actual language which is attributed to Hezekiah suggests the thought of a much later period, and it may be doubted whether he thought of Jahveh as the only God. He might regard Him as the most powerful of all, but such a doctrine is not monotheism. Even though He is thus the universal God, He still dwells upon the ark 'between the cherubim' or 'upon the cherubim' (the Hebrew construction is ambiguous; the latter is the more probable rendering). The cherubim appear to have resembled the composite creatures which are found represented in various portions of the ancient world. They had animal bodies, human heads, and eagle's wings, though it is possible that the conception varied from one period of art to another. They were probably Babylonian in origin, and the name they bear is certainly not Hebrew. They appear as performing two functions. On the one hand they have a position in relation to the Ark, over which their outstretched wings met (1 Ki. 6^{23-28}), and on the other hand the beings they represented formed the car on which Jahveh moved from place to place (Ezek. $1^{5\,ff.}$).

The reply was sent through Isaiah, and is combined with a poem,

---

[1] Compare Box's note : *Isaiah*, p. 146.

or rather with two, since vv. 29-31 seem to be separate from vv. 21–8. In all probability this should not be regarded as the original answer given by the prophet. A long poem of this kind is very unusual in the writings of the prophets, and is generally to be treated as a later composition inserted in the text by an editor. The real reply—or the substance of it—is to be found in vv. 32-4, and an oracle of Isaiah's may also have been preserved in vv. 29-31. The former section has points of resemblance with the great 'taunt-song' now preserved in Is. 14, which also is not generally held to be the work of Isaiah. Both are songs of exultation over the fall of a powerful enemy. If this is Isaiah's, it was probably not strictly an oracle or prophetic utterance, but a poem composed by the prophet after the departure of Sennacherib.

The rhythm of the poem is what is commonly known as ' Ḳinah ', i. e. an arrangement in which lines of four stresses interchange with lines of five. The latter usually predominate, and there seems to be no regularity in the combination of the two. It is possible that the whole has been worked over by editors or copyists, though the fact that it appears in the parallel passage in Isaiah (37^{22} ^{29}) shows that it was included in 2 Kings at an early period.

The poem opens with the scorn of Jerusalem, personified as a woman (this is the force of the phrase 'daughter of Zion'), for her enemy. He has made a mistake, and the God whom he has challenged is not the feeble deity of an ordinary people, such as those whom Sennacherib enumerated in his letter. In his pride the Assyrian has devastated Lebanon, the great storehouse for timber in western Asia. v. 24 suggests that an expedition to Egypt was also in prospect, and this may have been the case, even though it was not carried out till the reign of Esarhaddon. In v. 25 the poet begins a statement of his philosophy of history. The great mistake of the enemy has been that she supposed that her conquests were won by her own determination. This is not so ; all that has happened has been in accordance with the definite plan of Jahveh. He meant Assyria to conquer ; therefore she has conquered, and her opponents have had no strength to meet her. They have been as grass on the house-top, or as a field (so read in v. 26 instead of ' corn blasted ') before the east wind (a very probable correction for ' before it groweth up '. This is itself a conjectural reading ; the Hebrew has a phrase which is practically meaningless, ' before the stalk '.) All through Jahveh has known what the tyrant was doing, and his careless arrogance has met with the reward that was due to it. Now that Jahveh's purpose is fulfilled, the Assyrian will be removed.   He is no more than a half-tamed beast, who has done his work and now has to be taken back with hook and bridle to its stall.   The aim of the poem is to illustrate from actual history that supremacy of Jahveh in human affairs which was constantly urged by the prophets.

vv. 29-31 give a 'sign' to Hezekiah.   This is not a miracle that proves the power of Jahveh, it is something that will come to pass in the near future, when men will be able to recognize that Jahveh and Jahveh's prophet had foreseen and foretold the course of events.   It is clear that though Jerusalem was untouched, the countryside had been laid desolate.   The Assyrians have come before the harvest and destroyed the crops.   They have left too late for ploughing and organized sowing to be done, so it will only be in the third year that it will be possible for men to reap the fields and to resume the normal methods of life.   But the distress will last no longer than this, and soon Judah will be at peace.

vv. 32-4 give another answer, but to the same effect.   Jerusalem itself will remain untouched, whatever happens to the surrounding country, for before any effective assault can be arranged upon the city, Jahveh will interfere to save her.

The nature of that interference is explained in vv. 35-7.   The precise course of events has never been fully explained.   Sennacherib makes no reference to a disaster in Palestine, but this is not unnatural, and cannot be regarded as final evidence.   There is in Herodotus (II, 141) a story to the effect that he met the Egyptians in battle, and that an army of mice (rats?) gnawed the Assyrian bowstrings the night before and so brought about their defeat.   This, in combination with the Biblical account, has suggested to some scholars that the Assyrian army was attacked in Philistia by bubonic plague (always associated with rats, in modern as well as in ancient times), and was so swiftly devastated that it was found necessary to retreat. Sennacherib was assassinated in Babylon in 681.

20^{1-11} contain a narrative of Hezekiah's sickness and recovery.   It appears in a somewhat shorter form in Is. 38^{1-8}.   From this account the following portions are absent: The first part of v. 4, which in Isaiah begins 'The word of the Lord came to Isaiah'; from v. 5 the words 'the prince of my people' and 'I will heal thee: on the third day thou shalt go up to the house of the Lord'; from v. 6 'for mine own sake and for my servant David's sake'.   The story of the miracle

is greatly simplified and runs on with Isaiah's message, 'behold,
I will cause the shadow on the steps, which is gone down on the dial
of Ahaz with the sun, to return backward ten steps. So the sun
returned ten steps on the dial of Ahaz.' Finally, there is no reference
in Isaiah to the cure by means of a cake of figs.[1] In addition to these
variations in the text common to the two accounts, the Book of Isaiah
adds a Psalm appropriate to Hezekiah's condition.

The question of the relation between the two texts is a difficult one.
The prevailing opinion seems to be that the account in the Book of
Kings is an expansion, and that the earlier form was that to be found
in Isaiah. But it does not follow that this is necessarily the sounder
view, for though the narrative in Isaiah is smooth enough, it does
suggest contraction. In particular, the cake of figs incident has the
appearance of being primitive in the story, although the extended
conversation between the prophet and the king is probably redactional,
i. e. due to an editor. It is not likely that anybody would state cate-
gorically 'this shall be the sign unto thee . . .' and then proceed to
ask what sign would be preferred.

It is difficult even to guess at the date of this event. The mention
of fifteen years in v. 6 suggests that it took place either in 711 or in
701. In both years there was danger from Assyria. Sargon was in
Palestine in 711, and in the course of his expedition took and sacked
Ashdod (cf. Is. 20[1]), whilst his great attack on Judah was made in 701.
It is also hardly possible to identify the disease from which Hezekiah
suffered. Bubonic plague has been suggested, but there is no mention of an epidemic—the form which this disease usually takes.

The story is a simple one. Isaiah is sent to Hezekiah to tell him
that his sickness is fatal. The king meets the news with tears and
prayer, for to ancient Israel there was no hope beyond the grave, and
the best for which a man could look was a long and prosperous life
on earth. Isaiah left him, but had hardly reached the middle court
(the marginal reading of the R.V. is almost certainly correct here)
when he was bidden to return and announce a reprieve. To this is
added a promise of safety from the Assyrians. Then (and the incident is surely more in place in the Isaianic form of the narrative?) the
prophet gives Hezekiah a choice between two 'signs'. Shall the sun
go forward or backward on the 'steps' of Ahaz (possibly some form

---

[1] For an exegetical commentary on the passage the reader is especially
referred to Sir G. A. Smith's chapter in the *Expositor's Bible* on Isaiah, entitled
'An Old Testament Believer's Sickbed; the Difference Christ has made'
(ch. xxv).

of sun-dial, on which the length of the shadow was measured by steps).
Hezekiah feels that the latter would be the more miraculous, and
chooses it — an interesting light on the ancient mind, for both would
seem equally impossible to a modern observer.   This is accordingly
done.

20$^{12-19}$ give the story of the embassy of Merodach-baladan (so read
in accordance with the text in Isaiah ; the name in Babylonian appears
as Marduk-apal-iddina) of Babylon to Hezekiah.   The occasion here
stated is the recovery of Hezekiah from his sickness, but it is much
more probable that this was merely a pretext.   Merodach-baladan
was one of the bitterest enemies that Assyria ever had.   Twice he
rebelled against Sargon (in 721 and 710) and, though treated with
unusual leniency, was again in arms against Sennacherib in 702.   It
may well be that in 705 he sent to Hezekiah to try to persuade him
to make trouble for Sennacherib in the west.   The embassy can
hardly be connected with the events of 702-701, for by that time
Merodach-baladan had been finally overthrown.

Whatever be the actual cause of the visit, the Babylonians were
allowed to inspect the whole resources of the kingdom, and the narrative continues with an account of Isaiah's condemnation of his recep-
tion.   The words put into his mouth are a prophecy of the final
captivity of Jerusalem which is to be carried out by the Babylonians.
There is no parallel of any kind to such a prophecy on the part of
Isaiah, and this may be the interpretation placed on Isaiah's protest
by the compiler.   The extract from the prophetic annals ends with a
promise that the disaster will be postponed till after Hezekiah's death
in recognition of his piety and fidelity.

20$^{20-21}$ are the final note taken from the royal annals.   Mention is
made of what was the most enduring monument of Hezekiah's reign,
the aqueduct which was cut to carry water from the so-called Pool of
the Virgin into the city.   It was for its age a magnificent piece of
engineering, as the portions still in existence show.   A tunnel had to
be cut through the solid rock of the hill on which the Temple was
built, and this is still to be seen.   An inscription which was discovered in the tunnel has unfortunately been erased, but it was carefully
copied and is still known.   It describes the completion of the work of
the tunnel, and is the earliest monument of Hebrew writing that has
been recovered from Jerusalem, apart from a few seals and gems.
The pool mentioned within the city is the Pool of Siloam, and the
purpose of the whole was undoubtedly to provide Jerusalem with
water in case of siege.

**21^{1–18}.   *The Reign of Manasseh of Judah.*

In the eyes of the compiler Manasseh is to Judah what Jeroboam I had been to Israel, and his sins were held to be the direct cause of the Exile.   No king in the south is more strongly condemned, for he seemed to adopt every method that he could to violate the Law as

The Siloam tunnel.
Photograph by Fr. Vester & Co.

understood by the compiler.   The narrative falls into two parts, vv. 2–9 giving a description of the sins which he committed and the remainder the judgement that was passed on him and on his country as a result of them.   It appears that the first part has been worked over by the second compiler, who was responsible, amongst other features, for vv. 4 and 6, in which there are constructions which are

extremely awkward in Hebrew if they are to be read continuously
with vv. 3, 5, 7 ff.

The sins ascribed to Manasseh (including those mentioned in v. 6)
are (1) the worship of other deities than Jahveh, (2) human sacrifice,
(3) the use of magic and necromancy, (4) the profanation of the Temple
by the insertion of heathen symbols within its precincts.   The objects
of worship enumerated under the first head are said to be Canaanite
in origin, and include the Baal and the Asherah, but the mention of
star-worship, which was originally a Babylonian cult, suggests that, as
in the case of Ahaz, the political situation may have affected the religious position of the king, and that this was really a result of Manasseh's subjection to Assyria.   Except in the general statement of v. 16,
there is no other reference to human sacrifice in the case of this king,
and the later editor's mention of the sin may have been an interpretation of that verse.   Necromancy and divination alike were strictly
forbidden in Israel because both recognized the existence of, and
offered some sort of worship to, other beings besides Jahveh.   In the
account of the last form of sin the phrase 'graven image of the
Asherah' requires some attention.   There is evidence to show that
the Asherah, originally a simple wooden pole, was personified and
regarded as a goddess.   On the other hand, most of the Biblical
references do not suggest that this view prevailed in Israel, and the
Chronicler, who took his account of Manasseh's sins from this passage, had 'graven image of the idol', which may have been the
original phrase here (see 2 Chron. 33⁷).   To this list of ritual sins
should be added the moral crime mentioned in v. 16.   The reason for
the wholesale slaughter thus described is not stated ; early Jewish
tradition says that it was a religious persecution, and that, amongst
others, Isaiah himself was put to death.

The remaining verses, 10–15, are best ascribed to the second editor,
since they seem to presuppose the Exile.   As a punishment for the
sins of Manasseh Judah is to suffer the fate of Israel.   The first metaphor of v. 13 must not be pressed too far ; the line and the plummet
are not emblems of destruction, but simply means of expressing a
comparison.   The second is a striking figure for the completeness of
the destruction of the city and the deportation of its inhabitants.

The chronicler adds further details of the life of Manasseh, describing his capture by the Assyrians and his temporary imprisonment in
Babylon.   There, it is said, he repented, and prayed for forgiveness.
On his return, he carried through a reform of religion, and restored
the conditions which had prevailed under Hezekiah.   Whilst it is not

The inscription found in the Siloam tunnel

The work was started from both ends, and the two tunnels were being driven past one another, when the workmen heard the picks of their fellows working through the rock, and cut sideways to meet them

always safe to accept without reserve statements in Chronicles which have no parallel in Kings, it is possible that in this case there was an actual historical event underlying the narrative. In 677 Esarhaddon held a great court—what would be called in India a *darbar*—at Carchemish. Amongst the twenty-two western princes who did homage to him there Manasseh is mentioned, and his enforced departure on this journey may have been misunderstood by later generations as a captivity.

21^{19-26}. *The Reign of Amon.*

A notice which includes besides the usual formulas only a record of the fact that Amon fell a victim to a conspiracy, and that vengeance was taken for him by the people of the land. It would seem that in spite of his failure to conform to a high religious standard, he was not unpopular with the people as a whole.

22^1-23^{30}. *The Reign of Josiah.*

The greater part of this section of the history is devoted to the story of the discovery of the Book of the Law and to the reformation which resulted from it. It is usual to identify this volume with Deuteronomy or with the nucleus of that Book ; though doubts have been raised in recent years, there seems to be no conclusive evidence against the prevalent view. The narrative of the events leading to the discovery is to be found in 22^{3-10}. It begins with the repair of the Temple buildings in the eighteenth year of Josiah, i.e. 621, and the account may be compared with that of the similar work undertaken in the reign of Joash (12^{5-17}). The principal difference lies in the method of collecting the money. The priests of Joash found it necessary to place it in a special box whence it could be removed only by some properly authorized person ; and this does not seem to have been necessary in the days of Josiah. Certain similarities in the language make it probable that both narratives are taken from some set of annals, probably those of the Temple.

During the work there was found a book which proved to be a Law-book. It was a custom in certain parts of the ancient East to bury in the foundations of a new temple a document containing a description of the ritual or of some other feature of the temple, and it has been supposed that this was such a volume. But there is no evidence to show that the repairs went down so deep, and what followed in the actual reform does not suggest that the main subject of the volume was the Temple or its ritual. Certainly Deuteronomy

A vanquished people (perhaps the Jews) led away captive to Assyria
Photograph by ' Les Archives Photographiques d' Art et d' Histoire'

was not such a book, and if the discovery be rightly identified with Deuteronomy or with any part of it, it could not have been a foundation-volume. On the other hand it has been suggested that this was a pious fraud on the part of Hilkiah and his colleagues, and that they had really composed the book themselves and taken this opportunity of 'finding' it. This, again, is extremely unlikely. This was the eighteenth year of Josiah, and they had ample opportunity of producing the book earlier if they had so wished. It is true that the centralization of worship, which was one of the provisions of Deuteronomy, was definitely in favour of the Jerusalem priests as compared with the country priests. But Deuteronomy provided that the country priests should come to Jerusalem and share the offerings and gifts of the worshippers there, since their own livelihood was largely gone. This (23^9) was never carried out, and the reason seems to have been the hostility of the Jerusalem priests. It is not likely, then, that they were in any way responsible for the book. Its origin is far from being certain. It is generally held that it was compiled in the form in which Hilkiah found it during the reign of Manasseh. Or it may go back as far as Hezekiah, and be the code in which that king embodied alike his civil law and his ritual reforms. It is not likely to have been older than this, for it seems to show traces of the teaching of the eighth-century prophets, especially of Hosea.

Hilkiah handed the book over to Shaphan, the royal secretary, and when he next reported to the king on the progress of the repairs, he gave an account of its discovery and read it to Josiah. The result is described in 22^{11-20}. Alarmed by the threats of the book against Israel if she neglected the law, he instructed a body of his chief ministers to ascertain whether obedience at this late date would avert the penalties prescribed. The men selected included not only Hilkiah and Shaphan, but Ahikam, the son of Shaphan, Achbor, of whom nothing is known except that he was (probably) the father of the Elnathan mentioned in Jer. 26^{22} and 36^{12}, and Asaiah, who held an office of which the duties have not been exactly ascertained. They approached the prophetess Huldah, probably because she was the wife of a royal official, and therefore well known to all the court. Her answer is given in vv. 15-20. There are really two answers, the first (15-17) dealing with the people as a whole, and the second (18-20) addressed particularly to Josiah. The former is probably not in its original form. Josiah seems to have secured the co-operation of the people in his new policy, and this would have been difficult unless the divine message had contained some promise of safety for them if they obeyed the law. As it stands, this oracle of Huldah's is one of unqualified gloom, and would hardly have formed an incentive to reforming activity.

The second oracle is a promise to Josiah that he personally, on account of his character and life, shall not actually suffer as the rest of his people will. There is a certain awkwardness at the end of v. 18, for the phrase 'the words which thou hast heard' form an incomplete expression. Probably there is some error in the text, and the original form may have run 'Because thou hast heard my words' (so LXX), or 'Thou hast hearkened unto the words which I spoke'.

With ch. 23 begins the account of the measures taken by Josiah in accordance with the newly found law. The first step (vv. 1–3) was the summoning of a general assembly of Judah to Jerusalem, and the ratification in the Temple of a solemn covenant on the basis of the law. This is not a covenant in the sense of its being a bargain between two parties. It is rather a solemn undertaking on the part of king and people to observe the terms of the law. There seems to be some special significance in the king's 'standing by a pillar' (cf. 11^{14}), and the phrase used of the people 'they stood to the covenant' may imply some ritual which has no longer survived.

vv. 4–15 describe the purification of the worship of Israel. The passage may have been worked over by an editor still later than the second compiler of the book, but the reasons advanced for the excision of particular words are not convincing. It is of particular interest as showing the kind of worship current in Israel before the reform, worship carried on in large measure in complete innocence by men who were unaware of the fact that worship of this type was displeasing to Jahveh. But with the coming of Deuteronomy the whole situation had been changed, and much that had previously been accepted without question had to be swept away.

The work described was in the first instance confined to Jerusalem, and to the neighbouring cities of Judah. Orders were given to the two leading priests (the words 'the high priest' were not in the text used by the LXX and as a title were possibly not in use till after the Exile, but a body of priests like that of Jerusalem must have had a leader) to remove all idolatrous objects from the Temple itself. The charge was probably committed to them because the entry of laymen into the Temple itself might be regarded as sacrilegious. The first step was to remove all articles which had been used in connexion with the idolatrous worship. It will be noticed that here again, as in 21[7], the Asherim (still mere wooden posts, as v. 6 shows) were brought out and burnt in the valley of the Kidron, to the south-east of Jerusalem. For 'fields' the LXX seem to have read 'furnaces', and this may be original. Then followed the removal of the priests who had been especially appointed to conduct and oversee this worship in the cities of Judah. The intrusion of this feature of the reform in the midst of details that applied properly to Jerusalem alone has led to the suggestion that v. 5 was a later addition. But this is unnecessary, for there were probably such officials in Jerusalem, and their removal might lead the historian to anticipate this point in the purifying of the country worship. In this connexion it may be remarked that the word rendered 'planets' is of uncertain meaning, the most likely suggestion being that it is applied to the signs of the Zodiac, which were certainly worshipped in Babylonia. The Asherah itself was then taken out and burnt, its ashes being beaten into dust and scattered on the graves of the common people. Finally, the establishments of men and women connected with the immoral features in the worship of Jerusalem were destroyed. There is some uncertainty as to the precise function of the women mentioned; 'hangings' is a guess at the significance of a word whose literal meaning is 'houses'. Probably the LXX were right in reading 'tunics'.

Josiah then turned to the country outside Jerusalem. The local sanctuaries were abolished, their priests being brought to Jerusalem, though they were not admitted to the full privileges of the priesthood. These were, of course, the priests of Jahveh at the local sanctuaries, as distinct from the idolatrous priests mentioned in v. 5. This reform extended over the whole of Judah, from its southern limit in Beer-sheba to its northern frontier at Geba (to the north-east of Ramah), and included the abolition of the place sacred to the 'satyrs' or 'goat-demons' (so read in v. 8 for 'gates') near the gate of Jerusalem itself. He then defiled the 'tophet'—either burning-place or burying-place—in the valley of Hinnom where the human sacrifices of Manasseh and others had been offered, to prevent a repetition of the offence there. He returned to Jerusalem and did away with the emblems and instruments of the worship of the sun-god (probably another instance of Babylonian or Assyrian worship) and destroyed the roof-altars which still existed in the city. Emblems of various non-Israelite cults which dated back to the time of Solomon were

The Valley of Hinnom
Photograph by *Fr. Vester & Co.*

next abolished, and v. 15 describes an extension of the king's activities as far as Bethel. This probably means that the Assyrians were now too weak to maintain an effective control over the western parts of their dominions.

In vv. 16–19 a later editor has added a note to the effect that certain graves in the neighbourhood were rifled, and the bones found in them burnt on the altar. Apparently he failed to notice the difficulty of burning anything upon the altar after it had been destroyed, and merely wished to record the fulfilment of the prophecy described in 1 Ki. 13[1 ff]. With the same passage in mind he takes care to mention the fact that the bones of the Judaean prophet who had foretold the desecration of the altar at Bethel were not disturbed. As the text stands there is a very awkward gap at the end of v. 16, and the LXX were probably right in reading the verse '. . . which the man of God proclaimed when Jeroboam stood by the altar at the feast. And he turned and lifted up his eyes to the sepulchre of the man of God who had proclaimed these things.' vv. 19, 20 are also probably a later addition, based on the same passage, and are added with the desire to make Josiah's work appear complete.

vv. 21–3 speak of the Passover which Josiah celebrated in accordance with the law of Deuteronomy. The festival was certainly very ancient, and was possibly older than Moses. But in earlier days the regulations laid down in Ex. 20 seem to have been followed, making it a household festival. This time it is to be observed in Jerusalem alone, and it is in this that its peculiarity mainly consists. Another difference between the ritual described in Ex. 12 and that of Dt. 16 (the rule, apparently, followed by Josiah) is that in the former case the victim must be a sheep or a goat, and must be roasted; boiling is strictly and expressly forbidden. In Dt. 16 it might be an ox and boiling is prescribed as the right method of cooking it. Later generations of Jews followed the Deuteronomic law, and maintained that the regulations in Exodus applied only to the first celebration, the so-called 'Passover of Egypt'. But, from the way in which local observance is prohibited in Deuteronomy, it seems that this centralization was a novelty, and the strong probability is that it was kept in people's homes throughout the period of the monarchy. The fact that the date given for this Passover is the same as that of the discovery of the law suggests that the calendar in use by the annalist was that of the civil year which began in autumn.

The last feature of the reform is described in v. 24, and consisted in the religious purification of the houses of the people, amongst whom there seem to have been many who maintained private magical cults. With this verse goes also the approving formula of v. 25, which was probably written before the fall of Jerusalem in 585. On the other hand vv. 26, 27 clearly come from the Exile, and are due to the second editor, who felt that the sins of Manasseh and others were so terrible that even the reform of Josiah could not avert punishment for them.

The close of the reign of Josiah is described in vv. 28-30, which record his death at Megiddo. In Chronicles a battle is described, but there is no hint of such an event here, and the fighting may be an addition of the Chronicler's. But questions of detail are unimportant, and the main fact is certain. Josiah fell by Egyptian hands, and with his death perished Judah's last chance of prosperity and survival as a kingdom.[1]

23^{31-5}. *The Reign of Jehoahaz.*

The only feature of this short reign is the further interference of Egypt in the affairs of Judah. The new king, appointed by popular feeling, was unacceptable to Necho, who summoned him to Riblah in the far north of Syria, and thence sent him in chains to Egypt, where he died. It may be noted in passing that the words 'That he might not reign in Jerusalem' do not properly belong to the text here, but have been introduced from Chronicles. It is impossible to check the compiler's estimate of Jehoahaz's character, but it is worth noting that both Jeremiah (22^{10-12}) and Ezekiel (19^{1-4}) speak of him with some sympathy.

In vv. 34 ff. the narrative continues with the new arrangements made by Necho for the government of the country as a vassal state. Subjection is implied in the new name that is given to the elder (half) brother of Jehoahaz, who had been formerly known as Eliakim but was now called Jehoiakim. He was placed on the throne, clearly to rule in the Egyptian interest, and his servitude was emphasized by the exaction of enormous tribute. His method of collecting it is described as though it were felt to be unnecessarily oppressive. The text is confused as it stands; probably we should read 'but he taxed the people of the land' and 'he exacted the silver and the

---

[1] For a discussion of the event see the historical introduction, p. 23 f.

gold of every one according to his taxation'. The last word properly means not taxation in our modern sense but 'assessment'. The narrative evidently stated that a systematic poll-tax was imposed, much as had happened in the case of Menahem of Israel a century earlier. Jehoiakim did not mean that the burden of tribute should fall upon himself, a policy fully in accord with his character as sketched by Jeremiah.

23³⁶–24⁷. *The Reign of Jehoiakim of Judah.*

The last verse is a general comment which however gives the key to the other statements included in the passage. Necho was defeated at Carchemish in 605 by Nebuchadrezzar, and though domestic arrangements prevented the Chaldean king from pushing his advantage immediately, only a few years had passed before the conquest of Palestine as far as the modern Wadi El-Arish was complete. Jehoiakim and his little kingdom of course experienced a change of masters, but it is not likely that the Egyptian court yet abandoned all hope of making difficulties for Nebuchadrezzar. For this purpose his best instrument was probably his own former vassal Jehoiakim. The list of neighbouring peoples who attacked Judah (for 'Syrians' in the list given in v. 2 we should probably read 'Edomites') suggests that Jehoiakim was isolated, and these marauding bands were perhaps enough for the time to prevent Judah from doing serious mischief. Before more drastic measures could be adopted Jehoiakim died and was succeeded by his young son Jehoiachin.

24⁸⁻¹⁷. *The Reign of Jehoiachin of Judah.*

Jehoiachin's reign was short. Not many days can have passed after his father's death before a Chaldean army appeared under the walls of Jerusalem. Nebuchadrezzar himself soon joined them, and three months after his accession Jehoiachin surrendered at discretion. He, his mother, his wives, and his court were all carried into captivity, and the Temple treasures—such as still remained—were rifled. 7,cco men capable of bearing arms and 1,000 craftsmen went with him (v. 14 is probably an insertion by a later reader who confused the two captivities). The figures themselves show how Judah and Jerusalem had been reduced by the troubles through which they had passed in the last generation. A last attempt was made by

Nebuchadrezzar to leave to the country a shadow of independence, and he placed a third son of Josiah on the throne, changing his name from Mattaniah to Zedekiah—again in token of subjection. The captivity of Judah had begun, and the best of the people had been carried away. The contrast between those who went and those who remained is strikingly drawn by Jeremiah (ch. 24), who compares the old court and ministry to a basket of very good figs, and their successors to a basket of figs so nauseating that they could not possibly be eaten. Both judgements have independent support. The history of the next few years, especially as reflected in the life of Jeremiah, is eloquent testimony to the rottenness of the new régime, whilst the prisoners included Ezekiel and possibly the author of Pss. 42-3. In the end it was in Babylon and not in Judah that the national life and faith were preserved, doubtless through these earlier exiles.

24^{18}-25^{21}. *The Reign of Zedekiah and the Captivity of Judah.*

Zedekiah was a full brother of Jehoahaz, and a half-brother of Jehoiakim. Fuller details of his reign are given in the historical portions of the Book of Jeremiah ; the narrative in Kings is confined to the last siege and destruction of Jerusalem. The accuracy of detail makes it clear that the greater part of this narrative, if not the whole, is from the pen of an eyewitness of the events described.

25^{1-7} are concerned with the fortunes of the king himself. Following on his last rebellion against Babylon, a Chaldean army invested the city in January 587, and surrounded it either with a wall or with a chain of forts. The Chaldeans had learnt the art of the siege from the Assyrians, the first people in history to develop military science. Escape and relief were almost entirely prevented, and it seems that the besiegers were content to let famine save their forces from the wastage of actual fighting. In July 586 supplies within the city failed, and the weakened garrison allowed a breach to be made in the walls. In the confusion Zedekiah and some of his forces succeeded in making their way out through a double wall to the south-east of the city. They fled towards the fords of the Jordan at Jericho, where the king was deserted by his guards and fell into the hands of the pursuers. The insignificance of Judah is emphasized by the fact that Nebuchadrezzar himself was far away in the north on the Orontes near Hamath, whence he could direct the whole campaign. A comparatively small detachment was enough to settle the fate of Jerusalem. Nebuchadrezzar held some sort of trial, condemned Zedekiah, executed his sons before his eyes, and blinded him, finally sending him away a prisoner in chains to Babylon.

25^{9-17} describe the fate of the city. A month after its actual capture an officer entitled 'Chief of the Guard' took charge of the final proceedings. The buildings were destroyed, and all of them that could be burnt was given to the flames. The walls were broken down, and all the people, both those who had remained in the city and those who had deserted during the siege (Jeremiah gives fuller details), were carried away to Babylon, only a handful of agricultural artisans being left behind to save the land from becoming a desert.

The narrator dwells with pathetic affection on the equipment and ornaments of the Temple. These were broken up and carried away as masses of metal, a spoil beyond enumeration. Most of the articles were believed to date from the time of Solomon, and though inroads had been made upon the treasures more than once, e.g. in the days of Rehoboam and of Ahaz, there was enough left to yield very valuable booty to the Chaldeans.

25^{18-21} describe a further punishment of the city. A number of officials and other representative men were taken to Riblah, and there put to death. In this Nebuchadrezzar was not unjust, and indeed for his age his whole conduct was marked by comparative clemency. But it was just the leaders of the people who had formed the anti-Babylonian and revolutionary party in the city. The king himself had been weak, and had yielded to them ; left to himself he might have remained loyal, but they were too strong for him. Their punishment, no less than the special favour shown to Jeremiah, suggests that the Chaldeans were not unaware of the internal politics of Jerusalem, and knew well who were their enemies and who could be trusted. The same suggestion is made by the further treatment of the land, over which Gedaliah, a scion of the house of Shaphan, already prominent in the story of Josiah's reform, was placed as Governor. The main Chaldean garrison was withdrawn.

25^{22-26}. *The Governorship of Gedaliah.*

These verses seem to be a condensed form of the narrative found in Jer. 39^{11}-43^{17}. Gedaliah's appointment seemed to be the opportunity for the life of Israel to make a fresh start. A number of leading soldiers had survived, probably including those who had escaped with Zedekiah, and these began to collect round Gedaliah. The narrative suggests that the new régime lasted only for a couple of months, but it is more probable that this is a misinterpretation of the facts. We gather from Jeremiah (where also the text simply speaks of the seventh month) that the community was well established, and was beginning to succeed in its agriculture. This was not the work of a few weeks, and it is possible that a year date has fallen out of both texts—or perhaps disappeared from that of Jeremiah before it was used by the compiler of Kings.

An Aramaic papyrus from Elephantine, containing evidence of a Jewish temple in the fifth century B.C. See p. 104.

But in any case the prosperity was short-lived. A man of the royal house named Ishmael, jealous perhaps that the authority had been given to an outsider, made common cause with the Ammonites, who sent him to assassinate Gedaliah. The plan was carried out with consummate treachery and barbarity. Numbers of wholly innocent people were involved in the slaughter, and Ishmael fled to Ammon. Those who were left behind felt that the Chaldeans might take indiscriminate vengeance, and that the safest plan was to make good their escape at once. Accordingly they fled to Egypt, leaving behind none who could be formed into an organized state.

This was the real end of the Judaean community. They might to some extent have recovered under Gedaliah; as it was, they disappeared from history. It is just possible that they—or some of them—passed right through Egypt and settled at Yeb, an island in the Nile just below the first cataract, for a Jewish community lived there which has left us a certain number of records dating from the fifth century B.C. They state that they were there before the days of Cambyses, but give no hint of the actual time or circumstances of their arrival. Under the Persian government of Egypt they formed a military garrison, but they may have been found there by the Persians and used to hold the Sudan. In that case (though the whole question is most uncertain), it is just possible that they were descended from the fugitives whose flight is described in this chapter.

25[27–30]. *The Liberation of Jehoiachin.*

Nebuchadrezzar died in 562, and was succeeded by his son Evil-Merodach (Babylonian Awel- or Amel-marduk). One of his first acts was to set Jehoiachin free from prison and to accord him royal honours. His motives are not obvious, but Babylon by this time contained a very varied population, and it is possible that the king hoped to secure the loyalty of an element in the country which in a very remarkable manner retained its distinctness and its solidarity. If any reliance is to be placed on later genealogies it seems that Jehoiachin married, and that his descendants continued to be recognized as leaders amongst the Jewish community. Certainly Zerubbabel, the builder of the Temple in 520-518, was believed to be his grandson. The release of the legitimate king of Judah must have raised hopes of a better time to come in the minds of the exiled Jews, and we may hold it as significant that the sad story of the declining kingdom closes with a hint of a brighter future.

'It is possible that they settled at Yeb (Elephantine), an island in the Nile just below the first cataract.'   See p. 104

Photograph by Sir Aurel Stein

THE BOOK OF AMOS

INTRODUCTION

LIKE most of the prophetic books, Amos contains three kinds of material: (*a*) the oracles, probably written down after being repeated orally for some time by those who had heard them and others; (*b*) narratives which describe his actions and words in the third person; (*c*) narratives which were due to the prophet himself, and may have been actually written or dictated by him. The greater part of the Book of Amos consists of passages of the first type, the second being confined to the story of the clash between Amos and Amaziah, the priest of Bethel, in 7^{10-17}, and the third to the accounts of the visions in chs. 7 ff. Some of the oracles seem to have received special treatment, especially those now found at the beginning of the book which refer to foreign nations. It almost looks as if these had once formed a separate collection, and as if they had been worked into a uniform shape; many students to-day believe that the oracle concerning Judah (2^{4-5}) is a later production which was appended to the original collection. Doubts have also been raised as to Amos's authorship of the oracles dealing with Tyre (1^{9-10}) and Edom (1^{11-12}). The grounds, however, are less serious than in the first case. It would seem that the editor who was responsible for the present form of the book adopted the initial formula of these 'foreign' oracles to introduce those which referred to Israel and formed the main portion of the material. Doubt has also been cast on the originality of the closing section, 9^{8b-15}, as it seems to many scholars that the strength of the prophet's denunciations would have been impaired if he had himself added these promises of prosperity.

Amos is our best authority for the social, economic, and religious conditions of the eighth century (see pp. 29 ff.). He himself belonged to the country in the south of Judah where agriculture was difficult, if not impossible, and men had to make their living from their flocks of sheep. The occasion of his utterances was a visit to Bethel, perhaps originally intended as a religious pilgrimage. He had known the life of Israel in the half-desert, and as a prophet was an enthusiast for Jahveh, and his observation of an entirely different civilization must have stirred him profoundly. He was not blinded by familiarity with the evils of the more highly civilized community, nor was he

THE WILDERNESS OF TEKOA
In such surroundings Amos was brought up
Photograph by Fr. Vester & Co.

rendered helpless by a sense of involuntary complicity, as others may have been who saw the rottenness of Samaria, but were not free to express themselves. To him the strongest contrast of all seems to have been the difference between the demands of Jahveh as he had learnt to understand them and the religious practices of the great cities. In the simple society of his own home Jahveh was the protector of morality; in Bethel He seemed to be its enemy. The worst iniquities of the agricultural community were committed in the name of religion, and men were found doing as religious acts, deeds which they themselves would probably have condemned in secular life.

From this contrast sprang his great message. Even in the highly complex society of northern Israel, the supreme demand made by her God was a life in which righteousness and justice reigned. Men thought that Jahveh was not interested in the way they treated one another, provided only that the external ritual was observed. Indeed, its maintenance might necessarily involve the neglect or violation of laws which were otherwise binding. Thus the civil code of Israel provided that if a poor man gave his outer garment in pawn, the creditor must restore it to him every evening, for use at night. If, however, it could be used for some religious ceremony in the temple, to spread beside the altar, the needs of worship were held to override those of common law (2^8). Ritual was more important than justice in the eyes of his contemporaries. Amos emphatically inverted this order, and said that ritual was worthless compared with justice. The existing conditions could have only one end—the final ruin of Israel. Amos saw only one chance, that Israel would seek Jahveh and learn to know Him as He really was. Then there.was a possibility that she might survive.

The work of Amos must clearly be dated in the reign of Jeroboam II. It seems likely, from the language used in 8^9, that the prophet had seen an eclipse of the sun which had been nearly total. This can have been only that which took place on June 14, 763, and his work is most probably, therefore, to be dated about 760 B.C. A visit to Bethel is mentioned, and some of his oracles were certainly delivered there, but though it is possible that all were uttered in the same place and on the same occasion, it is by no means certain. He may have paid more than one visit to the north, and his language at times suggests that he knew Samaria as well as Bethel, and had prophesied there also.

NOTES ON AMOS 3–7

3^{1–8}. *Jahveh the author of suffering.*

These verses form an oracle of which the main feature is an insistence on the relationship between cause and effect. If the effect be seen, then the cause may be inferred with certainty. If the cause be known, then there can be no doubt as to the effect. Amos expresses this in a kind of cumulative rhetoric, giving a number of illustrations which lead him at last to the conclusions which he would draw from the general rule which these illustrations exhibit.

v. 2 might be a title for the whole book. Israel had been in a special sense the people of Jahveh, and to her alone had He fully revealed Himself. But she could not count on a weak good-nature or an immoral partisanship. On the contrary, her special privileges implied special responsibility, and just because she had known better, her punishment would be far worse than that of nations who had sinned in ignorance. Jahveh would 'visit upon her' (the Hebrew idiom for 'punish her for') all her transgressions. She had had the best chance, and failure to take it would involve the worst disasters.

The very existence of suffering should prove to her that Jahveh was at work. 'Evil' (v. 6) does not mean moral or spiritual wrong, it means calamity or disaster. This is her own fault, and in this matter she ought to trace the hand of her God. There are no accidents. If two people are seen walking together over the lonely hill-sides of southern Judah, then the observer knows that it is not mere chance that has brought them together; they must have agreed to meet and travel in company. If a lion's roar is heard in the marshy jungles that fill the hollows in the hills, it is because he has leaped upon his prey. If a wild beast be heard to growl, the hearer knows that he has caught something, and is rending it in pieces. The vulture does not drop from the sky unless it has seen something to eat. If the watcher sees the spring of a snare start up from the ground, he knows that it has caught something. The moment the sentry's horn is heard from the outpost on the hill-top, there is tumult and confusion in the little village, for brigands are abroad and will soon be amongst the flocks and at the gates. Amos had seen nature, and from her had learnt the meaning of law, so he knew that the principle held good throughout, and if calamity befell a people it was not an accident—Jahveh was at work, and the disaster only proved it. In the same way there are some results that are inevitable.

No one can hear the roar of the lion without a shudder, and just as little can any man hear the voice of Jahveh and not prophesy. Amos, at least, cannot restrain his words.

3^{9-10}. *The destruction of Samaria.* The great nations of the world (for ' Ashdod ' we should probably read with the LXX ' Assyria ') are summoned to note the social sins with which the city is filled and to mark the utter inability of the people to act uprightly. Men have, as it were, saved up large stores of crime, and it is there for them to draw upon as they will.

3^{11}. *A fragment.* The compiler has rightly seen in this the inevitable result of the behaviour of Israel. The actual Hebrew text is a little uncertain, but there can be little doubt that the correct sense is given by the English versions. Amos seems to have been particularly impressed by the size of rich men's houses in the cities of northern Israel. Probably he himself was accustomed to houses which were little more than huts, made of wattled palm leaves and dried mud. Houses of brick, containing a number of rooms, appealed to him as the height of extravagance and luxury.

3^{12-13}. *The completeness of the destruction which will fall upon Israel.* The text is certainly corrupt at the end of v. 12, and it is unlikely that there was any mention of Damascus in the original words of Amos at this point, though it is not possible for us to make even a plausible guess at what he actually did say. The point of the oracle, however, is clear, and shows how readily and simply Amos could draw on his own shepherd experience. If a flock was entrusted to a shepherd, he was held responsible to its owner for the safety of every animal, and if any were found to be missing he had to make good the loss at his own expense. It was, however, recognized that he could not altogether prevent harm done by wild animals, and in such a case he was held to be absolved from payment. (Jacob claims it as a virtue that he had made no such excuse to Laban, Gen. 31^{39}.) But in order to secure this privilege he had to produce some portion of the torn animal to prove that it was not his carelessness that was to blame for the loss. Hence a shepherd would follow a lion that had stolen a sheep, and recover any fragment of the carcass that he could from the animal—a knuckle-bone, or the tip of an ear—with the marks of the lion's teeth upon it. He would not often get much more, and would not need more. The remnant of Israel will be just as small and insignificant a portion of the whole as the tiny piece that the shepherd brings to his master in evidence.

3[14-15]. *The destruction of the altar of Bethel and the houses of the wealthy.* The altar was a place of refuge, and he who would seek the special protection of Jahveh took hold of the projections which were called 'horns'. But—and it is significant that it is Jahveh who says this—so far from affording protection to other people, the altar at Bethel will not even be able to protect itself. An illustration of the futility of mere ritual and ritual practices which is quite character-istic of Amos. In v. 15 instead of 'great houses' a simple change

An ancient wall in Samaria.

Photograph by Fr. Vester & Co.

enables us to read 'houses of ebony', thus balancing the 'houses of ivory'. Again Amos shows how he is impressed by the luxury of Israelite dwellings.

4[1-3]. *The women of Samaria.* He seems to have felt that in the last resort it was the women who set the social standard, and that though they might not take an active part in affairs—and Jezebel had done even that—their selfish laziness and greed were really respon-sible for the worst features of life as he saw it. Like fat cattle from Bashan (one of the best grazing countries in Palestine, to the east of the Jordan), they care only for what they eat and drink, and are absolutely unscrupulous as to the means whereby their desires are gratified.

It is their nagging which drives their men-folk to commit the social iniquities which were sapping the life of the country. But when their policy, such as it is, comes to full fruition, they themselves will be the sufferers, and their corpses will be dragged like those of dead dogs through the breaches which the enemy has made in the city walls, and thrown to rot on the common dung-heaps. This seems to be what the prophet intended by the word given as 'Harmon', though it is possible that the text is here corrupt.

4^{4-5}. *A bitter denunciation of the ritual of Israel.* Ritual is only an excuse for wrong-doing, or possibly the prophet regarded it as being in itself wrong. Sacrifice, pilgrimage, and tithe are futile, even though the most scrupulous care be exercised by the worshipper to see that every detail is correctly performed. It may mean a surrender of things that people would like to keep for themselves, yet after all it is the easiest form of religion ; it is the kind of religion that men really like, and so they continue to maintain it regardless of the weightier demands of morality.

4^{6-11} recount a series of calamities which have befallen Israel, but have not brought her to repentance. She has failed to see that these are Jahveh's punishments for her sin. They are placed in ascending order of frightfulness.

v. 6. *Famine.* This is described as 'cleanness of teeth'. In accordance with the principle laid down in 3^{6}, that suffering proves the activity of Jahveh, Israel should have recognized in this calamity a call to repentance. But neither to this nor to the other appeals of the same kind had she responded.

vv. 7–8. *Drought, and its effect upon the people.* It is not unlikely that this has been somewhat expanded in course of transmission, and that the latter part of v. 7 was not included in the original oracle. Rain usually falls in Palestine at two seasons, the first in the autumn, and the second in February. These are the gentler 'latter rains', cool and refreshing, which serve to swell the grain and prepare it for ripening. The harvest is in May in the lowlands, and a month later in the mountains. If the latter rains fail, the harvest is sure to be poor. Moreover, the former rains are so violent as to rush swiftly off the surface of the ground, while the latter rains sink in more deeply and supply the wells. If the text be sound this failure was not universal, an occasional village retaining its water supply to a limited extent, and having to share it with their neighbours, so that none of them has enough. This too failed to bring Israel to repentance.

v. 9. *Blight.* The first word used seems to imply the scorching of plant life by the sirocco, the second to rottenness produced by too much moisture.   In addition to these dangers locusts have destroyed all the green things.   Yet Israel has not repented.

v. 10. *An epidemic.* The ancient world knew little about disease, and apparently suffered comparatively slightly from it, except in the

Women carrying water-jars to a well.
Photograph by Fr. Vester & Co.

form of epidemics.   These were therefore the more impressive, and from time to time swept the population off in thousands.   It is no fancy picture that Amos draws here and in 6^{9-10}.   Such epidemics seem to have been not infrequent in the marshy lands on the Egyptian frontier.   It is difficult to identify such diseases in the absence of careful diagnosis or description, but it seems clear that both typhus and bubonic plague were known in ancient times.   The plague of Athens in 432 and later was almost certainly the former, whilst the latter may have been the trouble that attacked the Philistines during the sojourn of the Ark in their country. Here, apparently, the disease had fallen on an army whilst it was actually engaged on an expedition. But this too has failed to bring Israel to repentance.

v. 11. *An earthquake.* This is possibly that to which allusion is made in the first verse of the book. In that case the ministry of Amos will have been a longer one than the surviving oracles would lead us to suppose, for his work began two years before it occurred. The destruction must have been appalling, for the language used, the very words employed, are those which describe the overthrow of Sodom and Gomorrah. Even without the mention of the names the Hebrew phraseology would inevitably have recalled that event. Yet all this has not brought Israel to repentance.

vv. 12-13. *Jahveh's coming imminent.* What more can Jahveh do? Famine, drought, pestilence, and earthquake are His messengers, and they have failed. The only measure that remains to Him is to appear Himself and take vengeance on Israel. As we find from other passages in the book, Amos was faced with a popular view of the 'Day of Jahveh' which was not unlike that held to-day by some of those who look for the 'second coming' of Christ. He Himself was to appear on earth, right all wrongs, take vengeance on the enemies of Israel, and establish her once and for all as the supreme if not the only nation on earth. Through Amos He claims the power to do this, the power of the Creator of the universe and its Lord, but His coming will be far other than that which Israel expects, and will bring to her what His messengers have failed to bring. She must prepare to meet her God.

5^{1-2}. *A dirge.* Amos sees, as it were, a funeral procession leaving a city, and as it approaches he raises the song of the mourners :

> Fallen is Israel, the virgin,
>   Never to rise ;
> Earthbound, with none to uplift her,
>   Prostrate she lies.

For it is the whole nation that lies upon the bier. Such dirges were a characteristic of Israelite funerals, and were usually sung by professional women, who combined with their poetic gift the knowledge of all the appropriate ceremonies and ritual necessary to secure a satisfactory burial.

5^{3}. *Destruction of the people.* This may possibly be a part of the dirge, but in that case it will have to be assumed that the introductory words have been inserted by the compiler, who did not see the connexion. It describes the fate of Israel by showing the effect of the coming disaster on the fighting force of the country. Ninety per cent. of all the warriors shall be destroyed. Though they are mentioned as being men of military power (this is implied in the verb 'went forth') it does not follow that the disaster contemplated was war.

5⁴⁻⁶. *Condemnation of worship.* These verses contain a denunciation of the religious forms existing in Israel in the days of the prophet, and call attention to the only hope of the people. Bethel, Gilgal, and Beersheba are famous sanctuaries, the former in the centre of Israel, the second probably near Jericho (though the name is a common one for sacred places, meaning simply ' circle '), and the third in the far south. None of these is of any use ; what is required is that men should seek Jahveh. They must learn to know Him and to appreciate His character and demands. Otherwise He may break out as fire and devour the house of Joseph (this is probably the correct order ot the words). It is noticeable that Amos speaks here and elsewhere of the 'house of Joseph', making no clear division between Ephraim and Manasseh. In fact he never uses either of these names. Joseph occurs three times, otherwise the name of the people is always either Jacob or Israel. This may be due to his being a southerner, and, politically, an alien.

5⁷. *Perversion of justice.* An isolated fragment of a passage which described the judicial corruption of Israel. This is, perhaps, the commonest form of social iniquity in the East, but it is not often that the administration of law is as corrupt as it seems to have been in the experience of Amos. In his day it was positively dangerous to go into a court of law, for justice had been turned (a strong word that might almost mean ' overturned ') into poison, and fairness was dead.

5⁸⁻⁹. *A fragment.* The beginning (and perhaps the end) of this oracle has been lost, but it clearly described the majesty of Jahveh. He is the Creator of the great constellations, and the Maker of day and night. The word rendered ' shadow of death ' probably means no more than ' darkness '; the traditional pronunciation and translation seem to be due to bad etymology. At the same time, His power extends to the human world.

5¹⁰. *Another fragment.* This refers to Israel or some class of persons in Israel, and comments on their utter intolerance of any kind of criticism. The ' gate ' is the public meeting-place in the East.

5¹¹⁻¹²ᵃ. *Exorbitant rents.* This oracle condemns the rapacity of the

Israelite landlords, who used to demand an extortionate share of the produce of the land from the tenant farmer. Their punishment will be that they shall not live to enjoy the fruits of their own labour. They take away what the peasant's toil has produced, and they in turn shall see the loss of all that on which they spend their own strength.

5^{12b-13}. *The ill-treatment of the poor.* This oracle gives another description of the treatment accorded to the lower classes by the wealthy and the officials. The R.V. are somewhat misleading in their connexion of v. 12 b with 12 a, for the verb 'turn aside' is in the third person and not the second. Nor is it necessary to add 'from their right'. The phrase means literally 'bend their way', and gives a picture of two men meeting one another in the city gate. One must give way to the other, and the wealthy man stalks proudly forward, while the poor man has to step to one side. So his track is crooked, while the others is straight. It is almost as if the one had shouldered the other into the gutter. At the same time it is not safe for the victim to make any protest or appeal; his best plan is to swallow ill-treatment in silence.

5^{14-15}. *The true demands of Jahveh.* This is the centre of the teaching of Amos. Israel claims that Jahveh is in her midst, and rightly, but His presence may be a danger unless she realizes the essential conditions of His favour. These are not ritual requirements but right feelings and relations between man and man. The condition of Israel has so deteriorated that terrible calamity is now inevitable, but there may be a remnant who will find prosperity if the necessary conditions are observed.

5^{16-17}. *Israel meets her God.* It is impossible not to recall the desolation of Egypt at the death of the firstborn, when Jahveh passed through the land. There is a reference to the professional mourners and dirge-singers, who are (exceptionally) men and not women.

5^{18-20}. *The true day of Jahveh.* Reference has already been made to the popular belief (see on 4^{12}), but here, for the first time, the subject is introduced into the text. People thought it was to be a day of happiness and triumph, a day of light and joy. On the contrary, it was to be a time of darkness, bringing upon men a doom from which there was no escape. Amos draws a picture of a man walking through the forest and suddenly meeting a lion. He turns in terror, and in his flight meets a bear—more terrible than the lion to the jungle-dweller. As a last hope he rushes into a hut for safety, and, spent with fear and exertion, leans his hand on the wall. But there is

AN EASTERN CITY GATE

a deadly snake in a cranny, and the death that he has twice avoided meets him at last. There is no escape for him, and there will be no escape for sinful Israel when Jahveh does at last appear. The Day of Jahveh is indeed a time of utter darkness, unrelieved by a single ray of light.

5$^{21-27}$. *Condemnation of ritual.* A somewhat longer oracle than usual, repeating the lesson that Amos has so often tried to enforce. Religiosity is no substitute for righteousness. Pilgrimage, solemn religious assemblies, gifts, even whole burnt-offerings—in these things Jahveh is not interested, and sacred music simply worries and irritates Him beyond endurance. There has been also the worship of false gods. v. 26 is in some disorder, but the LXX probably had the right text, '. . . Siccuth your king and the star of your god Kewan '— both, apparently, Babylonian deities. But this is of less importance than Israel's social and moral failure, and what Jahveh desires is a perennial stream of justice.

6$^{1-7}$. *The luxury and selfishness of the rich.* The passage seems to have been expanded by a reader at the end of the eighth century, for of the three places mentioned in v. 2, Calneh, a Mesopotamian city, was destroyed by Tiglath-pileser in 738; Hamath, on the Orontes, by Sargon in 720, i. e. two years after the fall of Samaria ; and Gath not until 711. But the rest of the passage awakens no suspicions. The picture is clear and detailed. We see the prominent people of Samaria, sure that no harm can befall them. If calamity is threatened, if some Amos foretells disaster, they say ' it will last our time ; there is no immediate danger', and thereby bring all the nearer that awful time when Violence shall ascend the throne and dominate the land. Meanwhile, they lounge in extreme luxury, eating and drinking of the best that the country can supply. Their inartistic and degraded tastes affect their music, and whilst it is really of the poorest quality, they pride themselves on its being the equal of any that David had. And whilst they are doing all this their people—Joseph—lies with broken limbs and shattered frame, and it is nothing to them. It is almost impossible to read this passage without recalling the French nobility in the generation which preceded the Revolution.

6$^{8-10}$. *A scene during pestilence.* A fragment from an oracle (v. 8) expressing Jahveh's loathing for the sinful people, followed by a prose account of a scene during a pestilence. Whole households are swept away, and where there is a survivor he hides in the far corner of the house. Men, including a relative, come to bury the corpses, and ask if any is left alive. The only answer is ' Hush ! ' It would in normal times be 'Jahveh bless thee', but none dare mention the Divine name now, for fear of attracting Jahveh's attention and bringing down yet further suffering.

6¹¹. *A fragment.* Destruction which will fall on the actual buildings. The reference is probably to an earthquake, which would work widespread destruction.

6¹². *Another fragment.* Apparently from an oracle which denounced the judicial corruption of the time. The first part of the verse is awkward Hebrew, and the sense is weak, for whilst no one would make horses gallop up a precipice, men did and do plough with oxen. A slight change—the division of the word rendered 'oxen' into two— yields the sense 'shall one plough the sea with cattle', which has every appearance of being the original text. It describes an absurdity, but it is not more absurd than the way in which the local judges turn law into poison which will slay all who put it to their lips.

6¹³⁻¹⁴. *Israel's 'jingoism'.* A portion of an oracle of which the opening words have not been preserved. Again the text seems to need correction, for the Hebrew is doubtful, and probably we should read for 'a thing of nought' the name 'Lo-debar', and render the word for 'horns' as another proper name, 'Karnaim'. Both are places known to have existed in Gilead, and were probably included in the territories recovered by Jeroboam II from the Syrians of Damascus. Amos sees that the triumph of Israel is only to be brief, for there is another enemy to face, Assyria, not named here, who will in the end harry the land from the extreme northern limit down to the frontier of Egypt.

7¹⁻⁸. *The first of a series of visions. A locust.* There is no reason to doubt that Amos was as clearly conscious of seeing the things described as of looking at the ordinary objects of daily life. This 'second sight' was characteristic of the prophetic experience, and was always held to be perfectly real, though it did not belong to the realm of ordinary life or to the things that ordinary men's senses would show to them. As Amos describes these visions there is some conversation between the prophet and Jahveh, so that the experience was one of hearing as well as one of sight. In one or two cases this develops into an oracle, and was possibly used by the compiler to introduce an utterance which he thought suitable to the occasion.

The first vision seems to have been that of a gigantic locust (for 'he formed locusts' we should probably read with the LXX 'the form of a locust'), which devoured the new grass springing up after the first mowing. This had gone to the king as tribute, and the farmers had as yet nothing for themselves and their animals. This means complete starvation, and Amos cries out that the land cannot bear it. And in pity Jahveh changes His mind. The thing has not happened yet, it has only appeared to the prophet in his vision as something which will come, and his prayer averts the calamity.

7[4-6]. *Jahveh summons a flame of fire.* The text is uncertain, but probably Amos did not use the word 'contend' here. The fire is no ordinary blaze, for it consumes the whole ocean and then starts to destroy the fields. Again Amos successfully intercedes.

7[7-9]. *A plumb-line.* Amos sees Jahveh Himself holding a plumb-line against a wall. He has repeatedly overlooked and pardoned the offences of Israel, but there is to be no more of this. He will see whether she is really 'upright' or not. The time has come for decisive action, and if it be found, as it certainly will, that Samaria is really a moral and spiritual failure, the punishment will not long be delayed. Even the powerful and conquering king will suffer, and will be carried away as a captive.

7[10-17]. *Amos and Amaziah.* This forms one of those narratives about the prophets which we not infrequently meet both in the Books of Kings and in the prophetic books themselves. It probably owes its present position to the fact that v. 9 is the only oracle in which Jeroboam is mentioned by name, and it was natural for the compiler to connect the two passages.

There are really two incidents, the first contained in vv. 10 and 11, and the second in vv. 12-17. In the former there is no direct contact between the priest and the prophet, and Amaziah simply sends to the king a report of the dangerous language which Amos is using. There would seem to be some ground for his action. He must have been a royal official, since the sanctuary at Bethel was the king's chapel, and would necessarily be concerned in the fate of the reigning dynasty. In days gone by the prophets had taken a prominent part in politics, and their disapproval of a king or of a family had proved dangerous. The house to which Jeroboam himself belonged had been placed on the throne through a revolution engineered by the prophets as a protest against the worship of the Tyrian Baal, and Amaziah may well have felt that this wild man from the southern deserts had similar designs on the house of Jehu. It is to be noted that the words he ascribes to Amos are not found in the recorded utterances of the prophet, but are a fair summary of much that does appear there. They may well have been actually spoken by him.

Perhaps we are expected to understand that Amaziah received

authority from the court for the expulsion of Amos, as described in the remaining verses of the chapter. He contemptuously classes Amos with the professional prophets, and tells him that Judah is the right place for such a man to earn his living. He addresses him directly as a ' seer', but a note in 1 Sam. 9⁹ shows us that the two terms had become interchangeable at an early date, the word for 'prophet' probably referring to his outward behaviour, the term 'seer' to his inward experience. In any case the royal sanctuary is not the place for him ; its religion is of a different type.

Amos replies that he is in no sense a professional prophet, still less a member of one of their more or less organized guilds. On the contrary, he had been a shepherd (so read for ' herdsman ' with LXX) until the moment when he first heard the actual voice of Jahveh and was driven thereby to leave his flock. It is this compulsion which has made him what he is, and having had this experience, he cannot possibly be false to it. As he said himself, ' The lion roars ; who shall not fear ? Jahveh hath spoken ; who shall not prophesy ? ' It is this sense of a direct and immediate commission which gives Amos his peculiar power, and made him a new feature in the religious history of Israel.

To this explanation Amos adds a word of personal denunciation of Amaziah. The fate that lies before him is that of captivity. Three aspects of this punishment are emphasized. The first is the desolation of his wife, who will be compelled to live the life of a common prostitute in the city to which she goes. The second is that the ancestral land which has probably belonged to Amaziah's family for generations is to be divided amongst others, and the third is that the priest himself, a holy person, who should never have any dealings with that which was not in itself consecrated, should actually die on ' unclean', that is foreign soil. The holy woman, the holy soil, the holy man—all these were to be profaned. We have no direct evidence to show that this prophecy was fulfilled in detail. The final captivity of Samaria did not come for nearly forty years, but the overthrow of Pekah may have been accompanied by a general desecration of Bethel. Even this would demand a period of probably about thirty years for the continued priesthood of Amaziah after the appearance of Amos at Bethel. But whether the calamity actually fell on Amaziah himself or not, it fell upon his house and on his successors. In Amos Israel had her warning and she refused to take it ; her doom, therefore, was certain, and the severest part of the penalty must have fallen upon those who were the religious leaders and should have brought Israel near to her God.

THE BOOK OF HOSEA

INTRODUCTION

THE work of Hosea is to be placed nearly a generation later than that of Amos. His main activity can hardly be dated before 740, and the fact that he makes no reference to the fall of Damascus, which took place in 732, makes it probable that the last of his prophecies was uttered before that event. The book which bears his name reflects throughout the condition of confusion and almost anarchy which followed on the death of Jeroboam II ; but the final overthrow of the northern monarchy, though imminent, has not yet taken place.

Hosea differs from Amos in several important respects. He is a native of the north and therefore sees her sins and her punishment not from the outside but as one who is personally involved. This gives him at once a sympathy and a passion which are together almost as near to remorse as to condemnation ; Israel's sins are to him as his own, and for them he himself repents. Further, his own history led him to a deeper truth than Amos ever attained. From the unfaithfulness of the wife whom he loved with his whole soul he learned what sin means to the heart of a supremely loving God. Amos had been chiefly concerned with the externals of life, the conduct of men towards one another. Whilst Hosea does not ignore the need for reform in this matter, his central thought is concerned with the relations and attitude of Israel to her God. Amos has much less to say than his successor in condemnation of apostasy, and while he does demand a return to Jahveh, lays far less stress than Hosea on the spirit which can make that return possible. In the last resort the essential need of Israel in Hosea's view is for a quality of soul, 'mercy' (yet far more than mercy), which will secure the right relation not only between man and man but also between man and God.

As in the case of other prophetic books, there are to be distinguished three types of material from which the volume in its present form was in the main compiled. In the first place we have oracular matter, and by far the greater part of the book is to be assigned to this type. In the second place there is narrative about the prophet, where he himself appears as the narrator—in Hosea found only in ch. 3. In the third place there are narratives which are somewhat similar to the last type, except for the fact that the story is told in the third person and not in the first. Again, this element is not extensive in the

Book of Hosea, being practically confined to ch. 1. Both ch. 1 and ch. 3 deal with the prophet's marriage, and commentators have found some difficulty in harmonizing the two. Some have even gone so far as to suppose that one account or the other is spurious, or that one is intended to be metaphorical. But as a matter of fact the discrepancies and differences between the two narratives do not seem to be unduly great if they are accounts of the same events as presented by different persons.

As in most cases, the oracles proper are in poetical form. The style of Hosea corresponds to his strength of feeling, and is passionate, almost tempestuous. Yet there is at times a sense of extraordinary tenderness, and there are few more beautiful or appealing pictures in literature than that of the father teaching his child to walk (11^3). Like all Hebrew poets, Hosea is rich in metaphor. Israel's sins are like the baker's furnace (6^{6-8}), her love like the morning cloud or the early dew (6^4), her political skill is that of a silly dove (7^{11}), her national stability that of a chip upon the waters ($10^{7\,\mathrm{mg}}$). The text seems to be frequently corrupt, but even where it is not, the gusts of feeling and rapid alternations of the prophet often make him difficult to read.

NOTES ON HOSEA 3, 5-6

3. *An account of Hosea's marriage.*

This section has aroused a good deal of discussion, both with regard to its relationship to the story told in ch. 1, and because of certain features of its own. Some students would regard both chapters as allegorical, having no basis in fact. Others believe them both to be records of actual events, and suppose that the narrative here should follow directly at the end of ch. 1. In that case it would seem that Hosea and his wife had separated after the birth of her children and that she had somehow fallen into slavery, from which her true husband redeemed her. Others, again, whilst accepting the narrative of ch. 1 as historical, think that ch. 3 is a later compilation with which Hosea himself had nothing to do, which was inserted in order to emphasize the relations between Jahveh and Israel. On the whole the simplest explanation of the facts is that suggested above, namely that they are both accounts of the same set of events, the one written from the point of view of an outsider, the other from that of the prophet himself.

The chapter falls into two parts, vv. 1-3 describing the marriage of Hosea, vv. 4-5 the lesson which is to be drawn from it. This latter is hinted at in v. 1, where the reason why Hosea has to give his heart to a woman of this kind is said to be the fact that Jahveh has given

His heart to Israel, and that she is no better than the poor woman whom Hosea takes. The prophet buys her, perhaps from the slave market, perhaps from a temple, perhaps (though this is less likely) from her father, in which case the price paid would be the ordinary gifts of the bridegroom. The purchase money is partly in coin and partly in kind, and the two sums were probably of equal value. The total would thus be about 30 shekels (£4 or a little less), the normal rate for a slave.

She does not attain full status in her new home at once. Because she is 'one loving a paramour' (so read for 'beloved of her friend' in v. 1), she cannot yet know the full measure of her husband's love. Probably, in view of v. 4, we should assume that something has dropped out from the last words of v. 3 and that the verse originally ended 'nor will I come unto thee'.

All this is a picture of the relations between Jahveh and Israel. The key-note of the teaching of Hosea is struck at once; he is primarily concerned with the treatment that the people have accorded their God. The place of the lover is taken by the Baals and the monarchy—to Hosea the northern dynasty was in its very nature wicked—and the husband is Jahveh. Therefore she must be for a time without those things which have made her political and religious life, kings, princes, and the paraphernalia of worship. She has indulged in 'cakes of raisins', which were probably eaten in honour of one or other of the Baals as a wine-god, so now she shall have no sacrifice or any material object to adore. The 'pillar' is a *menhir*, a plain upright stone which stood beside the altar, the 'ephod' and the 'teraphim' were probably large or small images which were used at the temples in divination. This means that she will be taken away from her land, and she will not even be in touch with Jahveh her own loving God. But this is only for a time, and eventually she will have had her wickedness purged from her (though some scholars doubt the originality of v. 5) and will be re-established with a legitimate royal house and a true spiritual relationship to Jahveh her God.

5$^{1-2}$. *Condemnation of the Government.* Little or no sense can be made of the Hebrew text of v. 2, and it has been suggested with a high degree of probability (the textual changes being very slight) that we should read vv. 1b-2:

> For a snare have ye been at Mizpah,
>   And a net spread upon Tabor;
> A deep pit at Shittim,
>   Though I rebuke you all.

The opening sentence is capable of more than one interpretation. It is usual to assume that 'unto you pertaineth the judgement' means that the sentence will be executed upon the priests and the court. But in view of what follows, it may be better to explain the phrase as meaning 'judgement is your proper business'. It is the function

MIZPAH.

Photograph by Fr. Vester & Co.

of the leaders of the people to secure justice (this applied both to the priests and to the king), and to do for their fellow-countrymen all that the Judges used to do in the days before the monarchy. Instead of fulfilling their proper function these men have been the ruin of Israel, and have hunted men down in order to destroy them. All three places mentioned are sanctuaries of one kind or another. Mizpah is in Gilead—there the rulers have laid traps for people. Tabor is not far from Nazareth—there a net has been spread. Shittim is the place where Israel sinned in the matter of Baal-Peor—there they have dug a pit to catch their game.

5³⁻⁷. *The chains of sin.* The use of the word 'month' in v. 7 has created difficulties, and it is probably due to textual corruption. No satisfactory restoration of the text, however, has yet been proposed. What is clear is that some terrible punishment is in prospect, and the details are not essential to the message. That message is quite characteristic of the prophets. The punishment that falls on men for their sin is not arbitrarily imposed by Jahveh, it is the inevitable result of the sin. Jahveh knows Israel, it is true, but it is not He who makes her recovery impossible. She has been guilty of apostasy, and has worshipped other gods, probably the Baals. Hosea applies to this the metaphor of marriage which he has used on other occasions, and it should be observed that such a metaphor was particularly suitable in the case of forms of religion which involved (as Baal worship almost certainly did) immoral rites. Now it is the sin itself which holds the sinner back, so that he cannot return to his allegiance. It is the pride of Israel which is the nation's own accuser, and their iniquity over which they fall. Until they have put away this thing from them, no sacrifice can restore the relationship between Israel and Jahveh. It is they who have forsaken Him, not He who has forsaken them, and they are bound by their own sin. This is the prophetic law of retribution, and illustrates the fact that these men saw the connexion between sin and the suffering which follows it as an illustration of the chain of cause and effect. If man sins, suffering of some kind is certain to follow.

5⁸⁻¹¹. *The judgement imminent.* Doubt has been raised in some quarters as to whether Hosea ever had anything to say about the southern kingdom of Judah. In that case the appearance of the name is due to textual corruption, and here and elsewhere 'Israel' should be read in its place. But this is far from being certain. In v. 8 for 'behind thee'—a cry of warning or alarm—the LXX read a verb implying panic. V. 11, as it stands, even in the R.V. (which is probably the best that can be made out of the traditional Hebrew text), can hardly be right, and it is better to follow the LXX and read:

> An oppressor is Ephraim,
>   He crusheth justice;
> For it is his pleasure
>   To follow a lie.

On the lofty heights of Gibeah and Ramah, both in the territory of Benjamin, and Bethel, here indicated by Hosea's scathing nickname, Beth-Awen (= House of Woe instead of House of God), there rings out the warning of the cornet (a curved ram's horn) and the trumpet (a straight instrument). An enemy is at hand, and all who would save their lives must flee instantly. Jahveh's 'rebuke' is at hand. That is to say He comes to settle the matter, to discuss it, to investigate

Site of Bethel.

Photograph by Fr. Vester & Co.

it, to pronounce and execute His decisions. There is no doubt as to the issue, for the ruling classes have been guilty of the worst of crimes. The removal of a landmark was an offence which incurred the heaviest of curses, cf. Dt. 19^{14}, 27^{17}. As Amos had seen, a generation earlier, the very foundations of justice were undermined by these people, and, worst of all, in their religious life they had deliberately chosen to adopt a worship which was baseless and false. For them the only possibility was destruction.

5[12–14]. *The failure and the stupidity of Israel's foreign policy.* It is possible that in the last clause of v. 13 the pronouns of the 2nd plural should be read as 3rd singular, to agree with the rest of the passage.

Israel has utterly failed to appreciate the meaning of her sufferings. Not seeing that it was Jahveh Himself who was bringing calamity upon her, she has tried to save herself by political means. The reference is almost certainly to the attempt of Menahem to secure the favour of Tiglath-pileser in 738 by sending him tribute. There is no reasonable doubt that the king of Assyria is intended, though the name Jareb is not found elsewhere. It has been plausibly conjectured that this is a misreading of an Assyrian title which meant 'Great King'. In any case the effort was futile, because it was made in the wrong quarter. It was Jahveh who was doing the harm, the human enemies of Israel were only His instruments, and no cure could be wrought by any one else.

5[15]–**6**[7]. *The shallow and inadequate repentance of Israel.* The words 'his going forth is sure as the morning' in v. 3 seem strange, and most modern scholars prefer to read with the LXX 'when we seek him we shall find him', the necessary alterations in the Hebrew text being very slight. The LXX again seem to have had the right reading in v. 5, where they render 'my judgements are as the light'. The phrase 'as Adam' in v. 7 is suspicious, the 'there' of the following clause seems to imply that a place-name preceded it, but no satisfactory suggestion has yet been made.

Jahveh is depicted as the patient lover who knows that sooner or later His erring bride will find herself in calamity, and will then turn back to Him for help. At last the repentance comes, and is expressed in familiar penitential language. Israel is so sure of His love that she takes her own iniquity lightly. 'He's a good fellow, and 'twill all be well' is the attitude she adopts. The language is exquisitely beautiful, but the sentiment is sentiment and nothing more. They are taking sin too easily. Hosea knows from his own experience what it really means, and knows that it is impossible for Jahveh to forgive as long as Israel fails to grasp the awful facts.

For it is not sacrifice, not ritual offerings or ritual prayers that Jahveh requires. There is a supreme quality of soul which adequately appreciates and duly responds to the appeal of personality. This is expressed by the Hebrew word *ḥesed*, and there is no one word in English that carries its meaning. Sympathy, kindness, mercy, love—it is all these and more, issuing always in practical life. It may be the attitude of the superior to the inferior, or that of the inferior to the superior, and it is applied both to relations between man and God and to relations between man and man. In so far as Israel has exhibited it at all—and in this passage it is probable that it is the religious and not the social aspect of the term that is in view— she has displayed it only in a superficial fashion. It has been like the dew which lies thickly over the ground at dawn but vanishes with the sun's early rays. What can Jahveh do? How can He give His people a sense of reality? That is the problem, and as Hosea sees it is insoluble. It is, perhaps, a little strange to find that the prophets are made instruments of punishment (v. 5), but (though the text is sometimes suspected) this is not wholly out of accord with Hebrew theory and history. The spoken word is held to be efficient in itself, and when the prophets have denounced Israel it is believed that the punishment has followed as a result of the utterance. Again, one at least of the great revolutions of Israel, that which placed Jehu on the throne and overthrew the house of Omri, was undoubtedly due to the political intrigues of the prophetic guilds led by Elisha.

And so the whole of this passage, indeed the whole teaching ot Hosea, is summed up in v. 6: 'I desire mercy and not sacrifice.' This is one of the greatest words in the Old Testament.

6[8-11]. *The iniquities of Israel.* Both text and rendering of v. 9 are uncertain, and it has been suggested that some such place-name as Machir once stood at the beginning and that the verse as a whole should run :

> In Machir are robber bands,
> A company of priests;
> On the road to Shechem they murder,
> For villainy have they wrought.

v. 11 may also be by a later hand, inserted to draw the contrast between Israel and Judah.

One of the most terrible features of the life of Israel in the eighth century was the appalling corruption of worship and religion. Gilead was one of the sacred cities, but it was spotted and splashed with blood. Elsewhere the very priests were the worst of brigands, and used their official position to commit robbery and murder, and the shrines themselves were at times little more than organized centres of immorality. It was the sense of this contrast between what he knew Jahveh really to be and the external forms of Israelite religion which made the real burden of Hosea's spiritual message.

THE BOOK OF MICAH

INTRODUCTION

OUR present Book of Micah is best regarded as a composite work. Three different short collections of prophetic utterances have apparently been placed together, and united—possibly by accident. The fact that the second and third of these are anonymous would tend to make this easier, and there are several other instances in the prophetic literature where this appears to have happened. A book which had no name prefixed would readily be assumed by a copyist to be a continuation of its predecessor, and he might not unnaturally write straight on. It is almost certain that this has happened not only in our present Book of Micah, but also in the Book of Isaiah and the Book of Zechariah. It should, however, be pointed out that this does not in any way affect the 'inspiration' of the documents concerned. A Divine message remains valid, whoever may have been the human agent through whom it was given to the world, and we have no right to assume that God could speak only through the limited number of individuals whose names we know.

The divisions in the case of the Book of Micah are to be found at the end of chs. 3 and 5. We have the strongest of reasons for attributing chs. 1–3 to Micah himself, for the last sentences of ch. 3 are quoted as his in Jer. 26[18]. But the tone, style, and general character of what follows seem rather to reflect the conditions of a later time. Chs. 4–7 include some of the noblest utterances in the Old Testament, but many scholars hold that they belong to another period than Micah's.

Assuming then that we can recognize in chs. 1–3 the undoubted work of the prophet whose name stands at the head of the book, we notice that the general conditions described are similar to those which Amos observed. The chief differences seem to be due to the different circumstances in which the two prophets lived and worked. Micah belongs to the agricultural country of the western slopes of the Judaean hills. His home is placed in Moresheth-Gath, probably a village on the Philistine border. He is thus familiar with the conditions of agricultural life in Judah, and he finds them no better than Amos had found them in the north. There is the same greed on the part of the wealthy landowners, the same abuse of the forms of law, the same oppression and desolation of the peasants. But Micah speaks in a tone even more bitter than that of Amos; he is, apparently, himself one of the sufferers from the iniquities of the social order. He has not the breadth of vision nor the deeper insight of his great predecessor, but nevertheless his message is substantially the same. From the reference in Jer. 26[18] it would seem that he spoke of no mitigation of the sentence passed by Jahveh ; he felt that the doom was inevitable.

The actual date of his prophecy is uncertain. The mention of Samaria seems to place a part of his activity, at any rate, before 721 ;[1] but there is a general tendency to assign the greater portion of his work to rather later times, and to locate him between 715 and 701. A part of the difficulty in dating him accurately is the fact that he is so little interested in the wider movements of international politics. He is deeply concerned with the sufferings of the agriculturists in his own village and immediate district, but his references to the capital are less striking than those of any other Judean prophet, and he does not so much as mention Assyria, the great world power and the worst terror of Israel and Judah in his days.

NOTES ON MICAH 1[1]–3[12]

1[1]. *Superscription to the whole book.* As is usual in the prophetic books, the first verse is simply of the nature of a title. Micah's home has already been mentioned, and the three kings are named as indicating the period within which the activity of Micah fell. There is, as has already been said, a good deal of uncertainty as to the exact events to which his prophecies referred, but it is unlikely that any of them went so far back as the reign of Jotham. Probably this note was the work of the final editor of the book, who was not very sure of the dates of the kings.

1[2–9]. *The coming of Jahveh to judge Israel and Judah.* It is possible that we should read only one of the divine names Lord God (i.e. Lord Jahveh) in v. 2. In v. 3 the Hebrew words for 'will come down' and 'will tread' are very similar, and may have been originally alternatives, both of which have found their way into the text. Doubts have been raised as to whether 5b (from 'What is the transgression of Jacob?') and v. 7, with its prosaic enumeration of calamities, belonged to the original text. It would certainly run more easily without them.

---

[1] This inference is not certain ; Samaria was not wholly destroyed by Sargon, and is mentioned in a later Assyrian inscription.

The whole oracle forms a magnificent theophany. In v. 2 all the nations of the earth are summoned to see the testimony that Jahveh bears against them. It is true that it is only Israel with whom He is to deal directly, but Micah has that outlook characteristic of the prophets, and still more manifest in Ezekiel than earlier, which makes him think of Jahveh as the greatest of Gods, and bids him announce that His dealings with Israel are intended as a lesson to the whole world. In v. 3 He comes. His home appears to be in the heavens, but to perform His will He descends to the earth, touching first the tops of the mountains. His coming is swift and terrible, and is heralded by appalling natural convulsions, melting hills, and bursting valleys. Then is His purpose made clear; He comes to take vengeance on His people for their sin. Details follow. Samaria is to be laid in ruins (some scholars would prefer to read 'country village' or 'wild forest' for 'an heap of the field'), and on her site vines may be planted. She was built on a hill-side, and the stones of which her houses and walls consisted were to be rolled down into the valley below, so that the very foundations—all that was to be left of her—should be visible, just as to-day many an ancient building may have its ground plan alone traceable from the foundations which remain. And though the prophet is deeply conscious of the sin of Israel, he cannot but be struck with sorrow, pain, and fear at the thought of the ruin of these noble monuments of human power and skill. For the tide of ruin pours southwards. Samaria is overwhelmed (this is seen prophetically, and the passage should therefore be dated before 722), and the trouble does not stop there, but rolls onwards till it reaches the very gates of Jerusalem. So he must mourn, with bared feet and scanty raiment, screaming and wailing in his grief like the jackal and the ostrich.

I$^{10-16}$. *The woe of the countryside.* In v. 10 the Hebrew word represented by 'not at all' probably conceals a place-name—Acco, Bokim, and Baca have all been suggested; the last is the most probable. The text of the latter part of v. 11 is very difficult, and is probably corrupt almost beyond hope of correction. The E.V. 'waited carefully' or 'waiteth anxiously' in v. 12 represents an emendation which is probably correct, the literal translation of the Hebrew text is to be found in the margin—'was grieved' or 'is in travail'. In v. 14 'thou shalt give' is better read as a Passive— 'there shall be given'.

The passage is one which speaks of the suffering which will fall on the district in which Micah's own home was situated. Moresheth-

Gath is one of the places mentioned, and all the others seem to have been within a few miles of it. The most striking feature of the passage is the number of puns or plays upon the names of these places. To the Hebrew mind this was in no sense humorous, and was quite consistent with the strongest expressions of feeling. Thus

Modern Samaria.

Photograph by Fr. Vester & Co.

the sound of the word 'tell' resembles the name Gath (the same phrase is used in David's lament over Saul and Jonathan, 2 Sam. 1[20]), 'Baca' or 'Bokim' would be a name that suggested 'weeping', Aphrah is practically the same word as 'dust', 'to the swift steed' is in Hebrew 'Larechesh'—an assonance with Lachish. In the case of Moresheth itself the suggestion is indirect and more delicate. The 'parting gift' is a term used especially of what is bestowed on a bride when she leaves the house of her father for that of her husband, and recalls the word 'Meoresheth', the Hebrew term for

a betrothed woman, 'A deceitful thing' is 'Achzab', and finally 'him
that shall possess thee' is similar in sound to the name Mareshah.

Little is said of the sins for which this punishment is to come.
There is a hint in v. 13 that it is the attempt to assimilate herself to
the 'higher' civilizations using horses and chariots which has been
responsible for the downfall of Israel. But in the main the passage
is simply an echoing cry of distress, rising from all these little
villages. It is not difficult to picture their distress, with the weeping
and the wailing, and the women plucking out their hair till their
heads are as bare as that of the vulture itself. The country has been
swept by marauding bands of enemies, and all the men worth
considering have gone into captivity.

2$^{1-5}$. *Oppression and punishment.* The text of v. 4 is obviously
corrupt, and editors generally resort to conjectural emendation,
making the verse run somewhat as follows:

In that day

> One shall lift up a taunt-song against you,
>   And utter a dirge:
> 'Our farm is measured with a line,
>   And none doth restore it;
> To our captors our fields are apportioned,
>   We are ruined, yea ruined'.

The first part of the passage—and possibly two passages originally
independent have been associated with one another—deal with the
sin, and the second with the punishment. The first word is a groan
over the oppressive squires who spend their nights thinking out
plans for robbing their neighbours, which they can proceed to carry
out as soon as the morning breaks. Their position as important
country magnates gives them the power to do this, and, as often
happens in the East, it is enough for them to want the property
of their poorer fellows, and they can take it when they will. The
treatment Naboth received from Jezebel is probably typical of much
that went on both in the north and in the south during the century
or two which followed her death. But Jahveh can think out plans
as well as they, and His plans mean the destruction of the oppressors
themselves in their turn. The result of His activity appears in the
dirge which these men will one day have to sing over their own
calamities, when the enemy will come and divide their land and give
it to others. The meaning and connexion of v. 5 with what precedes
are obscure, and many editors think that the verse is an accidental
addition from another source.

2[6–11]. *Another oracle on the same theme.* Again there are several alterations in the received text which most modern students believe to be necessary in order to recover the original sense of the prophet. Towards the end of v. 6, 'reach' or 'overtake' should be read instead of 'depart', and the phrase should be linked on to the first two or three words of v. 7. In this latter verse 'His words' is a more likely phrase than 'my words'. The first part of v. 8 is supposed to have run originally:

> And ye are a foe to my people,
> Against the peaceful ye rise;
> Ye strip from travellers security,
> — A captivity of war.

The passage opens with an imaginative and dramatic dialogue, in which an unusual and rather contemptuous word is used of prophesying:

A (addressing the Prophets), 'Do not prophesy !'

B (addressing A), 'Oh, let them prophesy.'

A (addressing B), 'They shall *not* prophesy of these things.'

And the speaker A goes on to give his reasons.   Israel is safe, no calamity can touch her, her God is on her side, and is a patient person who cannot behave as the prophets say He does. They cannot really be giving His message.   It is the feeling of the people who believe that the established order is of Divine ordinance, and that it is intended for their especial benefit. They can therefore continue in safety the kind of conduct which arouses the hostility of a Micah. They must learn otherwise. They have behaved to their own countrymen exactly as if they were foreign invaders. Peaceful travellers find that they are simply brigands who will kidnap them as an enemy takes men prisoners in war and sells them into slavery. Women are driven savagely from the homes they have loved, poor though those homes may have been. Children are ruthlessly torn from their parents, and the evicted and scattered families are allowed no place in which to stay. For this the ruin shall be swift and sure. Yet, though they will have nothing to say to the true prophet, the common drunken ecstatic can always secure a hearing—he is the prophet for them.

2[12–13]. *A final hope.* These verses are generally now regarded as an addition which presupposes the Exile, and therefore date from a time long after the days of Micah. There is one change in the text which is often made, most editors reading for 'Bozrah' a word which means 'in a fold'.

Jacob is scattered throughout the whole world, but that is not the end. A time will come when all shall be gathered again like a flock that has been dispersed and re-assembled. At their head is the 'breaker', i.e. the old ram who is the acknowledged leader of the flock, the 'bell-wether'. In this case the leader is Jahveh Himself, who has now superseded all earlier forms of government, and from now onwards takes the guidance and control of His people.

Ch. 3 consists of three denunciations of the leaders of the Jewish state. The first (vv. 1-4) and third (vv. 9-12) of these are concerned with the civil authorities, the second with the prophets. All three are couched in the strongest language, and it may be doubted whether the social iniquities of a landed aristocracy and of a privileged religious class have ever been more violently denounced.

3^{1-4}. *Official injustice and cruelty.* As elsewhere in the prophets, so here stress is laid on what is always in the East a primary function of government, the administration of justice. In every land and under all conditions this work demands high qualities, humanity, impartiality, incorruptibility, and a deep passion for righteousness. All this is implied in the words 'is it not for you to know judgement?' And against that ideal—knowing judgement—the prophet sets the actual life and practice of the rulers as he saw them. Their conduct seemed to him not even to be dictated by a cool self-interest, but by a real and passionate love of wickedness for its own sake, and an equally passionate hatred of good for its own sake. Their brutal cruelty is described in language which must be metaphorical, but is none the less true—flaying the wretched peasants, stripping the flesh from the skeleton and chopping up the very bones. But retribution will overtake them. Just as they have spurned the suppliant who has appealed to them for justice in his misery, so they in turn will fall before Jahveh when attacked by foreign enemies, and their cry will go unheeded. Their God will be as deaf to them as they have been to the sufferers and oppressed among their own people.

3^{5-8}. *The prophets.* The 'Lords spiritual' are no better than the 'Lords temporal'. The duty of the prophet was to transmit to people the message he had received from God, whatever that message might be. It was further believed in some vague way that the words the prophet uttered were in themselves efficient, and could produce the result described. But the kind of prophet who flourished in Micah's day allowed his own interests to dictate his message. If

men fed him—so that he could 'bite with his teeth'—the promises
he gave were pleasant and brought prosperity, but if no gifts were
bestowed, then the man would stir up a holy war and call on his
neighbours to persecute his enemy in the name of Jahveh Himself.
The punishment would be the deprivation of all prophetic rights,
privileges, and faculties. The prophetic vision would disappear, the
prophets would be made to exhibit signs of mourning of many kinds,
black raiment, the downcast face, and the covered lip. *They* have
ceased to win any answer from their God, whilst on the other hand
the prophet who, like Micah, has set his face against all falsity and
has spoken the truth, even though it meant dire calamity, will find
an increasing strength of spirit, as the true inspiration takes more
and more complete possession of him. He, at least, will 'declare
unto Jacob his transgression and to Israel his sin'.

3$^{9-12}$. *Summing up and sentence.* In v. 1 the Hebrew text begins
with 'He buildeth', not 'They build'. The E.V. translates a text
emended in accordance with the reading of the LXX and other
versions, and is doubtless correct.

In a few lines the iniquities of Israel are summed up, and vv. 9-11a
are a repetition of the last two oracles in brief. v. 11b adds a new
sin. These men—judges, priests, and prophets alike—appeal to
Jahveh for protection, and find their security in the thought of his
defence. Like the contemporaries of Jeremiah a century later they
say 'The Temple of the Lord, the Temple of the Lord, the Temple
of the Lord are these', and use their religion as brigands use their
cave. This is the crowning iniquity. It means that they are for ever
incapable of distinguishing between good and evil, of knowing right
from wrong. And the vindication of the righteousness of Jahveh
requires that they should be used to illustrate the lesson that they
cannot learn themselves. The world has a moral basis, retribution
is universal and inevitable, and for sinners such as they are doom
will be utter and complete.

THE BOOK OF ISAIAH

INTRODUCTION

THE Book of Isaiah, in the form which it assumes in our Bibles, is a prophetic library rather than a prophetic book. It falls obviously into three divisions. The first (chs. 1–35) and third (chs. 40–66) consist of oracular material, though in the former there is a good deal of autobiographical prose, whilst between them stands a fairly long biographical section of which the greater part is also found in the Book of Kings. It has long been recognized that the connexion between the second and third is of the slightest, and that the attachment of chs. 40-66 to the Book of Isaiah is probably accidental. They seem to consist, down to the end of ch. 55, of oracles mainly due to a single prophet who lived and worked in Babylon towards the close of the Exile, and from ch. 56 onward of the utterances of a prophet whose home was in Jerusalem at least a generation after the Return. For our present purposes, then, we have to consider only chs. 1–39, and even of these chapters the last four have been largely covered in the section dealing with 2 Kings. The remainder, chs. 1–35, presents us with what is, on the whole, the simplest and most obvious structure that we find amongst the prophetic books. The smaller collections from which the book has been compiled are clearly marked, and some have separate titles and short introductions. Thus ch. 1 is a general collection of oracles which serves admirably as an introduction to the whole book. The other groups are as follows:

Chs. 2–5. Mainly oracles concerned with the sins of Judah.

6–12. A collection of oracular and autobiographical matter concluding with a couple of short Psalms.

13–23. A collection of oracles directed against various nations, including, apparently, Judah in ch. 22.

24–27. An eschatological section describing the ultimate triumph of Jahveh and his enthronement.

28–35. An oracular collection concerned with Israel, and concluding with passages which promise a return from the Exile.

It seems unlikely that the whole of this material can safely be attributed to Isaiah the son of Amoz. The eschatological section, for instance, is probably some centuries later than this prophet, and is to be assigned to the fourth century B. C. It is true

that eschatology is not, as some have thought, a late development in Israelite theology (see Note on Eschatology, pp. 243 ff.),
but the kind of thought to which this section gives expression is
hardly early. The great Messianic passage in ch. 11 seems to
pre-suppose the Exile, for the tree of David has already been cut
down, and only its stump remains in the ground. In the
collection of oracles against foreign nations, those directed
against Babylon (chs. 13–14) and Elam (21^{1-12}) are most naturally
assigned to the time of the Exile, though it is sometimes doubted
whether the song over the fall of the tyrant in ch. 14 originally
referred to a Babylonian king, and not rather to an Assyrian
monarch. And finally chs. 33–5 seem to imply in large
measure either that the Exile is nearly over or that it is already
past—both points of view unnatural to Isaiah.

But when all allowance is made for these and shorter passages
of later date, there yet remains a considerable body of material
whose Isaianic authorship has never been seriously questioned.
From these it is possible to form a picture of the man. His
deepest passion is for moral holiness, and it is largely to him
that the world owes the moralization of the idea of sanctity. He
is as insistent as Amos or Micah on social righteousness, and
has an equally deep and fervid enthusiasm for his God. But he
has a wider outlook than any of his predecessors, and his view
of the world includes the great empires just as much as Israel.
He thus attains to a genuine statesmanship, though not such as
makes calculations as to the resources at the disposal of any of
the great powers, or elaborately discusses any given political
situation. He sees the whole of human history as the development of a divine plan, in which each nation must play its part.
That done the nation can be offered a new task, but if the work
has been performed with a lack of the moral principle which
Jahveh requires, then the tool will be thrown aside or destroyed,
to make room for another. At the same time Israel herself must,
if she desires safety, avoid entering the whirlpool of international
politics. As events showed, this was wise policy even from
a material point of view, but Isaiah's reason for advocating it
was not material. He was so convinced of the power of Jahveh,
and of His special relation to Israel, that he felt she did not
need any other alliance than that of her God. His statesmanship was built up on a foundation of faith.

He differs from Amos, Hosea, and Micah in one important
respect. Whilst he foresees calamity for his people as the
inevitable result of their sin, he also looks forward to a time
when suffering will have purged the nation. There will always
be a 'remnant', a small group of righteous survivors who will

form the nucleus of a fresh and better Israel. To his mind, Jahveh needed Israel for his own self-expression, and therefore could not suffer her utterly to perish, however severe the punishment might be. Closely connected with this idea, at any rate in thought, was the prospect of a Davidic king who was to restore the reign of righteousness and prosperity to Israel. Though he was still an earthly monarch, ruling over a physical Jerusalem, and apparently confined to a somewhat expanded Israel, Isaiah's picture of the coming Messiah gave the impulse to the growth of one of the great thoughts of his people, a thought which, after centuries of development, reached its culmination in the Christian experience of Jesus as the true 'Christ'.

NOTES ON ISAIAH 1, 6–10, 28–31

CHAPTER 1

The first chapter of the Book of Isaiah consists of a series of oracles which deal with various subjects, and have been placed together by an early compiler. They once, it seems, formed an independent collection, and were used by the main compiler of the book as a general introduction. Six separate oracles can now be distinguished.

1^1. *Title to the whole book.* This gives the general period of the work of Isaiah (all included under the term ' vision ', which here does not refer to any particular time or experience), and is generally recognized as being correct. Isaiah's initial vision is dated in the last year of Uzziah (6^1), and it is clear that some of his oracles must be put down to the reign of Hezekiah. To this last reign belong the historical events described in the biographical chapters, 36–9. There is no mention of Jotham elsewhere in the book, but the prophet's dealings with Ahaz have a certain amount of space given to them.

1^{2-3}. *The ingratitude of Israel.* This short oracle strikes the key-note for the denunciations of Isaiah. Israel owes everything to Jahveh, yet she has rebelled against Him.   Her people are His children, but the very cattle show more appreciation of their relationship to their owner than Israel does to her God.   The rhythm of the second part of v. 3 shows that the emphasis of the verse lies on the negatives :

> The óx knóweth his ówner,
>   And the áss his máster's críb ;
> But Ísrael doth *nót* knów,
>   My peóple doth *nót* consíder.

To the Hebrew mind 'knowing' a person implies far more than mere acquaintance. It involves a recognition of rights and claims, and a careful attention. We might almost render 'has no regard for', or 'is not concerned with '. The national sin lies in this rejection of all real relation between people and God.

1⁴⁻⁹. *The suffering and desolation that follow on sin.* This passage is usually dated in or about 701, when Sennacherib had laid waste the whole land of Judah. The figure is that of a man who has suffered from the attacks of some violent enemy, and is covered in every part of his body with wounds. It is not that of a patient who is afflicted with a disease (for 'festering sores' in v. 6 read the margin 'fresh stripes' or 'wounds'), and the choice of a parallel points to foreign invasion. The accuracy of the picture corresponds with the statement of Sennacherib himself. Jerusalem remains ('daughter of Zion' is a Hebrew way of personifying Zion), but she is alone in the waste, like a shed in a vineyard or a garden. This is the result of her sinfulness —she is 'laden with iniquity', and her calamities are the inevitable outcome of her conduct. Yet there is still something left ; Jerusalem is untouched, and here, for the first time in the book, we meet with Isaiah's doctrine of the 'remnant', to which allusion has already been made. But for that Judah would have disappeared as Sodom did (in v. 7 for 'the overthrow of strangers' many prefer to read 'the overthrow of Sodom ').

1¹⁰⁻¹⁷. *A denunciation of ritual.* This section was doubtless attached to the preceding by a collector of oracles, because it began with a reference to Sodom. But it clearly has no organic connexion with it, and may have been one of the earlier utterances of Isaiah, whilst vv. 4-9 form the latest section in the whole of Isaiah's work to which we can assign a probable date. Here Sodom is mentioned because of its wickedness rather than because of its fate. The passage enunciates a view of religion which must have been strange to Isaiah's hearers, and has never been easy to maintain in practice. It is not formal worship, but moral conduct, especially in social relations, which Jahveh demands. The various forms of worship are enumerated, the burnt-offering, which was wholly handed over to the god and his priests, the 'peace-offering', of which the fat alone was burnt on the altar, the observance of the New Moon and the Sabbath (the latter at this period, perhaps, observed as a monthly festival, that of the full moon). So far from being acceptable to Jahveh, these things are positively hateful—so are fasting (so read with LXX for 'iniquity' in v. 13) and the solemn assembly. When men see the face of Jahveh (the marginal reading in v. 12 is to be preferred) the last thing that He asks of them is this elaborate and costly ritual. The hands stretched out to Him in prayer are naturally covered with sacrificial blood. But He sees this, not as the blood of slaughtered victims, but of men, women, and children done to death by the cruelties of the social and religious leaders of the day. It is possible that we have here a protest (otherwise lacking in Isaiah) against the human sacrifices which cast so deep a stain on the reign of Ahaz. So the demand is that men shall cleanse themselves from moral pollution, and instead of wasting themselves and their substance on futile and irritating ritual, should right the wrong and seek the prosperity and happiness of those who are not in a position to win these things for themselves.

I$^{18-20}$. *The offer of pardon and the warning against refusal.* This is one of the most familiar passages in all the Old Testament. It is an invitation by Jahveh to go into the whole question of human sin and to settle it once and for all. But His offer still leaves to the guilty parties the option of refusal, and if that course is chosen, the consequences must be faced. Israel has no hope save in accepting what Jahveh is so willing to give her. Otherwise, the only prospect before her is one of utter destruction.

I$^{21-23}$. *The moral degeneration of Jerusalem.* Isaiah here adopts Hosea's figure of marriage for the relationship between Jahveh and Judah, but instead of connecting her sin with the Baals, he sees that it is in moral iniquity that she has found the lover she desires. Some commentators feel that there is a clause too many in v. 21 ; some would omit ' but now murderers ', others ' the faithful city '. A third alternative would be to leave out ' righteousness lodged in her '. The point in any case is clear. Jerusalem had been, so Isaiah feels, all that a city should be ; now she is all that a city should not be. Her silver has become dross, or perhaps the mixed ore from which it has originally been smelted ; her wine has been adulterated, though the exact significance of the word rendered ' mixed ' is by no means certain. Princes, who should have been the centre of loyalty, are traitorous, and, not content with accepting bribes in court, positively go in search of them. Once more a modern and Western reader is struck by the stress on legal process, and the difficulty of securing impartiality and incorruptibility.

I$^{24-28}$. *The prospect of reform.* This oracle is closely linked with the preceding, and the similarity is quite enough to account for the proximity in which they stand. It is recognized that there is some good in Israel, but Jahveh has many enemies, even amongst His own people. These He will destroy, thus purifying the true metal in the furnace (so many commentators read for the Hebrew word represented by 'throughly') from dross and base metal. The process is thus to be a painful one, but in the end it will succeed, and Jerusalem will once more be what she was in days of old, a 'faithful city'.

I$^{29-30}$. *Condemnation of tree worship.* This cult seems to have been one of the regular forms of worship taken over by Israel from the Canaanites. Sacred oaks are several times mentioned in the earlier books of the Bible ; the Oak of Mamre, associated with Abraham, was probably in the first instance a sacred tree. Gardens, too, had become holy spots. The judgement on these (read 'ye shall be ashamed' for 'they shall be ashamed') is to be that they will suffer as trees may suffer. The latter are not divine ; they are God's creation, and are dependent on Him for their life. So are those who worship them, and Jahveh goes out of their life ; they will be as the trees from which He has withdrawn His supporting hand.

I^{31}. *The result of iniquity.* The danger of sin springs from its very nature. Men or nations may have confidence in their own strength, but they must not think that they can sin lightly and have done with it. The sin itself will fall upon them, and will kindle them to a destructive blaze which none can quench.

CHAPTERS 6–10.

These chapters seem to have formed the original nucleus of the third of the smaller collections included in our present Book of Isaiah. Whilst it is possible that they include some prophetic material which is not to be attributed to Isaiah himself, no serious doubts exist as to the authorship of the greater proportion, and, indeed, there are only a few verses in the five chapters which have given rise to any question in the minds of competent students. On the other hand, chapters 11 and 12 seem to have originated in the Exile, and to have been attached as a sort of appendix to the collection by a collector. The great Messianic passage with which chapter 11 opens seems to presuppose the destruction of the Jewish monarchy ; the word for the 'stem' of Jesse means 'the stump that is left in the ground after the tree has been cut down '. Whilst the spirit and thought of these two chapters are in direct continuation of those of Isaiah, they seem to be applied to a later situation in the history of Israel.

The collection itself includes a good deal of autobiographical matter, a large part of which seems to be connected with the reign of Ahaz, and a number of oracles have been added to this to form the whole collection.

6[1-13]. *The first vision and call of Isaiah.* This chapter tells the story of the first great ecstatic experience of Isaiah, that which made him a prophet and summoned him to his life-work. The event is dated as having taken place in the last year of the reign of Uzziah, whose long reign overlapped that of Jeroboam II in northern Israel and marked the highest point of prosperity which the double monarchy ever reached. The prophet is either in the court of the Temple, facing the open doors of the sanctuary itself, or else actually within the building. If the latter suggestion be correct, it is probable that he had priestly blood in him, for though the rules were not necessarily as strict as they afterwards became, it is not likely that free access to the sanctuary as distinct from the open court was permitted to the general laity.

We may assume that Isaiah was there for the purpose of worship (though this is not stated) when the ecstasy fell upon him, and he became conscious of a world, real enough, but commonly hidden from human eyes. He saw Jahveh. Of the form under which the God of Israel was seen he offers no account, and indeed, it is a noticeable fact that of all the prophets who lived in more or less intimacy with the presence of Jahveh, Ezekiel alone even approximates to a description of His appearance. His state is kingly; He sits on a throne, and the purpose of such furniture is to-day in the East dignity rather than comfort. He is richly clad, and it may be that his garments are formed of the clouds of smoke rising from the altar of incense; it seems to the prophet that they fill the whole chamber. About Him are His strange attendants, the heavenly serpents. The name given to them, 'Seraphim', is that of the fiery serpents of Num. 21[4-9], and the bronze serpent made by Moses is a 'Seraph'. In Isaiah's early days this was the object of a recognized cult in Jerusalem, and it is not impossible that Jahveh Himself was held to be of this shape. Apparently they were serpents with human heads, hands, and feet, with wings distributed along their length, one pair being at the shoulders, and used to cover the face—even they could not bear to behold the full glory of Jahveh—one used for flight, and one veiling the feet. Their voices are human and intelligible, and their continuous song is praise of Jahveh's holiness. That is the key-note of the whole experience.

Its effect on Isaiah is immediate. Israel, like many other early peoples, believed that to see a deity was to die, except for certain privileged persons especially associated with him (or her). Such persons—whatever their precise function might be—were 'holy', and all others were 'unclean'. So the first thought that comes to

Isaiah is that of his own unfitness for such a sight, and therefore of the danger in which he stood. To his relief, one of the attendants of Jahveh takes from the altar a hot stone and lays it on his lips, with words which tell him that his disqualifications are removed. It is worth while noting, indeed it is fundamental to an appreciation of the meaning of the vision, that the 'uncleanness' is not a mere ceremonial unfitness, but a moral stain. It is not merely sin, it is iniquity that is removed from him. It is difficult to exaggerate the importance of the language. Every religion recognizes sin; it is that which is displeasing to the object of worship, or which interferes with the realization of the religious ideal. But in most religions, including that of early Israel, it has no moral content. A thing may be sin which does not affect the conscience in the least. Thus to the strict Hindu a breach of caste regulations is sin, though the act in itself may be harmless or even beneficial. On the other hand iniquity, i.e. acts which a man's conscience recognizes as morally wrong, may not offend the god at all, and are therefore altogether outside the pale of religion. As a rule 'holiness' and wickedness are far from being incompatible. But this vision shows Isaiah that his own 'sin' is not a ritual failing or incapacity, but his moral character. At once the conception of 'holiness' is lifted out of the sphere of the merely ceremonial into that of the moral, never to be lowered by any disciple of Isaiah's.

So ends the first element in the vision. Isaiah is purified, and is a fit person to be in the presence of Jahveh. Then he realizes that this quality which he has just won is not for his own use or advantage. He can now listen to Jahveh as he calls for volunteers to carry his message. At once the prophet responds, though the nature of the mission is not yet clear. That does not matter; the prophet is now Jahveh's man, and is willing to undertake any task that may be laid upon him. At first sight the charge is not merely difficult but terrible. His mission is to deaden the ears of Israel, to blind their eyes, and to harden their heart. But it must be remembered that the East does not readily distinguish between purpose and result, and all that can justly be inferred from the language addressed to the prophet is that he will find his people spiritually deaf and blind and unresponsive to what he has to say, so that they will not 'see with their eyes and hear with their ears' and be healed.

There follows a question on the part of the prophet, 'How long?' Is this to be carried to the extreme which will involve Israel in complete and absolute destruction? The answer is, unfortunately, uncertain, as a comparison between the A.V. and the R.V. suggests. vv. 11, 12 suggest a total desolation at least of the country districts, though the words need not necessarily apply to Jerusalem. v. 13, in which we should expect to find the decisive word, is obscure, and probably corrupt. For instance the last words, 'so the holy seed $\left\{ {\text{shall be} \atop \text{is}} \right\}$ the $\left\{ {\text{substance} \atop \text{stock}} \right\}$ thereof', were not in the text used by the LXX translators, and are probably a gloss, i. e. an explanatory note originally placed in the margin and accidentally included in the text by a copyist. The peculiarity of Hebrew syntax makes it possible that the opening words of the verse should be either a statement or a condition. If the former be right, then the hopeful tone of the A.V. is justified ; if the latter be the correct representation of the prophet's message, then the black outlook suggested by the R.V. must be accepted. In favour of the latter it should be pointed out that the word rendered ' shall be eaten (up)' comes from a root which means 'burn up', and elsewhere implies complete destruction. On the other hand the statement that the stump of the felled tree ('felled' of the R.V. is right as against 'cast their leaves' of the A.V.—if the text be sound) remains in the ground seems to suggest the possibility of a fresh growth. But this suggestion may be misleading, and the view now generally held is that the last verse really means 'If a tenth be left behind (as Amos 5³ hints), it shall be destroyed by fire, just as the stump of a tree that has been cut down is burnt away if it be too big and clumsy to be uprooted '.[1]

7¹⁻⁹. *Isaiah and the Syro-Ephraimite war. First utterances.* Two oracles (vv. 4–6 and 7–9) preceded by an historical introduction which, as our text stands, is from a biographical source, though some commentators think that ' Isaiah' of v. 3 is a textual error for ' me'.

vv. 1–2 give the historical circumstances. The fact of the coalition is familiar from Assyrian as well as from Israelite sources, and the effect on the mind of Judah, described in v. 2, is exactly what might be expected. The ' moving' or swaying of the mind of the king and of his people exactly expresses the state of panic into which they would naturally fall. The verses include the whole story of the war, for they mention the failure of the coalition, which, of course, was not apparent till after the events described in the following verses.

---

[1] The student is recommended to refer to Dr. G. B. Gray's fine exposition of the passage, *I. C. C., Isaiah*, pp. 99–111.

The entrance to the Virgin's Spring
Photograph by Fr. Vester & Co.

v. 3 introduces the first oracle, with an account of the meeting between Isaiah and Ahaz. The exact spot where the 'fullers' field' lay has not been identified, but it is fairly clear that Ahaz was engaged in a personal inspection of the water supply of the city. That has always been a difficulty with Jerusalem, and the inhabitants have had to depend either on stored rain water or on water brought by conduit from the one perennial spring in the neighbourhood of the city, that known as the Virgin's spring. This was connected with the city by an underground channel in the time of Hezekiah, but in earlier days the water was exposed, and was liable to be cut off by an invading army. As it was all that Jerusalem had to rely on, Ahaz was naturally anxious about it.

The first oracle (vv. 4-6) is a message of comfort to the distracted king. Incidentally we learn from it that the plans of the confederates did not involve the destruction of the city, but the substitution for Ahaz of an Aramaean sovereign, showing that, as a century earlier, Damascus was the senior partner in the alliance.[1] Isaiah is to take with him a son whose symbolic name 'a remnant shall return' implies both temporary suffering and final salvation, and has to say that the attempt to replace Ahaz will be a failure. Rezon (so his name should probably be pronounced) and Pekah are like a couple of sticks taken from a fire. They are still smoking, but there is no real heat in them, and in a few minutes they will be extinguished and cold. There is no need for Ahaz to take any action; the destruction of the rebels is inevitable and almost automatic.

vv. 7-9 contain the second oracle. The weakness of the allies is illustrated by the fact that Rezon and Pekah are at their head, implying a supreme contempt for these kings as individuals. The second part of v. 8 with its mention of 65 years is generally regarded as a gloss by a seventh-century scribe, who was aware of the activities of Ashur-bani-pal ('Osnapper', Ez. 4[10]), and applied the oracle to events of his own day. The point of the whole oracle lies in the last line—'If ye will not believe, surely ye shall not be established'—with its play on the words 'believe' and 'establish', which are derived from the same root in Hebrew. This is one of the earliest uses of the idea of faith. It implies something solid and durable, that on which a man may rest. It brings out the contrast between the two forces between which Ahaz stood. On the one hand are the

---

[1] A generation later the same method was adopted by the rebel princes of Palestine in the case of Ekron, whose loyal king, Padi, was imprisoned and handed over to Hezekiah for safe keeping, whilst a nominee of the confederates was set up in his place.

visible enemies, Rezon and Pekah, threatening but evanescent, on the other the eternal God of Israel, who alone can say 'It shall not stand, neither shall it come to pass'. Let Israel rest her spirit on the latter, and she may be assured that no harm can befall her.

7¹⁰⁻²⁵. *The sign of Immanuel and related oracles.* This section contains the account of a further sign to be given to Ahaz, possibly on the same occasion as the last message, certainly in connexion with the same political situation, and followed by four oracles in vv. 18-19, v. 20, vv. 21-22, and vv. 23-25 respectively. Like the sign of the name of Shear-jashub in the previous section, the new symbol consists of a name, together with some further details. It is not in any sense a miracle, but an illustration of what Jahveh will do in and for Israel.

This is described in vv. 10-17. Isaiah is sent to Ahaz, with the offer of any 'sign', miraculous or not, that the king likes to ask. It may be as high as heaven or as deep as Sheol (the marginal reading in v. 11 is probably correct). Ahaz refuses, professedly because this would be an act of distrust, but really, as Isaiah sees, because he intends to pursue his own policy, without guidance from the prophet. After an indignant outburst which, incidentally, throws some light on the character of the king's domestic government, a sign is given of Jahveh's own choosing. It is one which was for centuries misunderstood, and until modern times was applied by the Christian Church to prove the doctrine of the Virgin Birth of Christ. But the word 'virgin' in v. 14 is a mistranslation taken over from the LXX, which Greek-speaking Jews themselves rectified as soon as they found it used in Christian and anti-Jewish apologetics. The word does *not* mean virgin, though it might be used of a virgin. It means a woman who has already passed the age of adolescence. She may be already married, and might even be the mother of children—as long as she is not too old to bear children the term would still apply. The Revisers' marginal note suggests that they were not unaware of the facts, but in all probability they shrank from the theological storm which, forty years ago, would certainly have greeted the loss of an important 'proof-text'. The phrase 'butter and honey shall he eat' has also been the subject of some difference of opinion, some holding that it implies a life of poverty, others, probably correctly, that it involves the exact opposite, conditions of plenty both in field and wild. The 'sign' is nothing more nor less than a symbolic way of giving a fixed and dated limit for the fulfilment of the prophecy which Isaiah has to bring Ahaz. If a woman were to conceive now, by the time her child was born the country would have been relieved of the immediate fear of invasion, and the name she gave to it would indicate the general recognition of the fact that God had sided with Judah and rescued her. This gives an outside limit of ten months within which the failure of the confederates will be manifest. By the time the child is weaned the effects of the invasion will so far have disappeared that he can be brought up in simple luxury. When he knows how to 'refuse the evil and to choose the good', i. e. when he has clearly formed distinctions of taste as between things that are 'nice' and things that are 'nasty', he will be able to revel in rich curds and honey—a symbol of ideal prosperity in ancient Israel, as the familiar phrase, 'a land flowing with milk and honey', shows. For by that time the land (i. e. the combined kingdoms of Damascus and Samaria) at which Ahaz now shudders will be forsaken; its people will have been carried away into captivity. v. 17, with its threat of calamity greater than Judah has ever known since the days of Solomon, seems to have no connexion whatever with what precedes, and is frequently supposed to be an accidental insertion.

vv. 18–19 form the first of the appended oracles, and describe ruin which is to fall upon some country. If v. 17 is original, then the compiler thought that Judah would be the victim; if, on the other hand, v. 17 is out of place, then it will be Damascus and Samaria that are to suffer. Jahveh has at His disposal both Assyria and Egypt, and at His whistle both will come in swarms like flies or bees, and will cover the whole land.

v. 20 is another threat of calamity, which the compiler evidently thought applicable to the same victims as the previous oracle. The metaphor is different, and the completeness of the destruction and its shameful indignity are expressed in the figure of a complete shaving of the whole body. The value set on the hair and beard is exemplified in many places and in many ways amongst Semitic peoples, and such a figure suggests the last extreme of degradation.

vv. 21–8 contain an oracle with a very different message, fore-telling for the remnant (it is assumed that some terrible blow will fall) a time of prosperity. But the picture also suggests serious depopulation. One heifer and two ewes are to supply a rich abundance for the remains of the family. That means that the family must be very small. It may be remarked that this sense is a little clearer if, with LXX, we omit the words 'he shall eat butter'.

vv. 23–5 offer an additional picture of desolation. A vineyard whose vines were each worth a shekel of silver (this seems to be the meaning of the word rendered 'silverlings') was extraordinarily valuable. But after the calamity it will be so overgrown with weeds and jungle as to be full of dangerous animals, and no one will venture to set foot in it unless he is well armed. The same fate will befall the fertile hill-sides; the only living things that will dare to range them will be the cattle.

8[1-15]. *The sign of Maher-shalal-hash-baz and appended oracles.* The introductory prose passage, vv. 1-4, is of the autobiographical type, and is followed by three oracles in vv. 5-8, 9-10, and 11-15 respectively. They deal once more with a symbolic name, and once more refer by implication to the Syro-Ephraimite war.

Isaiah is bidden take a large tablet, probably of smooth clay, such as were used for documents of certain kinds wherever Babylonian influence penetrated. On this he has to write in ordinary characters, i.e. in the common Hebrew letters, and not in the cuneiform script which was possibly still used for some kinds of state documents, a name with the words 'belonging to' before it. This was the usual formula for seals, and it seems clear that Isaiah's instructions meant that he was to prepare a seal which should be used for stamping and identifying any property belonging to the owner of the name. But no such person seems to have been known to Isaiah, and accordingly he gives to his next son the name on the seal, and he, like his brother, becomes a 'sign'. Incidentally we observe that Isaiah calls his wife a 'prophetess'.

It is in the name that the significance of the whole lies. 'Maher-shalal-hash-baz' is curious in that it is derived from two languages. 'Maher-shalal' means in Hebrew 'speed spoil', and 'Hash-baz' means exactly the same thing in Aramaic. That is to say part of the name applies to Samaria and part to Damascus, and the message of doom is delivered to them both. Before the child can talk at all— 'Father' and 'Mother' are the two first words a child usually says— the implied prophecy will be fulfilled. Isaiah's action in preparing the seal has been carefully recorded and attested by witnesses of high standing and repute, so that there will be no doubt of Jahveh's share in the events. In all probability the incident of the making of the seal took place before Ahaz appealed to Assyria, and was a part of the general attempt the prophet made to persuade him to rely wholly on Jahveh instead of placing his confidence in political alliances.

The oracle contained in vv. 5-8a, on the other hand, presupposes that advances to Assyria have already been made. The text seems to have suffered through additions by copyists and editors. The words 'and rejoice in . . . Remaliah' are quite unsuitable to the tenor of the passage, and the Hebrew is very awkward. Some scholars would emend this to read 'and melt before . . .'; others would omit the whole clause. Possibly in v. 7 the words 'the king of Assyria and all his glory' are a marginal comment which has been accidentally inserted in the text.

The waters of Shiloah are a stream rising below the Temple hill and forming the so-called Spring of the Virgin. They are naturally somewhat insignificant, and are used here to imply the small national life of Israel, concentrating on its sanctuary and its God. Ahaz has rejected Jahveh and turned to Tiglath-pileser, but the only result will be the flooding of Judah by the Assyrians, here introduced under the figure of the Euphrates.

8b–10 seem to have little or no connexion with what has gone before. The figure is that of a great bird which spreads its wings over the whole country. Such a metaphor usually implies protection, and is hardly suitable to the Euphrates, even when the Euphrates is itself symbolic of the king of Assyria. It is also noticeable that the words 'God is with us' (disguised as a proper name, 'Immanuel' in v. 8) appear at the end of vv. 8 and 10. The probability, then, is that vv. 8a–10 are a fragment of a Psalm which had a regular refrain 'For God is with us'. A part of one verse and the whole of the next have been alone preserved. In the tone of the late exilic or post-exilic community the Psalmist calls on all nations to be submissive and subservient to Jahveh, or they will be destroyed by Him. The original was quite possibly a song of victory over some Israelite triumph which is not now to be identified.

The oracle contained in vv. 11–15 is a warning to Isaiah and those like-minded with him not to share in the popular attitude of the moment. It opens with a personal statement of the way in which this truth was revealed to the prophet himself through the ecstasy—'with a strong hand', or 'with strength of hand'. The exact point of the first part of v. 12 is not clear. The second part seems to refer to the general fear of the confederate kings, though they are not really terrible, as Isaiah well sees. But why should the word 'conspiracy' be introduced in the previous line? Many commentators would emend the text, though it cannot be said that any great improvement is secured by the corrections suggested. Perhaps there were spy panics in Jerusalem, and people on every hand were 'detecting' traitorous dealings with or inclination towards the enemy. It is in truth Jahveh who is to be feared. 'Sanctuary' may be a mistake for a word meaning 'snare', and this would add to the list of perils encountered by those who refused to accept His guidance. It must never be forgotten that the best of things, if misused or neglected, may become the most serious of dangers.

8¹⁶⁻¹⁸. *The preservation of the message for the future.* To all appearance the work of Isaiah was a failure, both from the political and from the religious points of view. Indeed they were one, for in turning to Assyria for help, Judah was definitely rejecting the help that might have been given her by her God, and was therefore turning her back upon Him. Yet the prophet knew that his message was the true one, and that in days to come the remembrance of it might help his people to win again what they had lost in the days of Ahaz. So in this short autobiographical section—possibly only a fragment—he describes his method. Just as deeds are signed, sealed, and put away for the use of a later time, so he will shut up (read 'I will bind up' for 'bind up') the testimony and seal the teaching (so R.V. margin, rightly) in the minds of his disciples. There is no suggestion here of a written prophecy. That idea had apparently not arisen, though it may have come to Isaiah in later life. It is in the memories of a group of men whom he could trust that the truths he had uttered were to be enshrined. In the meantime he could await the good time of Jahveh. This is his faith, a certainty of his God, and the conviction that His truth will one day take its proper place in the world, which brings with it a great patience to his soul. As an earnest of greater things to come, his name and those of his two sons are 'signs'—and, in a sense, 'wonders' in Israel. That is to say, they are a testimony to, and a reminder of, the teaching he had to give Judah. His name is 'Jahveh saves', an eternal truth. One of his sons is called 'A remnant shall return', a call to hope in the darkest hours of national and individual life. The other is named 'Speed spoil, speed spoil', a testimony that Jahveh will intervene for the sake of His people in years to come and that calamity will fall upon their adversaries.

8¹⁹⁻²⁰. *A warning against 'Spiritualism'.* Amongst all early peoples there seems to be a strong belief in the ability of certain persons to consult the dead. The procedure appears to be much the same everywhere; the 'medium' falls into an abnormal psychological state and whether there are unaccountable material phenomena or not, words pass from the medium's mouth which are attributed to a spirit which has for the time being taken possession of the body. Such spirits in ancient Israel were called 'familiar spirits', i.e. the ghostly dead (not the living that are connected with them, for all these words refer to the spirits themselves and not the medium), 'wizards'—rather spirits who make themselves known to the medium, 'chirpers' and 'mutterers'—words which have reference to the actual sound of the abnormal voice. The consultation of these spirits was forbidden in the interests of true Jahveh worship, not because the practitioners were believed to be deceivers but because they were believed to be genuine. Necromancy was therefore apostasy, for Jahveh would have no rivals in the worship of His people. Here Isaiah (though some would deny his authorship of the passage) contrasts the two cults. On the one hand necromancy is 'seeking unto the dead on behalf of the living', on the other hand the only faith that has a 'morning', i.e. that has a future of light before it, is that which says 'To the teaching and the testimony'. God does deal with men in direct ways, and tells them all they need to know by recognized means, such as scripture or prophetic and priestly teaching. The last words, 'surely there is no morning for them', are sometimes taken with v. 21, and in that case the preceding clause should be rendered 'surely it is thus that men should speak'.

8²¹⁻²². *A desolate man in a desolate land.* Like the fragment which precedes and the fragment which follows, it is quite impossible to date this or even to be absolutely certain of its authorship. Here some unnamed person—unnamed as far as the extant fragment goes—finds himself in a desert, loses all hope, and finally seals his own doom by cursing God and the king—there is no help for him in heaven or in earth. For the state of mind which leads to this deadly sin, the appeal of Job's wife to her husband may be compared.

9¹. *Another fragment alluding to the rescue of Galilee.* This was doubtless attached to the preceding fragment because of the occurrence of the words 'gloom' and 'anguish', though it may be a prose note appended to the previous verses by one who had seen the dawn of a brighter day for lands that had been as the desert described in v. 21. Zebulun and Naphtali were laid waste and depopulated by Tiglath-pileser in 732 B.C., and whoever wrote these words must have seen the land begin to recover, many years after that event. This does not absolutely preclude Isaiah's authorship, though making it unlikely. Unfortunately, we have as yet only the scantiest references to northern Palestine between the captivity of Samaria (721) and the governorship of Nehemiah (444), and it is impossible to indicate any period between those dates to which this verse applies.

9^{2-7}. *The prosperity of Israel under the Messianic king.* This is one of the best-known passages in the whole of Isaiah's work. There have been students who have been disposed to deny Isaiah's authorship on the ground that it is Messianic, but further reflection has shown that this is unreasonable. Messianic prophecy must begin somewhere, and this passage has it in an early form. There is, therefore, no reason why Isaiah should not have originated the idea, which was to bear such rich fruit in later generations.

vv. 2–3 form a general introduction, calling people to exult in the happiness of the new time. This is to be greater than even the joy of harvest, the happiest occasion in the whole year for an agricultural people who win an uncertain living from the produce of the soil (probably we should read for 'thou hast multiplied the nation', 'thou hast multiplied the rejoicing'). The outburst of happiness is all the greater because of the contrast between the past and the present, for this is no less impressive than the contrast between absolutely thick darkness and the glorious light of noonday. Then in vv. 4–5 the immediate reason is given. Israel has been oppressed and tortured, and is suffering from war and cruelty. It may be that Isaiah has in view desolation wrought by the combined armies of Samaria and Damascus in 735, or it may again be a reference to the invasion of Sennacherib in 701. Of the two the latter is generally held to be the more probable, though there are those who would take the newly born prince of the following verses to be Hezekiah, in which case the earlier date would be more natural. In any case, Judah is now to be relieved of war, all its emblems and instruments are to be burned, and the oppressor himself is to be shattered and scattered as Midian had been before Gideon in ancient days (Jud. 7).

Then follows the further reason. A royal child is born, to whom various names symbolic of his character and activities are given. The meanings of these names are far from clear, and there has been a great deal of discussion over some of them. The first is that which implies that the new king is to be a marvellous counsellor, that he is to be possessed of that practical wisdom in politics which is so highly valued in the East. It would probably be reading a good deal too much into the second name to assume that it implies actual divinity, in that case another Hebrew word would probably have been used. The term 'God' is used by Jacob of Esau in Gen. 33^{10}, and is probably used here to raise the idea of heroism to the highest power. At the same time it must be recognized that this is no ordinary monarch, for the next title is 'eternal father', i.e. one who will for ever exhibit over his people the characteristics of a father, a frequent metaphor for a kindly monarch. The features of his reign are to be peace in rich abundance, righteousness, and justice. Clearly the picture of the Messianic king, though he is still a human prince of the Davidic line, has a strong eschatological background, since he is to reign endlessly and will therefore have no successor. At the back of the whole lies Jahveh, whose passion for His people is the motive which impels Him to give this assurance of final blessedness, to be reached on earth, and, indeed, in Jerusalem.

9^{8}–10^{4}. *A group of oracles of destruction.* It seems probable that $5^{25\,f.}$ once belonged to this same group, but has been accidentally displaced. In the present passage there are four of these oracles, 9^{8-12}, $^{13-17}$, $^{18-21}$, 10^{1-4}. The group presents the appearance of a poem of four regular stanzas, each ending with the refrain 'For all this is His anger not turned away, but His hand is stretched out still'. It is, of course, possible that this refrain was added in some cases by the collector, who wished to make a small homogeneous group out of the oracles, but, on the other hand, Isaiah himself may be to some extent responsible for the compilation.

The first oracle in the group, 9^{8-12}, is an attack on the proud security of the northern kingdom, and must therefore be dated before 721. Damage has been done by earthquake (cf. Am. 1^1) and by foe, but instead of learning the moral lesson which these calamities should have brought home, Samaria has used her disasters only as an excuse for the exhibition of more pride and luxury. Instead of mud bricks baked in the sun, men will use for the new houses costly hewn stones, quarried and brought from a distance; instead of the cheap and worthless sycomores that have been destroyed by the invading army, cedars, the trees most highly valued by the ancient Israelite, will be planted. From her sufferings Samaria has learnt nothing and forgotten nothing. Therefore a further penalty has been exacted from the northern kingdom. Its precise character is a little obscure, because the words rendered 'the adversaries of Rezin' are almost certainly corrupt, and while most editors seem to agree in thinking that what Isaiah really said was 'his adversaries' or 'the adversaries of Israel', the error may be greater than this. In any case it is curious to notice that amongst the enemies who are the instruments of this further punishment the Assyrians are not mentioned. Is it possible that there was an abortive attempt to restore the life of northern Israel after 721,[1] and that this was finally frustrated by a combination of the

<hr>

[1] Cf. note on p. 71.

other Palestinian states? The objection to this lies in the mention of Syria, though here again it is possible that the ruin wrought by the Assyrians in 732 was less complete than we have hitherto supposed. A time when Syrians and Philistines together were in a position to oppress Israel is difficult to find within the period of Isaiah's prophetic activity, and the prophet may be going back to events earlier than even the reign of Jeroboam II to find an illustration of the truth expressed in his refrain.

The second of these four oracles is contained in vv. 13–17. The people have again failed to learn from experience, and a new calamity has befallen them. In a single day there has come upon them disaster so wide and complete that great and small, rich and poor, prosperous and miserable—all have suffered. v. 15 is almost certainly a marginal note, accidentally incorporated in the text interpreting v. 14. Here the blame is laid on those who should have been the leaders and teachers of the people. Because they have not guided men rightly, those who were committed to their charge have had to pay the penalty; even the weak and helpless among them, the typically defenceless classes, have not been spared. At the same time the prophet makes it clear that this is not a case of the innocent suffering for the guilty. The whole nation is involved in the sins which are responsible for the calamity. In character all are 'profane', which, in the light of Isaiah's conception of holiness we must interpret in a moral sense—i. e. their actions are wicked and their words are foolish. What can God Himself do with a nation like this?

vv. 18–21 depict a state of civil war. Both in the northern kingdom itself and in the larger whole which is composed of Israel and Judah together, a fire is blazing, a fire due to the sin of the people themselves, which, now finding its true fulfilment, burns with twisting columns of smoke over the whole land. It would seem that in v. 19 the metaphor changes, though it is not clear what the original text was. The word rendered 'burnt up' has really nothing to do with burning, and is probably due to textual corruption. It is also possible that instead of the very awkward 'as the fuel of the fire', which goes back to the metaphor of v. 18, we should read 'as devourers of men'. Only the slightest alteration of the Hebrew text is required to make this change.

Again, the last clause of v. 20 seems to be in itself corrupt; some early authorities omitted a letter and read (probably rightly) 'they shall eat every man the flesh of his neighbour'. If that be the true text, this clause would make a better balance placed at the end of v. 19. The figure is thus one of domestic war and cruelty raging on every hand, and may well be a reference to the confusion which followed the death of Jeroboam II, with a hint at the attack of Pekah on Judah.

Unlike the first three oracles, that contained in 10^{1-4} does not deal with a whole nation, but with a class within the nation, and describes their fate when the judgement already predicted arrives. 'They that decree decrees' are, of course, not legislators but judges, and those who write them down are officials of the courts. We have, therefore, another of the too familiar complaints as to the maladministration of justice, presenting the features which we have seen elsewhere in the prophetic books. The Day is coming; that is assumed, and the Day will find them helpless in their turn, trying to hide themselves and having no refuge save amongst the captives and the slain. v. 4 should read :

> To avoid crouching under the prisoners,
> And falling under the slain.　(Gray's rendering.)

This seems to imply that the Day will involve a battle, and that the 'desolation', or rather 'storm', is a metaphor for war. Eschatological pictures usually included some such event, and the prophet seems to have in mind some well-known view of the end of things. The popular mind, no doubt, thought of Jahveh as fighting for Israel, and conquering, capturing, or killing foreigners. But the prophet sees, like Amos, that the wicked in Israel are Jahveh's real foes, and that their inevitable doom is that which they expected to fall upon others.

10^{5-11}. *Jahveh's purpose with Assyria.*　This is the first of a small collection of oracles extending down to the end of the chapter, in which the prophet deals with Assyria. Here the stress is laid on a philosophy of history. There is a moral purpose behind all international relations. Assyria has been able to do her work because Jahveh has willed it so. He has needed to vindicate His character on a people—His own people—who had proved themselves 'profane', and were therefore the object of His fury ('the people of My wrath'). He has therefore let the Assyrians loose amongst them (so rather than 'I will send him against' them) to do their worst. But the instrument has imagined itself to be independent and self-determining, and thinks that its treatment of Israel is comparable to its treatment of other nations whom it has overthrown. It has not realized that in crushing Samaria and in ravaging Judah it has to deal with a God who is interested in them more than in the other victims, and who can at His will control the physical forces of the world. It is possible that vv. 10–11 (which appear to be in prose, and not, like the rest of the oracle, in poetry) are an expansion by a later hand of the thought of v. 9.

10^{12-15}. *Another oracle on the same theme.* The actual oracle is contained in vv. 13–15; v. 12 is an editor's introduction. Here again the boastful pride of Assyria is vividly depicted. She compares herself to one who has found a nest from which the parent birds have been driven, leaving eggs or young to the spoiler, and not daring to make a movement or utter a sound in their defence. She insists that this is all her own doing, and this attitude is to some extent illustrated by extant Assyrian records, though as a rule the credit and glory are assigned to the god Ashur. But it is not even Ashur who is responsible; it is Jahveh, and that will appear in its time. Assyria is only a tool, and for her to claim independence of action would be as foolish as if the stick were to assert that it controlled the actions of the man who wielded it.

10^{16-19}. *The punishment of Assyria.* 'Glory' was the aim of the Assyrian kings. Now glory suggests light, and light there shall be, but not that which Assyria expects. On the contrary, it shall be the light of a great fire, whose consuming flame is none other than Jahveh Himself, 'the light of Israel and his Holy One'. The world empire may be a great forest of noble trees, but it shall all serve as fuel for the mighty conflagration. The meaning of the last words of v. 18 is very uncertain. It is not at all likely that the rendering 'as when a standard-bearer fainteth' is right, and even the marginal reading of the R.V. 'as when a sick man fainteth', with its reference back to the metaphor of v. 16, may not be the prophet's real thought. v. 19 is now commonly supposed to be an editorial addition or a marginal comment which has found its way into the text.

10^{20-23}. *The prospect for Israel.* This section is based on that which precedes—and on one or two other passages. It is now generally supposed that it is of the nature of an editorial addition to what precedes, for it suggests confusion of two distinct ideas held by Isaiah and others, one being that Israel should attain to greatness of numbers, and the other that they were to suffer for their sins so severely that only a small fraction of the people would survive. These are not in themselves incompatible, but the way in which the attempt is made to combine them is quite unlike Isaiah's methods of thought. Various dates are assigned to the passage by different scholars, but nearly all agree in ascribing it to a generation long after the time of Isaiah.

$10^{24-27ᵇ}$. *A promise of deliverance.* Again we have a prose passage,

which is usually assigned to a later time than that of Isaiah. It orms
an exhortation to Jerusalem not to fear the Assyrians, for Jahveh has
nearly reached the end of the punishment which He has determined
for His people, and is about to lay Assyria herself low. As far as the
subject-matter is concerned, there is little in this which could not have
been said by Isaiah in 701, and it may be that an original oracle of his,
dating from that time, has been expanded into prose. It will be
noticed that an appeal is made to history. Jahveh has done such
great things in the past, notably in the deliverance of Israel from
Egypt, and again from the invading hordes of Midian, that His people
may safely rely on Him to repeat His mighty acts, and shake the
burden from their shoulder and the yoke from their neck. It is probable that the passage originally ended, ' his burden shall depart from
off thy shoulder and his yoke from off thy neck shall be destroyed ',
the last words ' yoke (second time) because of the anointing ' being an
erroneous rendering (possibly with slight textual mistake) for the
words which originally stood at the head of v. 28. They therefore
belong to the next section.

10^{27c-32}. *The advance of the invading army.* In stirring and impressive language the prophet describes the progress of the enemy, probably Sennacherib in 701.   The last three words of v. 27 (see above)
should perhaps be read 'He is gone up from before Rimmon'.
Rimmon is probably the modern Rammân, four or five miles north
by east of the ancient Michmash.   The other places mentioned, in so
far as their sites have been identified, all lie between Rimmon and
Jerusalem.   Aiath is the place also known as Ai, and from there the
invader has taken the shortest route to Geba, where he is only six
miles from Jerusalem.   For some miles round the country is desolate
because the inhabitants have fled in terror, and cries resound from
one hill village to another (in v. 31 the margin ' answer her ' is to be
preferred to the text ' O thou poor ').   The next morning the enemy
will appear threatening before the walls of Jerusalem herself. It may
be remarked that in several cases there are plays upon the names
mentioned, such as occur in Mi. 3.

10$^{33-34}$. *The fall of the forest.* This short oracle or fragment is fitly
attached to the preceding, though it formed no original part of it.
Again the Assyrian power is compared to a forest, though this time
the means of its destruction is not fire but the axe. ' By a mighty
one' in v. 34 can hardly be right, and most moderns read 'with its
mighty ones ', i. e. with its mighty cedars.

So this collection of oracles on Assyria concludes.   The original thesis is maintained to the end. Jahveh did indeed use Assyria to perform His purpose of punishing Israel for her apostasy, religious and moral, but when that was once accomplished, He would not suffer her to reach the summit of her selfish ambition. Whilst the historical details are obscure, the outstanding fact remains. Israel in the north was conquered and desolated, in the end even Judah was laid waste, but Jerusalem proved inviolate as a city, and beneath her walls the

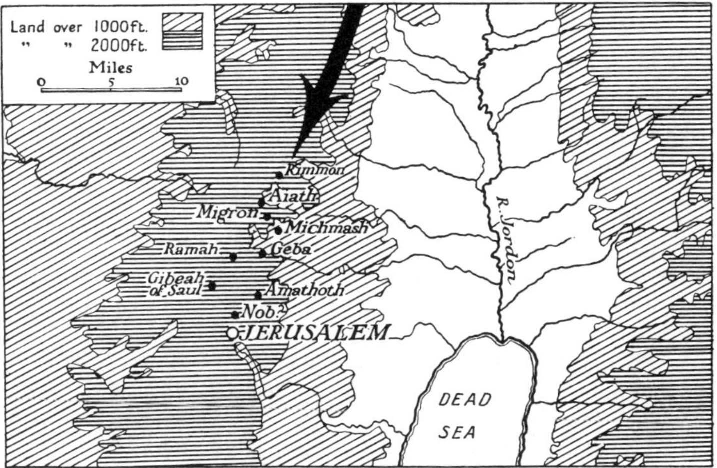

Map illustrating the Assyrian march on Jerusalem.

progress of the Eastern conqueror was stayed. A remnant was to remain, and in long time was to learn the lesson which all the history of the age might have taught, and in learning it was to hand on a unique and priceless truth to all future generations and peoples.

CHAPTERS 28–31.

These chapters, to which portions of ch. 32 should be added, form the basis of the sixth collection now incorporated within our Book of Isaiah. Whilst some of the oracles included must have been uttered before 721, there are others which seem to date from a later time, when Hezekiah was dallying with that Egyptian alliance which eventually brought so much ruin and destruction on the peoples of Palestine. The various oracles included in these four chapters, with the exception of a few additions to individual oracles and one or two pieces which appear to come from a later date, are almost universally recognized as being the work of Isaiah himself.

28[1-4]. *Denunciation of drunkenness in northern Israel.* The prophet first draws a picture of some drunken revel, in which the participants are garlanded with flowers. The orgy has lasted all night, and the flowers are beginning to fade. This is typical of the speedy end of the glory of Ephraim. She has already been overcome (the prophet uses a very strong word which literally means 'hammered') by wine, and that has deprived her of strength to stand against the forces that are moving against her. These will come down on her like a sudden sweeping storm which will carry away and destroy everything before it. The figure changes, and Israel is as attractive to the invader and as short lived as the first luscious figs of a new season. The moment they are seen they will be devoured. Just as little hope has Israel of long survival. One more vivid picture is added to the gallery in which the prophets from Amos onwards have portrayed for us the thoughtless selfishness and the insecurity of the northern kingdom.

28[5-6]. *An eschatological appendix.* This can hardly have been originally attached to the preceding verses, and is often assigned to a date later than Isaiah. The eschatological note is struck at the outset, and possibly this is a fragment of a poem which had nothing to do with its present context, but was placed here by a compiler on account of the similarity of language. Here Jahveh will be the crown of His people's pride, and will become a spirit of judgement for him that sitteth in judgement. Once more the stress is laid on the importance of the judicial functions in the Israelite community, and the need for Divine inspiration to perform those functions correctly.

28[7-13]. *Isaiah's dealings with the drunkards of Jerusalem (?).* The scene has apparently shifted from the north to the south. But Judah is no better than Israel, and a picture similar to that of vv. 1–4 is given. But this time the prophet himself is present to rebuke the revellers in person, and has to meet their mockery. He speaks to them as he sees them staggering and lurching about the room, probably in the Temple itself, in which they have been feasting, even when they are called upon to give decisions on civil cases in the name of Jahveh. With them are associated the prophets, men who have the God-given power of vision, but are too drunk to use or interpret it aright. In answer to his remonstrance there rise from the tables the jeers of the men he is rebuking. He is talking to them as to babies, and in strange language they imitate the gurgling of infants. The meaning of the words 'line upon line, precept upon precept' (if that is what the Hebrew is intended to convey) has always been found obscure. The words are chosen not for their meaning, but for their sound :

Káw lakáw, sáw lasáw, káw lakáw, sáw lasáw, z'ír shám, z'ír shám.

To them it sounds as if the prophet were talking a strange language— as indeed he was, though not in the sense they intended ; it was the substance of Isaiah's message that was foreign to these men, not his words. He has offered them the only true road of safety, that of peaceful confidence in Jahveh, and they have refused to take it ; on the contrary, they have made it a basis of reproach. For this very reason the authentic communications of Jahveh are no more to them than mere drunken babblings. If men will not accept the voice of God for what it is, then it not merely fails in its purpose, but becomes a positive danger.

28¹⁴⁻¹⁵. *The covenant with death.* It is difficult to say how far political and religious ideas are interwoven in these verses. It is probable that they represent words uttered at the time of the Egyptian alliance, and that the prophet is telling his fellow country-men that Egypt is no safer as a friend than death. But there is more in the language than this, and it undoubtedly implies necro-mancy, though this may have received an added impulse from association with Egypt. What the 'statesmen' of Judah have done is to seek security from the dead, and to win their satisfaction from a vision which has brought them into touch with those who are in Sheol, the abode of the dead (the margin has the right word). From these practices they have gathered an assurance that all is well with them, and that no harm can come to them from the forces of Assyria.

28¹⁶⁻²². *Jahveh's judgement on this covenant.* Necromancy is the kind of apostasy to which a superficial mind will resort in moments of panic. Jahveh's offer of security is quite different. Deep below the surface, where none can see it, He has laid a solid foundation, tested and valuable. The man who understands Him will 'believe', will recognize in this foundation a valid basis for life even though he may not see it, and that basis will take from him all panic fear and hasty ill-considered action. (It may be remarked that some modern students think the word 'make haste' inapplicable here, and prefer to read 'be ashamed' or 'give way'.) The building to be erected on this foundation is a spiritual one, and the mason's line employed in its construction is justice, the plummet righteousness. In contrast to the permanent security afforded by this method the prophet speaks of the failure of the current policy. When the ruin comes it will be found that the measures taken will be perfectly futile. The destroying host will sweep over the land, every day a fresh wave will break upon the country, and the 'message', i.e. that which comes from the dead with whom the leaders of the people are in touch, will be a thing of horror instead of comfort. Practices of this kind can give a false security only; they cannot alter facts. If a bed is too short or a blanket too narrow for a man, no amount of necromancy will make these things large enough. Just as panic fell on the enemies of David in the valley of Gibeon, so Jahveh will work, it may seem in barbarous fashion, against His own people of Judah, and the end of all this mockery will be utter and inevitable ruin.

28$^{23-29}$. *The adaptability of Jahveh's methods.* The methods of agriculture are very varied. At one time a farmer ploughs, at another he sows, at another he reaps or threshes. And the instruments are adapted to each operation. (In v. **25** the words rendered 'in rows' and 'in the appointed place' are not represented in the LXX, and are probably a later insertion. The ancient husbandman did not plant corn in rows, he scattered it broadcast over his fields. Cummin and 'fitches' are aromatic plants like caraway or anise, 'spelt' resembles wheat.) In all this he is acting on instructions given him by Jahveh, who thereby illustrates His own methods of dealing with men. A charge of inconsistency might have been brought against Him on the ground of the different treatment Israel and Judah had received. Samaria was no more wicked than Jerusalem, yet the former had been destroyed and the latter had, for the time at any rate, escaped. Should not the punishment have been identical? No, says Isaiah. Jahveh has no one invariably rigid rule for handling all men in all circumstances. He is not a machine, He is a person, and deals with individual men and with individual communities on individual lines. The principles underlying His action are uniform and unchangeable, but the forms in which they manifest themselves will vary with every different case.

29$^{1-8}$. *The humiliation and salvation of Jerusalem.* The passage opens with a 'Woe', like ch. **28** and some other sections in this division of the book. The city is addressed as 'Ariel', i.e. probably 'Altar-hearth'—the essential importance of the place lies in the fact that there Jahveh has His home. She is reminded of the days long ago when David encamped against her and took her. Once more she is surrounded by armies, but this time it is no prince of her own people who is in command. Jahveh now takes David's place (read (in v. 3 'like David' for 'round about', following the LXX), and the armies which He directs are those of Judah's foes. She is brought down to the very dust, slain as it were and buried, so that her utterance is from the grave and her voice like that of a ghost. Some would

Farmer ploughing in modern Palestine.
Photograph by Fr. Vester & Co.

regard the first part of v. 5 and vv. 7 and 8 as the addition of a later commentator who knew his history. This may be true of v. 8, but it is less certain in the case of 5a and 7. If they be accepted as part of the original oracle we see how suddenly the tumult is stilled, silenced by a yet greater outburst on the part of Jahveh, who appears in His most tremendous manifestations for the rescue of His people. His 'visitation' is usually to punish Israel, but if His purposes can be thereby served, it means her redemption. So here; like chaff before the gale her foes are swept away, and vanish as the dream world in the morning sun.

29⁹⁻¹². *The fate of wilful blindness.* An original oracular fragment in vv. 9–10 has been expanded by the insertion of two explanatory glosses in v. 10, 'the prophets' and 'the seers', and the addition of two prose verses which illustrate the conditions described. The leaders of the people have been struck with staggering amazement, and behave as though drunk (all the verbs in v. 9 should be read as imperatives). But it is not drunkenness that has fallen upon them, it is the strange condition of insensibility, sometimes resembling deep slumber, which Jahveh casts on men when He is about to perform some special act upon them. It may be that in its original form the oracle, after this powerful introduction, went on to describe what it was that Jahveh was doing to them, but beyond the fact that it is now impossible for them to see or understand, no details remain.

29¹³⁻¹⁴. *The dangers of insincerity.* There is probably a reference here to some form of foreign worship which was carried on alongside of the proper worship of Jahveh. But the God of Israel was a jealous God, and could brook no rivals. Hence He would punish, and that in strange ways, which would be past the understanding of Israel, and would leave Judah helpless in their presence.

29¹⁵⁻¹⁶. *Hiding from Jahveh.* What we have here can be regarded only as a fragment, and most commentators to-day believe that even v. 16 is no part of the original oracle, but has been written to fill up a gap. In v. 15 it would seem that the politicians were carrying on their intrigues in the hope and belief that they were in some way screened from Jahveh's sight. This is now generally assumed to be a reference to the Egyptian alliance strenuously opposed by Isaiah, who claimed to know and to express the true will of Jahveh. Probably he discovered the treaty only after it was actually accomplished. The first sentence of v. 16 is not open to such difficulties as the remainder, and the oracle may well have continued with further illustration of the confusion, the 'inversion' of reality implied in the conduct of the Jewish princes. But the latter part of the verse certainly has the air of a later comment.

29¹⁷⁻²¹. *The overthrow of all tyrants.* This section has apparently been attached to the preceding as giving an illustration of the 'perversity' or rather 'inversion', the 'turning of things upside down' alluded to in v. 16. It begins with such an inversion; the great forests are to become garden land and the gardens to become forests;

MODERN CARAVANS.   Two methods of carrying goods

Photographs by Mr. R. Gorbola

the deaf are to hear and the blind are to see. There are also spiritual
and moral aspects of the case, for the oppressors—who do not seem
to be foreigners—are to be destroyed, and the scoffers are to cease
The conditions reflected seem to be such as prevailed after the return
from captivity.

29[22-24]. *The redemption of Jacob.* This passage again may be
regarded as a continuation of the preceding, purposely given its
present position by the collector. But the tone and language are
nearer to those of prophecies dating from the end of the exile than to
those of the post-exilic period. The shame of Jacob is over ; Israel
can once more hold up her head, and look on the world round about.
What she sees is a vast increase in her own people, which makes her
recognize that Jahveh has been working for her whilst she has been
in the veiled darkness of distress. She will now praise and glorify
His name. Even those who made the greatest mistakes have been
endowed with intelligence, and the grumblers listen to reason.

30[1-5]. *Denunciation of the Egyptian alliance.* Jahveh is Israel's
Father ; so Hosea had stated the relationship, and others before him.
Yet her conduct had been unfilial. She had rejected the advice—or
rather had not really sought it—that she might have had from Him,
and has trusted in political measures. These had involved certain
religious rites, and Isaiah speaks of offering libations in which Jahveh
had no part. The king of Egypt in question is not easily identified.
It may have been Sabako, who, till his defeat by Sargon, ruled over
the whole country. That appears to be the meaning of the mention
both of Zoan in the north and of Hanes, which seems to have lain
in the far south of the country. Some would read Tahpanhes for
Hanes, and thus see an allusion to the little kingdoms of Lower Egypt.
Or it may be that the actual sovereign is left intentionally vague ; the
whole of united Egypt would be of no use to Israel, for the only result
will be disaster and shame.

30[6-7]. *An oracle on the beasts of the Southland.* This is an oracular
fragment dealing with the same theme as the last, though not from
the same oracle. Treasure is being sent to Egypt, loaded on the
backs of asses and camels, probably either as tribute or as a bribe.
The animals have to pass through the desert that lies to the south of
Judah, known as the ' Negeb ' or Southland, peopled by all manner
of strange and deadly creatures. The word represented by ' whence '
can hardly have that meaning, and it is conjectured that (by a very
slight change) we should read ' roaring ', an adjective going with ' lion '.

Yet all this expenditure of wealth is meaningless—Egypt cannot or will not help. There is some doubt as to the exact form and meaning of the latter part of v. 7, some modern students preferring to regard the line as a later addition, and even then as having been erroneously copied. At the same time the name 'Rahab', that of the great primeval monster who preceded creation in the old story, serves well to indicate the mass of Egypt, a country of which the southern portion is of considerable length, but very narrow, being confined to the strips of fertile land that border the Nile. Further, the epithet 'that sitteth still', which practically means 'idle', is well applied to a country which was never of the slightest real help to her allies in the long period of struggle during which Assyria was reaching the height of her power.

30$^{8-11}$. *The writing of an oracle.* Isaiah's message had met with no response from his immediate auditors. They are not interested in truth for its own sake, and have tried to stop the vision of the seer and the utterance of the prophet where these do not coincide with their own wishes. If the men of God would prophesy 'smooth things', they would listen, but all Isaiah's dwelling on 'the Holy of Israel' irritates and wearies them. So he is bidden to commit an oracle to writing—apparently only a short one, since it is to be written on a 'tablet', and then in a 'book'. We have no means of deciding which of Isaiah's numerous oracles was the one intended; some have conjectured that it was vv. 15-17, but there is no direct evidence on the point. The object of writing it down is that a later generation will be able to read it, and will know that the inspired man has spoken the truth of God. This is the earliest reference we have to any attempt on the part of a prophet to commit his oracles to writing, and it may be noted that apparently Isaiah has to retire to his own house to do this work, for the word rendered simply 'go' more properly means 'go in'.

30$^{12-14}$. *The penalty of rejection.* This section is closely connected in thought with the preceding, and may have been the actually written oracle. Because Israel has refused to listen to Jahveh and has preferred diplomacy (most modern students read 'wile' for 'oppression'), their ruin will come upon them, as complete as that of a high wall which collapses suddenly and is smashed into small fragments, none of them big enough to serve as a ladle to carry fire or water.

30$^{15-17}$. *Security, true and false.* In this oracle Isaiah reiterates the

idea which underlies his political attitude. It is only by coming back
to Jahveh, and by rest in Him, that Judah can find safety. Hers
must be a policy of non-interference ; she must keep quiet and avoid
panic. This, however, is not what the Government has done. Isaiah
plays on words here, "'on horses will we speed'; so your flight
shall be speedy! and 'upon the swift will we ride'—so swift shall
your pursuers be" (Box). The Egyptian alliance meant cavalry,
which always seems to have had a fascination for Israelite monarchs.
But the result would be that they would meet people stronger in
cavalry than the Egyptians, and their resort to mounted troops would
result in military disaster.

30^{18-26}. *Consolation and prosperity.* Israel is no longer an independent state in rebellion ; she has lost her freedom, but is now
penitent and about to be restored. Consequently many editors prefer
to regard the passage as due to a later prophet than Isaiah, and think
that it may have been inserted here to fill up a gap left by some
accident in the text.

Jahveh is more ready to grant favour than His people are to receive
it. There is a day of calamity to come, but when it does arrive
Israel will find it a day of mercy. Affliction is now present, and
Judah suffers famine as in a siege, but these things will pass away
when the real spiritual return manifested in the destruction of idols
has taken place. Blessings will be immeasurably multiplied.

30^{27-33}. *The overthrow of the Assyrians by Jahveh.* The Isaianic
authorship of this oracle has been doubted on grounds of style and
thought. If it be by the prophet himself, it must date from about 701,
when the armies of Sennacherib actually threatened Jerusalem. It
describes in noble and passionate language the appearance of Jahveh
in all His majesty—that seems to be implied in the use of the word
'name'—from His distant home, presumably in Sinai. (A similar
picture is drawn in the Song of Deborah, Jud. 5.) A cloud gathers
on the southern horizon. It draws nearer, and is seen to be flashing
with fire, the fire of the fury of Jahveh, whilst His rage is audible in
the crashing thunder. As it is about to break there comes (as usually
before a thunder-storm in the east) a blast of wind which falls with
the suddenness of a winter torrent, in whose bed a man may without
warning find himself up to the neck in the swirling waters. This is
Jahveh, coming for vengeance, to sift His foes in a sieve and to lay
his halter on their jaws.

From the darkness rises a song, as swift and spontaneous as that

SIFTING THE CORN AFTER THRESHING

Photograph by Mr. R. Gorbold

which breaks from the people on the eve of a festival, Passover or
Tabernacles. But it is not a chant of joy; it is the war-song of Israel,
and above it rolls the thunder in which the majesty of Jahveh is
recognized, whilst the lightning shows the fall of his punishing arm.
At length the full fury of the storm breaks, with a cloud-burst and
the battering of hail.

In the midst of this Israel gives battle, and the tumult of war is
added to that of the elements. The Assyrian army is panic-stricken,
and suffers fearful losses in its flight. The bodies are taken up and
carried to Tophet, the burning-place in the Valley of Hinnom, greatly
enlarged to meet the unusual need, and as the storm dies away the
smoke of burning pyres suggests the breath of Jahveh now showing
itself as a river of sulphurous flame.

31^{1-3}. *Against the Egyptian alliance.* This passage contains perhaps
the clearest of all Isaiah's statements of his 'political' creed, and
shows how far he was from being a mere statesman in the ordinary
sense of the word. He had often spoken before on the question of the
proposed alliance with Egypt, and he has now to say that the will of
Jahveh is unchanged. 'It would be wise', men seem to have said,
'to form an alliance with a great military power like Egypt, strong
in horses and chariots, or else we shall be unable to meet the
Assyrian armies.' So men look to (so read with LXX in v. 1 for
'stay on') horses instead of looking to Jahveh; they rely on their
own wisdom instead of consulting His. Yet now, as always, He can
and will bring calamity on evil-doers, and is in Himself a sufficient
protection against the enemy. A central thought of Isaiah's is that
the ultimate considerations, in public as in private life, are never
merely or even mainly physical; they are always spiritual. The
contrast between 'flesh' and 'spirit', between 'God' and 'man', was
no new one. But Isaiah's use of the distinction is profoundly important in the history of religion. He does not compare Jahveh with
the gods of Egypt, and say that He is the stronger; even if he does
not deny their existence he passes them over in silence. For him
and for Israel there is only one God, Jahveh. The mistake that the
government of Judah was making lay in thinking that any material
measures could repulse the Assyrians; one power alone, that of
Jahveh—whom the government had totally neglected in this connexion—could afford protection to the state. The Egyptians were
not courted because of their superior spiritual resources, but because
they could throw into the field masses of cavalry and chariots.
A nation that leaned on such support would find that it would give

way, and both would fall with a crash. It was only the issue of Sennacherib's expedition that taught Judah the lesson which was repeated two hundred years later by Zechariah: 'not by might nor by power, but by my spirit, saith the Lord'.

31[4–5]. *Jahveh, the unassailable.* The remainder of ch. 31 consists of a number of fragments, probably Isaianic, which have been placed together by a collector. It seems that even in these two verses portions of two different passages have been combined, for the metaphors do not fit one another. In v. 4 Jahveh is likened to a lion which cannot be frightened from its prey. The shepherds are the Egyptians, whom Jahveh will not allow to save Judah from his wrath. But in v. 5 Jahveh is the protector of Jerusalem. Probably the break comes after the words 'As birds flying' in v. 5, for birds on the wing are hardly a suitable emblem for protection.

31[6–9]. *The overthrow of the Assyrians.* v. 6 seems to stand by itself, and has the appearance of being a fragment of a longer piece. The margin is right in reading the 3rd plural for the 2nd in the verb, but probably the text is right in taking 'children of Israel' as a vocative. Who, then, are the 'they' who have revolted? Possibly the king and his princes, but any answer to this question must be conjectural.

v. 7, again, seems to have no connexion with its neighbours. The word rendered 'for a sin' is absent from the LXX and is probably an explanatory note inserted in the text from the margin. The change of persons is very awkward, and beyond the fact that the verse records the abandonment of idolatry by some one, it is difficult to see its meaning or place.

vv. 8–9, on the other hand, stand together, and seem to be from an oracle of about the year 701. The lesson that they teach is that of vv. 1–3, for they announce the destruction of Assyria, but by no human agency. Not merely destruction but complete subjugation, even slavery, is promised, while v. 9 indicates the complete moral disintegration of the invading armies. The fulfilment of all this men rightly saw in the overthrow of Sennacherib's host.

THE BOOK OF ZEPHANIAH

INTRODUCTION

THE book which bears Zephaniah's name consists of a number of oracles most of which describe a calamity about to fall upon Judah and the surrounding peoples, though in the last chapter there is a promise of restoration and salvation for some at least of the inhabitants of Judah. The instrument of punishment is to be a foreign invader, and the period is three-quarters of a century later than the time of Isaiah. The conditions suggested imply a date rather before the Reform in the days of Josiah than after it. In fact the most probable date for the activity of this prophet is during the first half of the reign of Josiah, and in that case the enemy whose ravages are in view is probably the same as that referred to in some of Jeremiah's earlier oracles. This is commonly, though not universally, identified with the Scythian people, a wild horde of northern savages who are said to have broken into the midst of the civilization of western Asia between the years 631 and 604. This date is borne out by the superscription of the book.

Zephaniah's pedigree is traced farther back than that of any other prophet, and the list of his ancestors ends with the name of Hezekiah, who may quite possibly have been the king of that name. In that case the prophet will have belonged to the upper classes, but this does not prevent him from seeing the iniquities of his order. He speaks in a vivid and passionate style, and, like his predecessors, lays stress on the social and ritual iniquities of his people. He is much concerned with the coming Day of Jahveh, and has a stronger eschatological tone than any other pre-exilic prophet. Apart from this he has little or nothing to add theologically to what Amos and Hosea have said already, and from this point of view is perhaps the least important of our canonical prophets. The text, especially in chs. 1 and 2, is very corrupt, and is never easy to translate.

As in the case of practically all the prophetic books, it is probable that an original nucleus of Zephaniah's oracles has been augmented by the addition of anonymous material. The extent of this is differently estimated by various students. Some, believing that eschatology is a comparatively late development in Israelite thought, would eliminate all that gives the work of

Zephaniah this peculiar cast. Others, with perhaps more justification, recognize that such pictures are very ancient in Hebrew
thought, and reduce the amount of later material accordingly.
The judgement of scholars is on the whole against the originality
of the close of ch. 3, from v. 14 onwards.

NOTES ON ZEPHANIAH 1

The superscription in v. 1 needs no further comment. There
appears to be no ground for doubting that it represents a reliable
tradition.

vv. 2–6. *A universal catastrophe.* This has a special bearing on
Judah, or perhaps the intention is to limit to Judah (as far as this
oracle is concerned) a disaster which at first appears to be universal.
It is possible that the oracle has been expanded by later copyists.

v. 2 gives out the theme of the piece, and the key-note is the word
'consume'. This literally means 'gather', and suggests the sweeping together of a mass of rubbish for destruction. This is somewhat
elaborated in v. 3, and it is possible that an original list, ending with
'the fishes of the sea', has been expanded. In any case the expression 'the stumbling-blocks with the wicked' is awkward, and a slight
change enables us to read 'and I will cause the wicked to stumble'.
In v. 4 the particular application to Judah is introduced, and it is made
clear that this is punishment for ritual sins. Baal worship, and the
assimilation of Jahveh worship to that of Baal, alike are to vanish,
together with other forms of apostasy. It is to be noted that the
'Chemarim' are priests, usually heathen priests. They are connected
with the illegitimate cultus. 'Malcam' is the god of Ammon.

With v. 7 begins a series of oracles all dealing with the coming Day
of Jahveh.

1^{7-9}. *Jahveh's sacrifice.* It is not impossible that v. 7 was originally isolated, and that the oracle in vv. 8 and 9 was attached to it by a
compiler because of the recurrence of the metaphor. It is a grim picture. Jahveh is making a sacrifice (this is common to all three verses).
He has summoned all the enemies of Israel to share in it, for this is
the type of sacrifice in which the greater part of the victim is eaten by
the offerer and his friends and household. The victim is Judah herself. Part of her sin consists in her adoption of foreign (and therefore
heathen) ways at court, part of it in adherence to heathen customs
such as leaping over the threshold of a temple or house, part of it

lies in the social injustice rampant in Judah. A terrible but probably accurate picture of pre-Deuteronomic Jerusalem.

I^{10–11}. *Every quarter of Jerusalem is affected.* The verses consist of an enumeration of the various points in Jerusalem from which the cry of suffering goes up. These seem to be mostly on the north side of the city, though the sites are not all certain. The 'fish gate' is certainly the northern gate. The 'second quarter' is probably a northern suburb, for Jerusalem seems to have grown northward throughout its history. Where the Maktesh is we do not know, but it is suggested with some probability that it lay in the Tyropoean valley. In any case it seems to have been the market-place in Zephaniah's time, for the 'Canaanite' is a general term for merchant, as the parallel in the second half of the verse shows.

I^{12–13}. *The doom of the sluggish.* This oracle depicts Jahveh searching the city, even lighting up its darkest corners. He is seeking a particular class of men, those who have 'settled on their lees', a metaphor taken from wine coagulating when exposed to the air. Such people are becoming dense and thick of heart and mind. They have developed a practical atheism, refusing to believe that Jahveh will ever interfere in their affairs. Such an attitude can lead only to calamity. This spiritual sluggishness must end in disaster, and the lazy, selfish, dishonest luxury will end in an invasion which will sweep away all they have.

I^{14–18}. *Calamities of the Day of Jahveh.* The last oracle of the chapter, which describes the various forms of calamity which will appear on that day. It was the model and source of the ancient hymn 'Dies irae, dies illa'. The text has awakened suspicions, especially in v. 14. In the latter part of the verse the E.V. hardly makes sense. We should render 'Hark!' instead of '*even* the voice'. The 'there' seems to be due to actual corruption of text, and many editors would read 'also'. In vv. 17 and 18 the sudden introduction of Jahveh in the third person is strange, since it is He who speaks elsewhere. 'Because they have sinned against the Lord' may well be a marginal note that has crept into the text, and in v. 18 editors prefer to alter the words so as to produce a speech in the first person throughout.

The whole picture is one of calamity, ruin, and terror. The language recalls that of Amos in dealing with the same subject. Darkness, cloud, tumult, noise, slaughter, panic flight, and in the end destruction,—these are what the day of Jahveh brings.

THE BOOK OF DEUTERONOMY[1]

NOTES ON DEUTERONOMY 12, 18–19

DEUTERONOMY 12

v. 1 is introductory to the whole of the legal section of the book, and is couched in terms which are characteristic alike of the style and of the point of view of the whole.

vv. 2–14 contain the fundamental law of the single sanctuary. This is emphasized in two ways, (*a*) by contrast with the Canaanite practice (vv. 2–7), (*b*) by contrast with the habits of Israel during the period of the wanderings (vv. 8–14). In vv. 2–3 an account is given of the promiscuous worship of the inhabitants of the land, who had altars ' on the high mountains, and upon the hills, and under every green tree'. As a matter of fact, practically all the available evidence goes to show that this was also the custom in Israel down to the time of Josiah, except for a short period in the reign of Hezekiah. Every village and town would have its sanctuary where sacrifice was regularly offered, though certainly some sanctuaries were more famous than others. These are all regarded, probably rightly, as Canaanite centres of worship, and the greatest care is to be taken to destroy them. All symbols and objects used in the cultus are to be destroyed. The altars, built of stone, are to be broken down, their ' pillars '— upright single stones of the kind to which archaeologists give the name *menhir*—are to be broken, possibly by heating them and then pouring cold water on them, the ' Asherim '—resembling the ' pillars ', except that they are made of wood—are to be burnt, and the images, probably of snakes or bulls, carved in wood and overlaid with precious metal, are to be chopped in pieces with axes. Then in vv. 4–7 comes the contrast. Israel is to have only one sanctuary, and thither are to be brought all sacred dues of every kind. It is interesting to note the various forms of dues to which the writer refers. There are first the ' burnt-offerings ', of which the whole is appropriated to sacred purposes, and is actually burnt on the altar. The ' sacrifice ' is a common meal, in which God, priest, and worshipper shared. The same portions as in the ' burnt-offering ' are consumed on the altar, the greater part is eaten by the worshipper and his guests, while

[1] For introductory remarks on the Book of Deuteronomy see note on ' Deuteronomy and the Deuteronomists '.

the priest has a share, a single 'helping' taken from the vessel in which the whole is cooked. The nature of the other dues is indicated by their names, except that of the 'heave offering', which was probably a daily contribution taken from the family's ordinary store of cereal food. All these are to be offered at the central sanctuary *and nowhere else.*

vv. 8–14 are little more than a repetition of vv. 4–7, but with a different preamble, showing that the practice enjoined was consciously an innovation. The purpose of the writers made it necessary for the command to be put into the mouth of Moses and traced back to the desert period, in order to ensure its validity. To the modern mind this savours of fraud, but it has to be recognized that the ancient world looked on many matters with different eyes from ours, and the writers certainly believed the command to be just as valid as if it had actually been given through Moses at Horeb.

vv. 15 ff. introduce a further modification of the ordinary life of Israel. It seems to be a universal idea amongst early peoples that the eating of the flesh of the domestic animals is always a sacramental act. This is probably due to a belief that the animals, like the men, are under the special protection of the tribal god or spirits. Wild animals are in no such position; if they are connected with any spiritual power at all it is with the spirits of the desert. Hence game may be eaten whenever found, the only stipulation made being that the blood shall be poured out on the ground. Hence whenever the Israelite would eat beef or mutton (usually, we may guess, goat-mutton), i.e. 'on every impulse of thy appetite' (so render rather than 'after all the desire of thy soul'), he was compelled to offer sacrifice. This was possible and easy as long as the local sanctuaries existed, but, as vv. 20 f. point out, a central sanctuary would be so far from many places in the country as to make journeys comparatively rare. Adherence to the old rule would then mean that beef or mutton could be eaten only once or twice in the year, and this difficulty had to be met. The method was to secularize the flesh of the domestic animals, and emphasis is laid on the fact that the ceremonially impure were as free to eat it as those who were in a condition to partake in the cultus. It is thus reduced to the level of game. As before, the law is repeated, being stated once in vv. 15–19 and once in vv. 20–8.

Two restrictions are further added. In the one case the eating of blood is strictly forbidden. This must be drained out of the carcass and allowed to soak into the ground, a rule which seems to have held good even in the case of wild animals captured and killed for food. Further, the permission to eat flesh at home does not include any animal slain in pursuance of ritual regulations. The whole cultus, including the communion sacrifices in which the worshipper shared, was confined to the central sanctuary. But the flesh of domestic animals was no longer necessarily sacrificial; it might be profane and eaten under secular conditions.

Note should be taken of the special mention of the Levite in v. 19. In this book all Levites are competent to act as priests, but not all have their home in the sacred city. The abolition of local sanctuaries, where the priests had lived mainly if not entirely on the flesh and other forms of food brought as sacred dues, left them without means of support. They are therefore—though other provision is eventually made for them—particularly commended to the care of the laity. It was no part of the purpose of the Deuteronomists to starve them out as a class. There is some uncertainty as to what they actually were in origin. That there was originally a tribe of Levi is beyond dispute, but there are hints in the older literature which suggest that this tribe had disappeared at an early stage of the occupation of Canaan. Amongst certain peoples of the Arabian peninsula there was a class of priests to whom the name *lawi* was given, and it has been suggested that in Israel also the Levites were originally priests, confused with an extinct tribe of similar name by later generations. The evidence, however, is far from being conclusive, and, in the absence of more definite information, it may be better to retain the traditional view that the Levites were the original clansmen of Moses himself. It is at least clear that to the Deuteronomists the terms Levite and priest covered exactly the same group of persons.

vv. 29–31 constitute a warning against the adoption of Canaanite religious customs in connexion with the worship of Jahveh. That which is especially mentioned is the practice of human (probably infant) sacrifice. This from time to time took place in Israel, e. g. in the days of Ahaz and Manasseh, and it has been held with some reason that the earlier laws actually contemplated the offering of human as well as of animal first-born. Collateral evidence is furnished by such a passage as Ez. 20$^{24-6}$, and the special mention of the practice here hints that it was an element in the cultus which had been taken over from the original inhabitants of the land—as it may well have been. It is, however, now definitely and finally prohibited. The last verse of the chapter (E.V.) is a warning to observe the law.

The Jewish division of the Hebrew Bible made this the first verse of ch. 13, to which, perhaps, it more properly belongs as an introduction.

Deuteronomy 18, 19

As has been seen in dealing with ch. 12, the law of the single sanctuary inevitably carried with it further corollaries. Attention has already been called to the position of the local priesthood under the new regulations, and this is more explicitly dealt with in 18^{1-8}. Here it is provided that if they so desire they may leave their old towns and villages in the country and make their home in Jerusalem, where they are to share in all those portions of the sacred dues which fall to the priests. The old practice, as we learn from 1 Sam. $3^{13f.}$, had been for the priest or his servant to take haphazard whatever came up when he thrust his fork into the vessel in which the meat was being cooked. As even that early passage shows, the system was liable to abuse, and now the priests' portions of the ' sacrifice ' (i.e. the sacred meal) are strictly defined. Of these portions the local priests, now resident in the city of the central sanctuary, are to have their share.

18^{9-22} deal with the method of divine revelation of the future, a subject which in Israel was more or less closely connected with the cultus. For purposes of divination and magic men had been in the habit of consulting various kinds of practitioners, at least in pre-Israelite times. All the classes here mentioned are people who were controlled by or controlled some spirit, either one of the nondescript beings who inhabited earth and air or the spirits of the dead. All such practices are condemned. Necromancy or spiritualism (to give the practice its commonest modern name) is usually discredited to-day on the ground that it rests on fraud. In ancient times it was straitly prohibited on the ground that it was genuine. Israel must hold communication with no other non-human power save Jahveh Himself, and to deal with the spirits of nature or of the dead was a form of apostasy, and therefore was not to be tolerated. Israel must be ' perfect ' with Jahveh ; she must be wholly devoted to Him, and no other must share in her religious life (18^{9-14}).

The need felt by men for direct communication with the invisible world was to be met in other ways. The chief medium of communication was to be the prophet. It should be observed that v. 15 does not really refer to any particular prophet ; the word is quite general in its application, and we should do no violence to the sense if we used the plural instead of the singular. Jahveh would raise up prophets who should resemble Moses in their association with Him, and should speak His word (18^{15-19}). The Law itself was not the final revelation of Jahveh ; it required to be supplemented, and would be supplemented, by people who were in direct personal communication with Him. There was, of course, the danger that fraudulent and unauthorized oracles would be given, and to guard against this a very simple criterion is offered. If a prophet's predictions are fulfilled, then Jahveh is behind him : if they do not come true, then the man has spoken without the divine warrant (vv. 20–2).

19^{1-18} deals with the law of blood-revenge, and the special modifications necessitated by the law of the central sanctuary. Even as late as the time of Josiah it is clear that the old principles held good. When a man died, certain duties and responsibilities fell on his nearest surviving male relative, who became his representative (the Hebrew word is *gō'ēl*), and had to do for him certain things that he would have done for himself had he lived. As an illustration we may take the task of begetting children to carry on the name and line of the deceased, the principle on which the story of Ruth turns. If a man died a violent death, the duty of slaying the slayer was added to other responsibilities. The *gō'ēl* then became a *gō'ēl of blood* (E.V. 'avenger of blood'), and it was his recognized duty to hunt down and kill the person responsible for his kinsman's death, without inquiry into the circumstances. It must be remembered that the custom was a survival of a non-moral age, but the nobler feeling of the Deuteronomists recognized wide differences in degrees of guilt, and saw that a man, whilst the actual striker of the blow which caused death, might be morally innocent. Probably this distinction was not new, but the indiscriminate application of the law had been modified by the right of every man to take refuge in some sanctuary, and, by laying hold of the altar, to claim the protection of Jahveh. The responsible authorities could then investigate the matter and decide on the real guilt of the fugitive. At the same time, if the *gō'ēl* overtook and slew his victim before he reached this refuge, no blame of any kind attached to him. With the abolition of the local altars and sanctuaries the danger that might result to a perfectly innocent man from some accident such as the slipping of an axe-head from the handle (v. 5) was very greatly enhanced, and some substitute for the old local altar had to be provided. The remaining central altar was, of course, still valid, but, to meet the needs of men who lived far from it, three cities (afterwards increased to six) were appointed as ' cities of refuge '.

vv. 11–13 provide against abuse of this system. Even under the old arrangement a deliberate murderer was taken forcibly from Jahveh's altar (Ex. 21¹⁴) and put to death—presumably by the *gō'ēl*. The same rule is now to hold good, and the legal procedure is prescribed. The elders of the accused man's city are to send for him, if he be found guilty of murder in its extreme form, and he is deprived of the protection afforded to him by the city of refuge.

v. 14 is an isolated injunction, forbidding the removal of a boundary-stone or other mark. The importance of such a regulation in a country where the principal form of property is land is too obvious to need remark.

vv. 15–21 deal with the laws of evidence and perjury. The isolated evidence of a single individual is not to be accepted. ' Shall not rise up ' does not forbid a man to give evidence, but declares that such evidence shall not be regarded as decisive in settling a case. Two at least must testify, presumably on the same charge. The principle is a sound one, and has been widely adopted. It will be noticed that in so primitive a community as that of ancient Israel no definite provision is made for circumstantial evidence, except such as may be implied in the ' diligent inquisition ' of v. 18. As a matter of fact, in the modern East, circumstantial evidence is the only kind that can confidently be accepted—and that is frequently fabricated ! But such inquiry is enjoined only in cases where there is reason to suspect perjury. The penalty varies with that attaching to the case in connexion with which the perjury was committed. If it were a capital charge the punishment is death, if a charge which might have led to mutilation, the perjurer is similarly treated. This is in accordance with the ' lex talionis ' which is actually repeated in v. 21. It is noticeable that the case in which a man gives false evidence in order to secure the acquittal of the accused is not considered. The aim of the law is to protect others against the dangers, too common in the East, of a false charge, and therein illustrates the general humanitarian spirit in which the whole of this remarkable code has been drawn up. It is far more important, so the Deuteronomistic mind thinks, to protect the innocent than to punish the guilty, however desirable that may be.

THE BOOK OF NAHUM

NOTHING is known of this prophet beyond his name and the fact that his home was at Elkosh, a place which was probably in the south of Judah, though some traditions locate Elkosh in Galilee, others even in the neighbourhood of Nineveh. The book which bears his name opens with a poem which has probably suffered considerable mutilation, for it seems to have been originally an acrostic, in which each line began with its own letter of the alphabet. This can still be detected in vv. 3-8, but is difficult to find elsewhere. The acrostic occupies the greater part of ch. I, and is concerned with the coming of Jahveh to vengeance. The oracular portion of the book is all concerned with the fall of Nineveh, which is clearly imminent. It is therefore to be dated probably between 614 and 612. The style is extraordinarily vigorous and vivid, and it is probably to this fact that the book owes its preservation.

In general character it is quite unlike any other book in the prophetic writings. There is no denunciation of the sin of Israel, no appeal to repentance, no announcement of a judgement likely to fall on the people of Judah. Instead, we have a series of songs of ecstatic triumph over the ruin of an enemy, a loud burst of exultation over the destruction of an ancient oppressor. Nahum is perhaps a specimen (and if so, the only one left to us) of the type of popular patriotic prophet against whom the canonical prophets such as Jeremiah often had to inveigh. Yet we cannot regret the presence of the book in the Canon. Even if it has no direct lesson, it throws a brilliant light on the thoughts and attitude of the kind of prophecy which gladdened the hearts of men at the end of the seventh century.

The text seems to have suffered a good deal in the course of transmission, and some scholars would rearrange the last verses of ch. I and the opening of ch. 2, but the difficulties are more likely to be due to the accidents of compilation.

NOTES ON NAHUM 2

The chapter should rather begin (as in the Hebrew text) with the last verse of ch. I (E.V.). It is hardly prophecy or oracle in the usual sense, but a great paean of triumph over the fall of the tyrant city.

I¹⁵ (Heb. 2¹). *Judah is safe.* This calls for a message to be sent from distant Nineveh to Judah, telling her that now she can hold her festivals without fear, for the oppressor is gone. Perhaps the text of this chapter would run more smoothly if the first two verses were transposed, for v. 2 would make a good continuation of 1^{15}. Jacob has been ashamed and has lost his pride because of the calamities that have befallen him at the hands of Nineveh, when the Assyrians emptied him and cut his branches. The reference is possibly to the terrible campaign of Sennacherib in 701, which was still remembered.

$2^{1,\,3,\,4}$. *The actual assault on the city.* Nineveh is itself addressed. For 'He that dasheth in pieces' most moderns with a slight vowel modification would read 'the hammer'. Nineveh is scornfully bidden to take all precautions, keep a watch, gird herself, collect all her forces. For the foe is upon her, stained with her blood ; the city is forced, and the hostile chariots dash with lightning speed about her streets.

2^{5-8}. *The capture of Nineveh.* The text is possibly corrupt : 'He remembereth his worthies' is hardly what Nahum said. Probably the words have displaced a sentence which described the swift gathering of the heroes and captains to the walls to make their final attempt with battering-ram to beat down the gates whilst the penthouse protects them. A gate is broken open, apparently that through which the waters of the Tigris made their way.

In v. 7 the dismay in the city itself is shown to us. The queen (it seems almost certain that 'Huzzab' is a textual corruption which conceals a word meaning 'queen'), she who is most carefully secluded of all women, is dragged into the open and removed, while her maidens moan and beat their breasts. In v. 8 again we certainly meet with corruption ; the E.V. is an impossible translation of an impossible Hebrew text. Probably the original ran : 'And Nineveh is as a pool whose waters flee away,' i. e. though every effort is made to stem the panic flight of her warriors, yet they break out on all sides as the water of a lake which has broken the dam that held it back, and though men call to them to rally, they give no heed.

2^{9-10}. *The sack of the city.* Once more in v. 9 we probably have a corrupt text, which originally ran somewhat like : 'Take you plunder of silver, and plunder of gold, load yourselves with the burden of all pleasant things.' The work is soon done, and the city is empty, while such of its inhabitants as survive writhe and are livid with fear.

2^{11-13}. *World peace.* The poet reverts to the thought with which the chapter opens. A great relief has fallen on the world. As the lion fills his den with the flesh of his victims, brought home to feed his mate and his young, so Assyrian armies have brought to Nineveh the spoils of all the world. Now it is over. Jahveh has done what none other could have done. The task and the triumph are His, and humanity can once more breathe freely in its new security.

Assyrians besieging a city, using a movable tower and a battering-ram.

By permission of the Trustees of the British Museum.

THE BOOK OF HABAKKUK

Nothing whatever is known of this prophet except what may be gathered from the book which bears his name. That falls into two parts, chs. 1 and 2 consisting of oracular matter, and ch. 3 being a psalm, which has every appearance of having been taken from some collection similar to our Book of Psalms. In order to appreciate the critical problems which the book involves, it will be as well to take a cursory glance at its contents, at least at the contents of chs. 1 and 2.

1^{2-4} contain a complaint of the terrible state of suffering and oppression which the prophet sees around him. 1^{5-11} announce the coming of the Chaldeans, whose appearance and character are described. 1^{12-14} state the problem of the government of the world—why do the righteous suffer at the hand of the wicked? 1^{15-17}, presenting an oppressor under the figure of a fisherman, give an account of his success. 2^{1-4} record the answer which the prophet received to his 'complaint'. v. 5 (as it stands in our texts) is a warning against wine. The rest of ch. 2 is a series of denunciations of various classes of social sinners.

The difficulty presented by the book is to define the part played by the Chaldeans. Are they the successful sinners of whom complaint is made, or are they the avengers of the wrong that the prophet and his people have suffered? If the latter, then how are we to explain their apparent identification in 1^{13} with the 'wicked'? Would Jahveh's chosen avengers be so called? If the former, then what is the connexion between the first two sections? For the second certainly seems to imply that the Chaldeans are coming to punish the wrongdoers of vv. 2-4, and the 'woes' of ch. 2 seem to be directed against a people who had long been established in tyrannical power.

Various solutions have been offered, some scholars even going so far as to read 'Greeks' for 'Chaldeans', and assign the whole to the age of Alexander the Great. But perhaps the simplest solution is to see in the whole a group of oracles originally independent, whose present arrangement is due to a compiler. They may be of different dates and possibly from different hands, but there is no insuperable difficulty in the way of regarding them all in the main as the work of a single prophet.

In that case, since the Chaldeans are just rising above the horizon as a world-power, the date may be just before 605. It is also possible that the oppressor is the Egyptian power, represented in Jerusalem itself by Jehoiakim. The 'woes' of 2^5 ff. may have been denunciations of individuals, adapted by a compiler to a tyrannous nation. The language shows certain connexions with that of Jeremiah.

NOTES ON HABAKKUK 1-2

1^1 is the superscription of the whole book. The collocation of the terms 'burden' and 'see' is interesting. Both have their origin in the prophetic experience, though originally both probably represent different elements in it.

1^{2-4}. *A cry for justice.* The prophet and those for whom he speaks are weary of the tyranny which they have endured. They have cried 'Violence!'—the appeal of the victim, as to-day we might cry, 'Thieves!' or 'Murder!', but Jahveh has not interfered. Instead, He has left the sight of iniquity before the people's eyes (read 'must I' before 'look' in v. 3, with several ancient versions) and still the prophet sees trouble (there is no justification for the rendering 'perverseness'). Because Jahveh, who is the supreme lord of justice, is indifferent, iniquity is rampant without redress. Men enter the law-court, but the administration of justice is careless, and the judges are slow to reach a decision. Even when they do give a verdict, it is in favour of the wrong man—fear or partiality has been allowed to influence them.

1^{5-11}. *The coming of the Chaldeans.* As the text is arranged, this is Jahveh's answer to the cry for justice, an answer utterly unexpected and incredible. But the oracle may originally have been a warning addressed to the prophet's contemporaries. The language recalls that in which Jeremiah describes a coming enemy, Jer. 4^{13}, 5^6, &c. The terror of the army and its speed are described ; neither armed forces in the field nor fortified cities can stay their progress. v. 11 is very difficult, and is best read (altering the word rendered 'guilty'), 'Then he changeth his thought and passeth on, and maketh his strength his god', the verb forms being such as to denote swift and completely effective action.

1^{12-14}. *The great problem.* How, in the face of the righteousness and eternity of Jahveh, the ruler of the world, can the unjust continue to triumph over the just? Two remarks may be made about this problem. The first is that it could have arisen only as a result of such teaching as that of the eighth-century prophets. Unless a man believes that God is just, he does not find injustice difficult to explain. If the Hindu thought of the goddess Kali as the ruler of the universe, murder would be a natural and normal event, quite in keeping with cosmic law. It is only when a doctrine of the goodness of God, and the thought that He is for ever concerned in the affairs of the world, have taken a firm hold on men's minds that they can begin to find such a question as this puzzling. The second point to notice is that when once such a doctrine has been established this problem is bound to arise sooner or later. In Israel it proved to be the point from which all later advance in religious thought was made, and it led ultimately to a belief in the Resurrection. For this reason—since this prophet, as far as we know, was the first to ask the question—we have here one of the great turning-points in Jewish spiritual history.

One other point is of interest. In the second part of v. 12 the margin reads 'thou diest not'. This seems to have been original, but the idea of God's dying was so unthinkable to the Jewish mind that they would not write it, even in copying or reading the sacred text. So they altered it to 'we shall not die', but honestly recorded in the margin the original reading. There are eighteen such passages in the Old Testament, and they are called 'the emendations of the Scribes'.

1^{14-17}. *Triumph of the oppressor.* A fragmentary description of some tyrannical military power, perhaps the Chaldeans. They are pictured as successful fishermen who bring their nets ashore, empty them and cast them once more into the sea, and in their triumph they consecrate their implements to their god. Such consecration of arms is not unknown, though there seems to be no recorded parallel of fishermen dedicating their nets.

2^{1-4}. *The answer to the prophet's question.* It seems clear that this is connected with the statement of the problem in 1^{12-14}. The prophet first of all ascends his watch-tower, a metaphorical expression which probably means that he places himself in an attitude of receptivity, ready to accept whatever message Jahveh may send him. Then the reply comes. Sooner or later the problem will be solved, and man shall understand his fate. Jahveh, however, has His own time for the revelation, and will give it when and how he sees fit. The waiting may seem to be long, but the divine plans admit of neither haste nor delay. The first half of v. 4 is obscure and may be corrupt, but it

Fisherman casting a hand-net

Photograph by Mr. R. Gorbold

evidently is meant to indicate the impatient pride of the oppressor. With this is contrasted the attitude and fortune of the righteous in a very famous sentence, ' The righteous shall live by his faithfulness.' There are wide differences of opinion as to the exact meaning of these words. Some would see in them an eschatological reference, believing that the first part of the verse indicates the destruction of the wicked in the Day, while the second intimates that he who has throughout clung faithfully to Jahveh will win salvation. Or the words may give 'interim instructions' to the righteous. The time for the full revelation is not yet, and till it appears the righteous must be content to retain his faith, his confidence, his personal trust in his God. In any case it can hardly be claimed that the prophet has attained a final solution of his problem. That has never yet been fully reached, and perhaps never will be reached in our partial and limited view of what life means.

2^5. *The first Woe.* Most modern interpreters believe that the mention of wine is due to textual corruption, based on vv. 15 ff., and that the verse originally opened ' Woe to the treacherous dealer '. The reference may well be to the Chaldeans, who are then condemned because they are never satisfied with what they have, but are for ever seeking new conquests. Their appetite for fresh acquisitions is as great as that of She'ol, the place of the dead to which in the end all humanity must come. But in this, as in other of the ' Woes ', it is impossible to avoid the impression that we have here a denunciation of an individual for social wrongs, which has been adapted and modified to apply to a whole tyrannical people.

2^{6-8}. *The second Woe.* This has a short introduction, and gives the same impression as the last. A greedy money-lender is attacked for his ruthless avarice, and his doom is foretold through the vengeance of his victims. v. 8 applies this also to a sinful nation.

2^{9-11}. *The third Woe.* A similar denunciation to the last, except that the wrong done may be referred to dishonesty in trade, and that the purpose of the ill-gotten gains is the building of a house. The text of v. 9 is suspected by some scholars, but no suggestion has been made that would alter the essential meaning. The language recalls that found in an oracle against Edom preserved in Jer. 49^{16} and Ob. 3–4. The punishment is that the very materials of the building will cry out in protest ; the house will be haunted with the crime.

2^{12-14}. *The fourth Woe.* Another malediction on an unrighteous builder, recalling the condemnation of Jehoiakim by Jeremiah

Jer. 22¹³. v. 13 is the national application, and v. 14 is clearly a fragment of an oracle which is more fully represented in Is. 11⁹.

2¹⁵⁻¹⁷. *The fifth Woe.* The criminal here is one who has trapped his victims by making them drunk, and has then been able to fleece them at his will. But there is another cup beside that filled with the juice of the grape; there is the cup of the fury of Jahveh (cf. Jer. 25¹⁵ ᶠᶠ·). This in turn will be delivered to the oppressor to drink, and he will know the full results of his sin. v. 17, with its reference to the damage done to Lebanon, gives the national application. Mesopotamian armies, both Assyrian and Babylonian, frequently made havoc of the Lebanon forests, which were, as a matter of fact, the main source of timber for a large part of western Asia.

vv. 18–20 are a condemnation of idolatry. There is some reason to suppose that the verses are no longer in their original order, and certainly v. 18 would read more naturally after v. 19 than before it. The alternative is to suppose that v. 18 was an isolated sentence which was inserted by a compiler as being suitable to the subject. Contrasted with the idols is Jahveh, the living God, whose home is in Jerusalem. Before Him all nations shall rise and stand in silent awe. It is a little surprising to find idolatry condemned as early as the end of the seventh century. In view of the fact that this is the last of the oracles, it may come from a much later period than the remainder of these two chapters.

THE BOOK OF JEREMIAH

INTRODUCTION

Like several other books amongst the prophetic collections,
the Book of Jeremiah seems to have been woven together by
a comparatively late compiler from three literary elements.   He
had before him in the first place a collection, or, more probably,
several collections, of oracular matter attributed to Jeremiah.
These had already had a fairly long history, and some of them
included sections which few to-day can ascribe to the prophet
whose name they bear.   In addition to material of this type
there was a considerable amount of autobiographical prose,
which, in this instance at any rate, consisted mainly of the
substance of oracles delivered to the prophet, but apparently
modified in verbal form in the process of writing them down.
This fact suggests that if these sections are to be attributed to
Jeremiah (which is doubted by one or two modern scholars), he
either wrote them with his own hand or dictated them to a professional scribe.   These are divided into groups, each including
one or more original utterances which may have been entirely
separate to begin with, and some, possibly all, of these groups
have superscriptions giving a date or certain circumstances in
which the first at least of the component messages was presumably delivered.   It is, of course, possible that the superscription
of any given group was intended to cover all the matter within
that group, but this is not certain.   Passages of this type seem
to have undergone a good deal of revision at various times before
they came into the hands of the main compiler of the book, and
they have gathered a good many accretions on the way.   A third
type is to be found in a collection of narratives about the prophet,
evidently written by another hand, and to be attributed to some
one who was intimate with Jeremiah for a large part of his active
life, and who was in general more interested in what happened
to him than in what he said, though there are from time to time
brief summaries of his addresses and more personal communications.   This material also seems to have been divided into
sections, each having its own minor superscription, and is now
commonly held to be the work of Baruch, the professional

writer who was associated with Jeremiah during the latter part
of his ministry.

The compiler's method has been to take first the material of the
second type section by section.   To each group he has appended
one of his collections of oracular matter, as he found them
suitable, and has to some extent preserved the chronological

The Wadi Fara, near Anathoth.
Photograph by Fr. Vester & Co.

order of his prose collection, though there are one or two obvious
instances of displacement.   When the greater part of the autobiographical matter had thus been used, he employed for the
same purpose a few sections from the third type of material, and
finally placed at the end of the whole book what he had left
over of both prose types.   One oracular collection, however,
was left out and inserted at the very end.   This was a collection

of oracles against foreign nations which now occupies chs. 46–51.[1]
This, perhaps more than any other oracular collection in the
book, has suffered from latter additions, and whilst it would
probably be incorrect to ascribe the whole to later hands, as
some scholars have done, the nucleus of Jeremianic oracles
round which the whole collection has been built up was probably
comparatively small. The book concludes with an historical
extract taken from the end of 2 Kings.

The prophetic experience did not interfere with the expression
of a prophet's personality; it rather intensified it. And in
Jeremiah we have a man who appeals to many of us to-day more
strongly than any other character in the Old Testament. By
nature he was shy, shrinking, and retiring, with instincts which
would have led him to quiet family life. He was as capable as
Hosea of intense feeling, and indeed the two have much in
common. Both were filled with a passionate devotion alike to
their country and to their God, and both were compelled to look
forward to the destruction of their sinful people. It would seem
that Jeremiah was acquainted with the work of his northern
predecessor, and, at any rate in his earlier years, was influenced
by it. His home was in Anathoth, where he belonged to
a family of priests, probably those in charge of a local 'high
place', and he was therefore familiar with the baser elements in
the worship of Judah. We may thus trace back to his early
experiences his marked hostility to ritual and his repudiation of
the value of sacrifice.

Details of his life may be gathered from the book which bears
his name, and it is unnecessary to dwell on them here. From
his childhood he must have known Jerusalem, for Anathoth is
only a few miles from the city. Yet he always had a keen
interest in the country and the farm. He knew the ways of
the migratory birds and the habits of the partridge. The
charge of the lion, the speed of the leopard, the rapacity of the
wolf, and the howls of the jackal were familiar to him, and there
is a certain atmosphere of sympathy in his description of the
sufferings of wild things in time of drought. He was well
acquainted with the domestic beasts, the camel, the horse, and
cow, and understood their habits. But it is characteristic of
him that yet more of his metaphors are derived from the life of
men and women. His mind dwells on marriages, births, and

---

[1] It should be remarked that what is said here applies only to the traditional
Hebrew text. The Greek translation (LXX) was based on a text which placed
this collection in the middle of our ch. 25.

burials, and he often refers to social custom and criminal law. He speaks of the methods of getting and keeping water, of the medical practice of his time, of the traveller lost on the mountains, and of the common dealings at the market stalls. The operations of agriculture furnish him with frequent parallels, drawn from the corn, the olive, the almond, the fig, the vine, while the hunter,

Anathoth.

Photograph by Fr. Vester & Co.

the fowler, and the fisherman supply him with images of the dealings of Jahveh with His people, or the treatment of men by their brethren. Symbolic action was probably characteristic of all the prophets, but more of these acted metaphors are ascribed to Jeremiah than to any other, except Ezekiel.

Jeremiah holds a high place amongst the world's poets. No doubt his work sometimes seems uneven, but this may in part be due to the inclusion of material which was not his. The poetry that can certainly be ascribed to him is always vigorous, direct, and picturesque, and occasionally the intensity of his feeling raises his language to the loftiest heights.   There are few more impressive lyrics in all literature than the chaos vision in 4^{23-6}, or the image of Death the Reaper in 9^{20-1}.   His style is less obscure than that of Hosea, though his emotions are nearly as strong ; as an artist Jeremiah does not attain so high a level as Isaiah.   He would, nevertheless, have won an enduring position in literature independently of his position in the history of religion.

Apart from the prophecy of the New Covenant, to which reference has already been made (p. 146), Jeremiah has little to add to the theology of Israel.   Like his great predecessors, he thinks of Jahveh as the Creator, and ascribes to Him a high moral character and stringent ethical demands.   Hence there is nothing so horrible in the universe as sin, and appalling suffering is bound to issue from it.   But Jeremiah himself and his experience of God are a more important contribution to the growth of religion than any of his doctrines.   Instead of enjoying the life of happy domestic obscurity which he would have chosen, he was driven by the irresistible power of his inspiration to publicity of a kind most repellent to himself.   His message was always an unpopular one, and for forty years he had not merely to endure the final sorrows of the country that he loved so well, but to suffer persecution and sometimes to face spiritual despair.   The fulfilment of his words was delayed, and that brought to him and to others the thought that he was not really one of the God-chosen band of the true prophets.   Hence he had to endure scorn on every side, as well as the attempt to suppress his message, and there were times when he himself began to feel, knowing that Jahveh had surely spoken to him, that his God had deliberately trapped him into giving a false message.   In all literature there are few more poignant expressions of human agony of spirit than the section which opens with 20^7.

Yet it was this very bitterness of experience which after all gave him his supreme value for the world.   He stood alone with his God.   Religion was to him not merely a matter between the community and its deity, it was an intensely personal and individual relation between himself and Jahveh.   He is thus the first individualist amongst the world's great religious teachers, and it is this, more than any doctrine which he propounded, that gives him his place in the spiritual history of mankind. Whether the tradition which made him the original of the picture of the suffering servant of Jahveh in Is. 52^{13}–53^{12} be right or no, that description fits him better than any other Old Testament character known to us.   More than any other he bore his cross. And from the seed of his tears there has sprung a rich harvest of religious life. All that wealth of experience to which psalmist and saint have testified through the ages is dependent on the primary fact that God deals with men as individuals and not merely in masses. There is truth in the latter view, but it is not the whole truth, and it was the sufferings of Jeremiah that first made this clear. In a very real sense, he is the Father of all the Saints.

NOTES ON JEREMIAH 1–4, 7^1–8^3, 19–22, 36–44

CHAPTERS 1^1–3^5

1^{1-3}. *The superscription.* It gives the name of Jeremiah's father, and states that he came of a family of priests, probably the local priests of the shrine at Anathoth. The village lay a few miles to the north-west of Jerusalem, and was the home of the family of Abiathar after he had been expelled from Jerusalem by Solomon. Jeremiah may have been one of his descendants. Further, the dates of Jeremiah's prophetic activity are given, i.e. 626 B.C. to 585. They have been questioned, and it has been suggested that his work did not really begin till about 615, but the reasons advanced are hardly sufficient to justify us in denying the accuracy of the statement in these verses.

1^{4-10}. *Jeremiah's call.* This is his first ecstatic experience. He hears the voice of Jahveh telling him that from before his birth he has been destined to this particular work. He protests that he is an insignificant person (not necessarily a child; the word implies a subordinate, one who held no responsibility), and has neither the standing nor the equipment for such a task. Any fears he may have on this point are met by the assurance of support which he receives. Independent authority is not necessary to him, for it is not on his own errand that he is to go. One who is temperamentally a subordinate will suit Jahveh's needs, for He is behind all that the prophet has to say and do. At the same time support is promised. Jeremiah will have to face many terrible things and people, but he can rely on the strength of Jahveh.

Then in v. 9 comes a symbolic act. Jeremiah feels a Hand laid on his lips, and hears a Voice telling him that now the divine word has been placed in his mouth. With this may be compared the similar experience of Isaiah. The differences are—(*a*) it is glowing stone laid by a seraph on Isaiah's lips, (*b*) the object of the action is not so much

to place the words in Isaiah's mouth as to purify him, and so to make
him fit to respond to the call which follows (Is. 6⁶⁻⁹).

I¹¹⁻¹². *The first of a pair of testing visions.* This and the following
have a certain interest as suggesting one of the ways in which the
ecstasy might come upon the prophet. It seems that Jeremiah is
looking at the branch of an almond tree (Hebrew *Shākēd*, as the R.V.
margin points out), and with the fixed gaze he enters into a new
experience. The name of the thing obsesses his mind till he hears a
voice pronouncing a similar word, *Shōkēd*—' Awake ', and realizes that
Jahveh is speaking to him words in which the sound occurs. There
is more than a mere play on the words. Just as the almond tree is
the first to ' wake up ' after its long winter sleep, shared by all vege-
tation, so Jahveh Himself is not really dead, and after the long silence
of the Manasseh period He will show Himself to be alive and awake.
Jeremiah has had proved to him his own ecstatic powers, and has at
the same time received a divine message.

I¹³⁻¹⁴. *A similar vision.* A vessel is boiling on a little field oven,
consisting of three little walls, the south side left open. This shelters
the fire, and the vessel itself is tilted towards the south. A strong
north wind is blowing all the smoke and steam southwards. The
' seething ' cauldron is properly a ' cauldron blown upon (by the
wind) ', and the word ' blow ' gives the key to the vision. The LXX
text is almost certainly right in reading ' shall be blown ' for ' shall
break forth ' (lit., as the margin, ' shall be opened '). All this cloud
blowing southwards from the north typifies an enemy who shall come
from the north.

I¹⁵⁻¹⁶. *The foe from the north.* Here begins the oracular matter to
which the narrative of the call and the first two visions have been
prefixed from the first autobiographical section. The subject, the
coming foe from the north, who shall take possession of Jerusalem,
naturally attaches it to the last vision, though there is no reason to
suppose that it actually dates from the same experience. There is
nothing in the text to show who the enemy actually is, and two conjectures have been made. One is that it is the Scythians, the other
that it is the Chaldeans. In recent years some doubt has been thrown
on the accuracy of the narrative of Herodotus, and we are to-day
somewhat uncertain as to the Scythians. But if there is any particular enemy in view in 626 B. c. (the date of the preceding vision if not
of this oracle), then the experience of Jeremiah should probably be
allowed to weigh in favour of Herodotus' credibility. It is always

possible that Jeremiah recognized in later years that the ultimate foe
from the north was not the Scythians but the Chaldeans.   In any case
he had reason to suspect a calamity coming from that quarter, and the
cause, as his oracle declares, lies in the apostasy of Judah, probably
a reference to the conditions prevailing in the reign of Manasseh.

Almond tree in blossom in Palestine.
Photograph by Fr. Vester & Co.

I¹⁷⁻¹⁹. *A promise of support.*   Another ' personal ' oracle (of which
there are several in Jeremiah), repeating the promise of support and
at the same time giving a warning.   If the prophet does not use the
opportunities of courage that Jahveh affords him, if he flinches at the
sight of those who will be his foes, then Jahveh in turn will add to his
terrors, and will overwhelm him with panic in their sight.   But if he

shows them a firm front, then he will be inviolable. In fearlessness is his only security.

2^{1–3}. *Israel's early faithfulness.* Our text has a fresh superscription here, but the LXX seems to have had the original form, which omitted everything before 'saying' in v. 2, and for that substitute a finite verb 'and he said'. The oracle is a tender reminiscence, which recalls the tone and attitude of Hosea, of the happy nomadic days when Israel and Jahveh, newly wedded by their great covenant, were all in all to one another. Hers was the clinging, loving submission of the oriental wife, and His the chivalry of passionate devotion which would protect and, if need be, avenge on every occasion. In v. 3 'all that devour him shall be held guilty' fails to give the prophet's full meaning ; rather he says 'Israel is a holy thing, like the consecrated food that none save the sacred persons may touch. Just as calamity falls upon the layman who eats of the holy food, so would disaster in those old days have overtaken any who had touched Israel.' She was holy, Jahveh's chosen and separated possession, and all others interfered at their peril.

2^{4–8}. *Israel's infidelity.* v. 4 is introductory, possibly inserted by the compiler to emphasize the importance of the oracle which follows. The previous utterance had drawn an idyllic picture of the distant past, this one describes the descent to the present. In spite of all that Jahveh had done in bringing Israel out of Egypt and setting her in the good land, she had been unfaithful to Him. A breach had arisen between them—and it was not His fault. She had not only failed to acknowledge His goodness to her, she had foully desecrated with Canaanite ritual that fair home into which He had brought her. This was even more true of those who should have kept her in touch with Him, the priests and the prophets.

2^{9–12}. *Israel's apostasy.* The conduct of Israel is contrasted with that of other nations. None of them, unreal as their gods had been, had ever gone so far as to change their faith. The 'isles of Kittim' are the coasts of Cyprus (the 'far west' to Judah in the seventh century), and Kedar is a typical tribe of the eastern desert border. Between them they include the practical range of Jewish geography in Jeremiah's day. Nowhere has such a thing happened as that which Israel has done. Well may the very heavens be appalled and shudder with horror !

2¹³. *Broken cisterns.* Israel has forsaken the fountain of running water and preferred the stale rain-water that she has stored up in rock cisterns of her own making. It is unclean and dangerous at any time, but there is this additional fault, that there is a crack beneath through which the water drains away, and she is left without even the poor supply that she had gathered for herself. She has thrown away her own God, and the faith she has assumed fails her. There are no substitutes for God.

2^{14-17}. *The apostasy of Judah.* The text seems to need some attention. In v. 14 the A.V. 'spoiled' is better than the R.V. 'prey', unless it be remembered that it is the prey of an enemy, and not the prey of lions. v. 15 will hardly stand exactly as it is; lions do not burn cities, and this clause 'his cities are burned up' probably belongs to the end of v. 14. In v. 16 it is the margin which translates the Hebrew text, though it makes something rather like nonsense; the rendering in the text is due to a conjectural emendation which is probably right. Also the verbs in this verse denote a continuous process, not a completed one. The LXX is probably right in v. 17 in following a text which ran simply 'Dost thou not procure this unto thyself, in that thou hast forsaken me? saith the Lord'.

If Israel had been a slave, whether under the 'limited period' form of slavery current in Israel[1] or a born slave who could never hope for deliverance, the disaster that has fallen upon him might have been explicable. But Israel is a son—that is the implication. How then can a Father allow him to suffer so? The answer is that it is not the Father's doing. The wilful boy has had his way, and cannot escape the consequences.

2^{18-19}. *Foreign entanglements.* Another oracle of the same type, but with more explicit reference. Whether the association with Assyria and Egypt was political or whether it was religious is not clear, probably the two went to some extent together. Either would mean apostasy, and for that Israel must suffer. Again the LXX has a variant text, but it does not seriously affect the application or the meaning of the oracle.

2^{20}. *A rebellious people.* The verbs should be read in the second person, as in the R.V. margin. Israel has refused to be a slave, but instead of liberty has chosen licence. The language strongly recalls phrases common in Deuteronomy.

2^{21-22}. *The bad vine.* There was nothing wrong with the stock from which the vine came, but when it sprouted it turned to rotten-ness (so read for 'into the degenerate plant of'). It is not Jahveh's

---

[1] Cp. Ex. 21^{1-6}, Dt. 15^{12-18}.

fault that Israel is what she is ; she is so foul that no means known to man can ever purify her.

2$^{23-25}$. *Israel's lust and its consequences.*   In one of the strongest metaphors in Jeremiah, backsliding Israel is likened to a young she-camel or other domestic beast ('wild ass' is probably an error for 'cow') which in her lust has broken away from the encampment or the farm, and will not return till she has satisfied her desire.   The last verse is a dramatic plea to Israel not to wander thus, and her answer is that it is hopeless—she *must* have her way.

2$^{26-29}$. *The results of apostasy.*   Israel has said to the Asherah ('a stock') 'thou art my father' and to the *menhir* (see note on Dt. 12$^{2-3}$) 'thou hast borne me', but the time will come when she will need real help.   Then to her horror she will find her mistake.   These deities with which she has crowded her cities will be helpless, and Jahveh Himself will give her no aid.

2^{30}.   An isolated remark of a kind which is familiar in the prophets. Israel should have learnt from her sufferings, but this she has refused to do.

2$^{31-35}$. *Israel's guilt.*   The first words of v. 31 are practically unintelligible, and are probably a marginal note which has been wrongly copied.   Again we have the plaintive theme, Jahveh has not wronged Israel, it is she who has broken away from Him.   In v. 34 (which should possibly be regarded as the beginning of a fresh oracle) a new form of denunciation appears.   There is a strong hint of social wrong.   There is blood on her skirts.   If she could claim that this was due to the just punishment of criminals caught in the act,[1] there might be some excuse for her, but this is not the explanation, there is too much of it.   She has committed murder; here is unmistakable evidence.   Yet she still asserts her innocence, and by her very persistence adds to the depth of her sin.

2$^{36-37}$. *Foreign entanglements.*   Once more a reference to association with Egypt and Assyria, and once more the prediction of sorrow and anguish as the only possible result.

3^{1}. *A parallel from Israelite divorce laws.*   When once a woman had been divorced and remarried, her former husband was the one man to whom she could never go again (Dt. 24$^{1-4}$).   Israel has been yet more terribly separated from her Husband, and that by her own act ; can she think of coming back to Jahveh ?   (The reading of the margin is undoubtedly the right one.)

<hr>

[1] Cf. Ex. 22^{1}.

3^{2-5}. *A similar oracle.* These verses repeat the same metaphor, only, if possible, in more lurid terms. In v. 4 the word 'father' is probably a later insertion, and the LXX were right in reading the last words of the verse 'the darling of thy youth'. The withholding of the showers, too, in v. 3 looks suspicious. The LXX had 'and thou hadst many shepherds for a stumbling-block unto thyself', and inasmuch as the Hebrew words for 'shepherd' and 'lover' are very similar, they may have had the original text with this variation. In any case it is the amazing effrontery of Judah that is so striking. She has not merely yielded to the seduction of a tempter, she has gone out into the roads and captured people, like an Arab brigand, and has forced them to give her what she asked.

So ends this first collection of oracles. It will be noticed that many if not all of them are of a similar type, and they show in a marked degree the influence of Hosea. Thus they probably belong—most of them—to the earlier life of Jeremiah, though we are not justified in arguing that because they stand first they are therefore to be given the earliest date. Some of them, at any rate, would well fit the period of the Deuteronomic reform, and if Jeremiah was one of the adherents and preachers of the newly discovered law, it is quite possible that we have here his judgement on the worship of the local sanctuaries which he knew so well. He, at least, was under no illusions as to their character, for one of them was in his native village.

CHAPTERS 3^{6}–4^{31}

3^{6-18}. This is a prose passage of the autobiographical type, which has been used by the compiler as an introduction to a series of oracles which extends down to the end of ch. 6. It contains several sections, and probably has received non-Jeremianic additions. This is generally agreed, but it is not easy to say where the later stratum begins. It seems likely, however, that vv. 6–10 form the first nucleus. They tell the story of the religious history of Israel in the form of the parable of the two sisters. The elder, Israel, fell into sin, and was destroyed. Her younger sister, Judah, instead of taking warning, committed even more sin than Israel. The passage formed the model for Ez. 23.

vv. 11–13 continue the parable, but with a message of consolation for the exiled North, which is invited to return. Inasmuch as there is no suggestion of Judah being in exile, there is ground for assigning the passage to Jeremiah, especially as the promise of restoration involves a genuine repentance and a recognition of her sinfulness.

vv. 14–17, on the other hand, unless a break is to be made at the end of v. 15, must be exilic or post-exilic. Like the preceding section, they contain a promise of restoration, with an assurance of a proper government. But in v. 16 comfort is offered to those who mourn for the destruction of the Ark. Jerusalem is to take its place as a centre of the religious life and thought of Israel.

v. 18 appears to be a final addition, promising the restored Judah that the other tribes also will be added to the new community. Then and only then will Israel be complete.

3^{19} and ^{20} look like isolated sentences, but may be connected. The first speaks of Judah as a daughter, and hints at the law of inheritance. If there were no sons, then the daughters would share the family property, care being taken that they should not marry outside their own clan. But here the case is different. It is assumed, as in the case of Job, that there are sons as well as daughters, and in this case it would be only by special grace on the father's part that the daughters should share in the property. Jahveh has thought of treating this daughter, Judah, as a son, but her character renders that impossible.

3^{21}–4^{2}. *The repentance of Israel in answer to the appeal of Jahveh.* 'A voice' should be taken as an interjection—'Hark! on the bare heights weeping is heard, the supplications of the children of Israel'. This cry of penitence is heard by Jahveh, who calls them to return. The reply comes in vv. 22 f. In v. 23 the word 'from' should probably be omitted along with the italicized words (so LXX)— 'Truly in vain are the hill, the tumult of the mountains'. They recognize that the worship of the local sanctuaries is useless for spiritual purposes, and the sense of their sin is strong upon them. But again the message is brought to them that if they are really willing to come back to Him, using His name in the oath (one of the ways of accepting the authority of a god) and observing it, then they shall have such prosperity as Jahveh alone can give. Other nations shall so recognize that Israel represents the perfect type of success that when they wish to call down blessings they will use the name of Israel—'May you be as prosperous as Israel' will be their phrase.

4^{3-4}. *Break up the fallow ground.* The religious soil which Israel has been cultivating is that of the Canaanite faith. This is foul and overgrown with rank weeds. Let them try the ground that they have left so long untouched, the pure faith of their ancestors, making their religion not a matter of external material observances, but of

Winnowing corn

Photograph by Mr. R. Gorbold

an inner heart-faith.   That is the only way in which they can escape disaster.

4[5-8].   *The foe from the north.*   This is the first of a series of oracles dealing with the danger which threatens Judah.   Some commentators believe that all are concerned with the coming of the Scythians, and have been modified later to suit the Chaldeans.   This is not likely, however, to have been true of all the oracles involved, though perhaps the greater number were uttered in some such time of foreign invasion.   This certainly seems true of the present passage. Clearly an enemy is coming from the north, and the whole country-side is in flight.   They hasten from all the open villages into the fortified cities, and there is a feeling that Jerusalem is the only safe place.   All over the country guide-posts are erected, showing the way to the capital.   For a ravaging foe breaks on the land like a lion springing from his thicket-lair.   It is a time for lamentation and mourning, for even if men escape with their lives, their homes are left desolate and waste.

4[9-10] seem to contain a scrap from the autobiographical matter which has been separated from the rest, possibly by the compiler himself.   It complains that this disaster is not what Judah had been led to expect.   It is possible that at this time Jeremiah himself shared the doctrine, so common among his contemporaries, that Jahveh would not suffer his own land, especially his own city, to become the prey of a foreign enemy.   The reference to the prophets in v. 9 suggests that the popular ecstatics were encouraging this belief, and that Jeremiah still was disposed to recognize in them the truly inspired agents of Jahveh.   If that be so, then we may guess that here for the first time he entered on a conflict which was to last all his active ministry.

4[11-12].   *The storm of war.*   An oracle which likens the coming enemy to a sirocco from the desert.   In the agricultural life, wind has its helpful uses, for the work of winnowing the corn would be impossible without it.   But this is no such wind ; its violence is such that it would carry off the grain with the chaff—a picture which needs acquaintance with the life of the country for its full appreciation.

4[13-14].   *Swiftness of the enemy.*   An oracle which compares the speed and fury of the invaders to that of the thunder-cloud or the vulture.   It closes by calling attention to the real cause of the trouble, Judah's sinful heart.

4[15-18].   *Another oracle, emphasizing the same point as the last.*

Panic-stricken messengers are racing southwards, but so fast is the approach of the enemy that the news of the assault on Dan in the far north is immediately followed by that of the attack on Mount Ephraim, seventy miles to the south. The enemy is moving as fast as the courier. Every walled village is surrounded by packs of howling enemies (probably we should read 'panthers' for 'watchers' in v. 16 and 'jackals' for 'keepers' in v. 17). This is what apostasy has brought on Judah!

4^{19-21}. *Jeremiah's sorrow for Judah's suffering.* A passionate cry of anguish from the heart of the prophet himself, as he sees wave after wave of destruction crashing over his people. Not only does the passage illustrate his sufferings, it also gives a perfect picture of his patriotism. Jeremiah was not a patriot of the Nahum type, who could say only smooth things to delight people's minds. But he went further than denunciation. He identified himself with his own nation, her sorrows were his, he himself knew the bitterness of remorse for her sins—sins in which he had no personal share. This is the true patriotism.

4^{22} is an isolated fragment, having no connexion either with what precedes or with what follows. It may none the less be Jeremiah's, for it expresses a point of view which he had often to adopt. All Judah's intellectual strength is used for evil; she is clever enough there, but when it comes to questions of righteousness she is an utter fool.

4^{23-26}. *Chaos.* This is one of the most impressive oracles in all the prophetic literature. The prophet is looking out over the country, and suddenly the whole scene dissolves into the wild chaos that preceded creation. There is no light, no life; instead there is a mass of heaving mountains and tossing hills from which all semblance of an orderly universe has vanished.

4^{27-28}. *Jahveh's designs are unchangeable.* The destruction which falls on Judah is a part of the immutable plan of Jahveh for the right government of the world. He has worked out His designs, and there is no power in heaven or earth that can induce Him to change them.

4^{29-31}. *The flight of the people.* We are back once more in the actual scenes of invasion. Cavalry are thundering down the valleys of Judah, and the village population has betaken itself to any refuge it can find in the thickets or in holes of the rocks. There is no means of escape for Judah. In former days she had cajoled the foreigner and charmed him into false friendship by the harlot's art;

here is a foe whom she can neither conquer nor seduce. Her agony is upon her, and her pangs; she must go through the whole terrible experience.

CHAPTERS 7^1–8^3

This collection forms the third of the groups taken by the compiler from the autobiographical prose which he had before him. Like most of the others, it contains several distinct sections, which may have originated in oracles delivered at different times and under different circumstances.

$7^{1–2}$ form the superscription and give the circumstances of at least the first section. The events are more fully described in ch. 26, which is an account of the same utterance, with a description of its results for the prophet, written by the hand of the biographer, whom we commonly identify with Baruch.

$7^{3–15}$. Jeremiah's 'Temple Address'. He takes his stand, apparently on some great festal day, at the gate of the Temple. He has to deal with the belief, which had received some justification from the prophetic utterances of an earlier generation, that the Temple, being the home of Jahveh, was inviolable. He has to insist that this is true only as long as Judah satisfies the moral implications of her association with Jahveh. Otherwise she is simply using Him and His house as brigands use their cave, a place of refuge where they may find security from punishment and a safe base for future operations. They are 'delivered to do all these abominations', the iniquities in Church and State that had characterized the last seventy or eighty years. As a further warning they are told to consider the old sanctuary at Shiloh, which had fallen to the Philistines either in the days of Eli or in those of Saul, probably the former. That, too, had been a Temple, a house of Jahveh, and He had not shrunk from destroying it utterly rather than allow it to be associated with the kind of wrong which old Israel had perpetrated. The northern kingdom that had once made Shiloh its sanctuary had now vanished. So also would Judah vanish unless she mended her ways.

$7^{16–20}$ are a personal warning addressed to the prophet himself, to the effect that the matter has gone too far for intercession by himself or any other to be of the slightest use. The apostasy has been flagrant and open, and has constituted a direct challenge to Jahveh, which he cannot fail to accept. Complete and absolute destruction is the only possible issue of the situation.

7^{21-28}. This passage seems clearly to point to a time after the appearance of Deuteronomy. That law had secularized the flesh of the domestic animals, and had to some extent done away with the ancient communion sacrifice in which the worshipper shared the flesh of the victim. Now, says Jeremiah, apply the same principle to all sacrifice, even that which should be wholly given to Jahveh or his representative. Sacrifice was never a part of the divine ordinance in the days when the great Covenant was first established between the people and their God. What He then asked, and what He still asks, is self-consecration and obedience, and sacrifice is dangerous inasmuch as it seemed to offer men a possible substitute for true religion. Into this trap Judah has fallen, and there can be no hope for her until she realizes her position and puts things right.

7^{29} is an isolated scrap of oracular material which has somehow found its way into the midst of this group of prose passages. It bids Judah mourn and raise a dirge over her losses, for her very life is dead. The shearing of the hair is a widespread mourning custom.

7^{30-34} deals with a particular element in the religious horrors of the recent past. In the valley of the Kidron human sacrifice had been offered in the time of Manasseh, and it had thus become a sacred spot. But in the end the slaughter in Judah would be so great the ordinary burial-places would be filled, and men would have to use the valley of Hinnom for the purpose. This is quite in accord with the method said to have been adopted by Josiah in desecrating the altar at Bethel (2 Ki. 23^{16}).

8^{1-3} is a passage allied to the preceding, inasmuch as it speaks of burials. But the connexion is rather different; here the bodies are taken from the graves, and the purpose of the action is to illustrate the desecration which awaits their corpses, not that which is to fall upon a sacred place. Veneration for a burial-place is still a leading characteristic in the thought of the East, which is even more horrified by the violation of graves than is the West. To those who heard Jeremiah speak, this must have been the final horror in a situation which on other grounds made death preferable to life.

CHAPTERS 19–22

19^1–20^6 is the first passage of any length that we have from the pen of the biographer. Though there is no superscription, the use of the third person in 19^{14} makes this clear. The whole centres round a symbolic action performed by Jeremiah. He is told to buy a flask of clay and take with him some of the most important men in the city to the eastern gate overlooking the valley of Hinnom. The name of the gate is not quite certain ; it may be rendered either 'sun-gate' or, more probably, 'pottery-gate'. There he is to deliver a speech which predicts the ruin of Jerusalem because of her sins, and he is to emphasize what he says by flinging the flask away on to the heap of broken pottery which lay outside the gate. The meaning of this symbolic action is sufficiently obvious, even without the gruesome details given in v. 9.

From the gate above the valley of Hinnom Jeremiah returned to the city, and repeated the substance of his message in the Temple (19^{14-15}). This brought him into conflict with Pashhur, the chief of the Temple police. Amongst the duties of his office, as we gather from Jer. 29^{26}, was the task of keeping the place clear of 'madmen and prophets', and he arrested Jeremiah, placing him for the night in the stocks. In the morning he released him, but Jeremiah gave him a new name—'Terror-around', symbolizing the destruction that would fall upon him and the government which he represented.

20$^{7-10}$. *Jeremiah and Jahveh.* This forms one of the most terrible passages in our Old Testament, approached only by some of the more stirring utterances in the Book of Job. It must be remembered that men had not yet realized the full moral character of Jahveh, and still attributed to Him qualities and actions which a later age would rightly abhor. They thought, for instance, that He might use the prophetic inspiration to entrap men to ruin, and had, indeed, a special term which they employed in this connexion. It appears in the narrative of Ahab and his prophets (1 Ki. $22^{21, 22}$), and again in Ezek. 14^9. In the former of these passages the prophetic inspiration is used to entrap and destroy the king, in the second it is the prophet himself who is the victim. Jeremiah uses it here. That is to say, he believed himself to have been enticed and trapped to his own ruin by Jahveh, through that very inspiration which ensured his close association with his God. This does not necessarily represent his permanent attitude, but there were times of depression when the terrible thought dominated and overwhelmed him. It is from such a moment that this utterance springs. Deuteronomy had doubtless given expression to a widely accepted view when it offered fulfilment as the test of the truth of prophecy. For many years Jeremiah had foretold the destruction of the city and the people, and it had never come. This roused men's scorn, and, with a brutality which to a humaner age seems only revolting, they had held him up to derision.

They felt that others might safely put him to death since Jahveh had thus doomed him. Whilst conscious of this, he had been even more occupied with the inward struggle. The burden of the ecstasy lay upon him and he had tried to shake it off, but all in vain, and in the rending conflict of the spirit the 'I must' had conquered the 'I will not'. The English language is inadequate to depict the agony of soul which this amazing passage records.

20^{11-13} offer a series of isolated expressions of triumph. One of them (v. 12) is found also in 11^{20}, and all were probably introduced here in order to modify the blackness of the last fearful utterance—and that which follows.

20^{14-18}. *Jeremiah curses the day of his birth.* There can be no doubt that the passage forms the basis for a similar though more elaborate utterance in Job 3. The curse is a double one, and it may be that something has dropped out in the latter part, originally, perhaps, a separate utterance. The day itself is cursed, though the precise form which the curse will take is not stated as it is in Job. Then comes the messenger who brought the news to the child's father, thinking to give him tidings of gladness. Possibly, as has just been suggested, something has fallen out or been deliberately omitted before v. 17. It could hardly be expected that the messenger should have killed the child before his birth, and yet v. 17 seems to imply that both mother and child might have died before her delivery. We are thus led to suspect that the real subject of the verbs in v. 17 was Jahveh Himself, and that the scribes refused to write the words which cursed Him. Yet such is Jeremiah's mood that even this does not appear impossible.

21^{1-10} is another section from the biographical writer. It is dated during the last war with the Chaldeans, and describes a message sent by Zedekiah to Jeremiah, asking for Jahveh's decision on the whole campaign. The answer is one of complete destruction. The very weapons of the Jewish soldiers will of themselves turn against their holders, and even Jahveh will be on the side of the enemy. Famine and pestilence will be added to the horrors of war, and in the end Zedekiah himself will be carried into exile. Then (vv. 8–10) Jeremiah added words of advice to the people. The only safety for the individual was to desert at once to the Chaldeans. Those who did that might lose all they had, but would at least save their lives.

21^{11-14}. A succession of oracular sentences of which those in v. 12 are an appeal for social righteousness in the manner of Amos and the remainder a threat of punishment. The first half of v. 15 (down to 'saith the Lord') does not appear in the LXX.

Ch. **22** is a collection of material dealing with the kings of Judah. The compiler seems to have drawn on more than one type of source, and there may be comparatively late accretions. Thus vv. 1–5 are from one or other of the prose types, and demand social justice as the price of the continuance of the line of David. No date is given, and no individual king is suggested.

22[6–9]. *An oracle against an unnamed king.* He is compared to Lebanon, and threatened with destruction. To this have been appended two verses in prose (vv. 8–9) which describe the wonder of other nations at the penalty that has fallen on Jerusalem.

22[10–12]. *Jehoahaz.* v. 10 is oracular, the rest a repetition of the same thought in prose. There is a real pathos in Jeremiah's feeling for this man. He seems to have been lovable, for the people chose him to succeed his father in preference to his elder brother, and in Jeremiah's lament there is a touch of tenderness. What he might have been or done we cannot guess ; all we know of him is his fate.

22[13–19]. *Jehoiakim.* Two oracles are included here : the first, vv. 13–17, being a condemnation of Jehoiakim ; the second, vv. 18–19, a prediction of his end. The first of these is remarkable for its character. It draws the contrast between Jehoiakim and his father, and while it is clear that Jeremiah admired, respected, and loved Josiah, it is noticeable that his opinion of him was based on social and moral grounds rather than on his religious policy. He was essentially a democratic king, and his main concern was the doing of justice to his people. Jehoiakim, on the other hand, was the oriental sultan who took Solomon as his model, and strove to outstrip his father in buildings. His works were, no doubt, magnificent, but they were erected by means of forced labour, and Jeremiah would have none of the splendid palaces of Jehoiakim, because they meant injustice and oppression to the people. As a rule the oriental thinks and speaks of the subjects as the 'servants' or 'slaves' of the king; Jeremiah calls them his 'neighbours', and the term itself is significant of the whole prophetic attitude towards social relations.

vv. 18–19. *The coming fate of Jehoiakim.* There shall be no public funeral for him, with its normal accompaniment of lamentation and dirge. Instead, his corpse will be flung out into the streets, and the public scavengers will drag it away (as they still do animal corpses in the east) to be flung on some rotting dung-heap. This, the most shameful end that could befall him, was to crown the luxurious oppression and the ostentatious pride of Jehoiakim.

22[20–23]. *An oracle addressed to a woman, probably Nehushtan, mother of Jehoiachin.* The language recalls that which Jeremiah had used of Judah as a whole, and if it is to be taken as applying to the queen-mother, she must have been a thoroughly bad character, even when judged by the standards of her own time. She had shared in her husband's pride, and had made her home in his cedar palace ; she had been wanton, and she had constantly refused to listen to such advice as she might have had from Jeremiah and others of his kind. But her doom will reach her, and she will cover her face in shame.

22[24–30]. *Jehoiachin.* We have first a prose account of an oracle concerning him in vv. 23–27. However dear he may have been to Jahveh, however close his God may have been to him, he and his mother—apparently hers was the dominant influence during his short reign—will be carried away into an exile from which they will never return.

vv. 28–29 contain a dirge over Jehoiachin. The text seems to be corrupt ; all that the LXX had was 'Coniah is despised as a vessel wherein is no pleasure ; cast out is he and cast into a land which he knoweth not', a typical dirge couplet which may well have been the original form. v. 29 seems to have little or no connexion with v. 28, being simply an appeal to the land. It is noticeable that towards the end of many of the collections of oracles in the prophetic books the individual pieces become more and more fragmentary and uncertain.

v. 30 again contains another couplet, bewailing the fact that Jehoiachin was the last of his line, and would leave no child of his to sit on the throne. It is true that Zerubbabel's descent was traced to Jehoiachin, but he never sat on the throne, though it is sometimes suspected that he attempted to make himself independent. In any case, Jeremiah seems to have had little hope (if any) of a restoration of Judah from amongst the Babylonian exiles. The dramatic force of the little poem lies in the mention of David. He had been the founder of the dynasty, and, in a certain sense, the originator of the Hebrew monarchy, for Saul left no stable polity remaining after his death. For four centuries the sons of David had sat on the throne of Jerusalem. They had been men of different character, and had experienced varying fortune, but they had held their place, and as long as they were there Judah had enjoyed at

least the semblance of political independence. Now it was all over.
The lad was succeeded by his uncle, a step back in the line; with
Jehoiachin the royal house had reached its farthest limits and
its end.

Chapters 36–44

Ch. 36 begins the main block of the work of the biographer, which
extends down to the end of ch. 44. It is fairly typical of the style and
character of the whole, and this large section of the Book of Jeremiah
is one of the most interesting and important documents we possess
from ancient times. It is contemporary with the events which it
describes, and has the merit of being the work, apparently, of an
eyewitness. It is unofficial, and is therefore in no way affected by
the limitations or exaggerations of the state annalist. It is, further,
written round one of the greatest personalities of all time, and comes
from a most important period. Such evidence is always rare in Asia,
and apart from what is left to us of ancient Egyptian and Mesopotamian private material, there is nothing to be compared with it till
we reach the golden age of classical Greece.

The style is simple and straightforward, needing little comment.
Only an outline summary, therefore, will be found in the notes on
this section of the book. The text has probably suffered a good deal
at the hands of the copyists, and the LXX is appreciably shorter,
owing to the absence of a number of words and phrases which are
found in the traditional Hebrew recension. It is, however, very
rarely that we find a variation which makes a serious difference to
the sense.

Ch. 36 describes the circumstances under which Jeremiah's oracles
were first written down, and this is the first recorded occasion on
which any Prophet actually had a book of his utterances prepared,
though Isaiah had taken some steps to preserve the substance of
what he had said, and it is possible that both Amos and Hosea left
some written material. The date is 605, and the time was critical.
Nineveh had fallen some seven years earlier, and the last relics of
the old Assyrian Empire had now been crushed by Nebuchadrezzar.
Pharaoh Necho, in a vain attempt to restore the Assyrian kingdom,
had just met with a crushing and final defeat at Carchemish. An
invasion of Judah by Chaldean armies was to be expected, and
Jeremiah may well have thought that the earlier prophecies of the
foe from the north were to be fulfilled. In any case, practically all

that he might have said of the Scythians would apply with additional force to the Chaldeans.

He therefore summoned a professional writer, a man belonging to a class which is still a normal and necessary feature of eastern life, for reading and writing are the accomplishments of the few. The writing material was a 'roll', probably of the familiar papyrus type. Such rolls consisted of a number of sheets glued together at their edges to form a long strip. A wooden stick was added at each end, and on these the whole was rolled up. The scribe would unroll enough to give him room for one column of writing, and when that was finished would roll that up and unroll enough for the next column. If the sheets were of ordinary size, each sheet would be used for a column of writing.

For some reason which is still obscure to us, Jeremiah was unable to leave his house, and Baruch had not only to write the roll but to read it in the Temple on a fast day. The room he used for the purpose was that of Gemariah, the son of Shaphan, whose family seems to have been well disposed towards Jeremiah. Amongst those who heard was Micaiah, a son of Gemariah, and he reported the matter to the 'princes' who were gathered in the palace. They sent for Baruch to read the document to them, and felt at once that Jehoiakim must be informed. At the same time they gave him a friendly hint that both he and Jeremiah would do well to hide themselves. The roll was read in the king's winter chamber by Jehudi, and as he finished every three or four leaves, the king slashed them off with the knife he wore and flung them into the fire that burned before him. No doubt the language seemed to him to be dangerous and revolutionary, and he may well have recalled the part the prophets had played in the politics of the northern kingdom. But if he hoped to put an end to this 'alarmist' movement by his drastic action he was mistaken; the only result was the writing of a fresh roll, which Jeremiah and Baruch seem to have kept by them in order to make additions from time to time.

Chs. **37–39** give the story of the final siege of Jerusalem, especially as it affected Jeremiah. Ch. 34 belongs to the same period, and perhaps originally immediately preceded ch. 37.

37$^{1-5}$ state the circumstances of the siege. An attempt was made by Egypt to save Jerusalem, and for a time the Chaldean army withdrew. Jeremiah insisted that the relief was only temporary and that even though there were left in the enemy camp none but desperately wounded men, they would still be able to destroy the city (vv. 6–10). It is not surprising that this language was regarded as unpatriotic, and that Jeremiah's personal loyalty was suspected. He found it necessary to pay a visit to Anathoth on business connected with his ancestral estate, probably that to which reference is made in ch. 32. As he was passing through the gate of the city, he was arrested by the officer on guard and charged with desertion to the Chaldeans. It is clear from other passages in this section that large numbers of Jews had thus gone over to the enemy, and an official of the type of Irijah may be excused for suspecting Jeremiah's intentions. In spite of his denials Jeremiah was thrown by the nobles into prison (vv. 11–16). There seem to have been different grades of imprisonment, and it is clear that his sufferings in the house of Jonathan were severe, for when Zedekiah sent for him and consulted him, he pleaded that he might be granted some less rigorous treatment. There is a strong contrast between the attitude of Zedekiah and that of Jehoiakim, for though Jeremiah was able to offer the king only a warning of destruction, he secured the somewhat greater liberty of the court of the guard. Here it would seem that whilst he was still in confinement, and was unable to leave the court, there was free intercourse between him and any others who might wish to see and speak to him (vv. 17–21).

Jeremiah constantly advised those whom his looser confinement allowed him to reach to save their lives by deserting to the Chaldeans. Once more it was only natural that the officials should feel that such language was treasonable, and they urged Zedekiah to remove Jeremiah. With pathetic helplessness the amiable but feeble king gave his consent. Probably Jeremiah's bitterest enemies did not dare to kill a prophet of Jahveh outright, but their end could be secured without danger to themselves by starving him to death. In the court there was an old well, from which the water had been exhausted, though there were several feet of mud at the bottom. Into this Jeremiah was lowered and left to starve (38^{1-6}). From this position he was rescued by an Ethiopian servant of the court, Ebed-melech by name. The description of the methods adopted, with the special precautions that had to be taken show how deep and clinging the mud must have been. Indeed, unless it is several feet deep, mud is not worth mentioning in an oriental city (vv. 7–13).

Once again the king consulted the prophet, and swore solemnly that whatever the message might be no harm should befall him. Jeremiah gave to Zedekiah the same advice that he had given to others, 'Surrender, and you will be safe; maintain your resistance, and you are ruined.' But Zedekiah was afraid of the Jews, who had already deserted, and could not rid himself of the fear of their mockery. Jeremiah's reply was to describe a vision in which he had seen, not the apostate Jews, but the women of the royal palace being handed over to the Chaldean nobles, and singing a dirge as they went. But the king would not be persuaded, and his immediate care was to secure secrecy. With this in view he arranged that if Jeremiah were questioned by the nobles he was to reply that he had asked that he might be allowed to stay in the court of the guard, and not be sent back to the house of Jonathan. It is clear that Zedekiah had no heart for the rebellion, and left to himself would have made peace on any terms. The war was the work of the nobles, and they regarded even the king with suspicion as a possible traitor.

$39^{1–14}$ give an account of the actual capture of Jerusalem in language which closely resembles that of 2 Ki. 25. The original text of Jeremiah probably had only vv. 3 and 14, for the rest seems to be a later insertion, which was absent from the text before the Greek translators. The remaining verses of the chapter record a promise of deliverance made to Ebed-melech, who was to escape when others perished.

Ch. 40 is an account of the little attempt at reconstruction that was made after the fall of Jerusalem. When the affairs of the city were being settled, Nebuzaradan, the Chaldean officer in charge, gave Jeremiah a free choice, allowing him either to go to Babylon with the exiles or to remain with Gedaliah, the new governor. The latter was of the family of Shaphan, which had already befriended the prophet, and he chose to stay (vv. 1-6). Numbers of the peasants had been left behind, for it was no part of the Chaldean policy to leave the conquered territory desert, together with a few members of the old noble families. Gedaliah had taken up his residence at Mizpah, some five miles north of Jerusalem, and there began to draw together these remnants of the people, and set them to agriculture, always recognizing himself as under allegiance to Nebuchadrezzar. Fugitives who had found safety in Moab, Ammon, and Edom, believing that peaceful life was once more possible, began to make their way back. Two amongst the nobles need special notice, Ishmael, who had royal blood in his veins, and Johanan, who, after Gedaliah himself, seems to have been the most prominent member of the little community (vv. 7-12). Johanan had received information which showed that Ishmael was disloyal, and had, in fact, been sent by the King of Ammon to assassinate Gedaliah when opportunity offered. But Gedaliah, who was incapable of treachery, was of too noble a nature to believe in the falsity of another man, and though Johanan warned him and even offered to assassinate Ishmael, he refused to listen (vv. 13–16).

Ch. **41** tells the story of the tragedy which destroyed the Mizpah settlement. How long it had lasted we do not know. The record appears to allow it only a few months, but it is possible that three or four years elapsed. But in the end Johanan's suspicions were justified, and Ishmael murdered Gedaliah and his Chaldean bodyguard (vv. 1–3). Even this was not enough, and two days later he waylaid a company of eighty pilgrims who were bringing offerings to Jerusalem. From this narrative it appears that though Jerusalem was destroyed and the Temple burned, some kind of worship was still carried on in the city or on its site. Ten of the eighty escaped by paying a ransom ; the rest were slaughtered and their bodies flung into a pit. Then Ishmael gathered together all whom he could find, and started for the land of Ammon, taking with him the royal princesses and the rest of the Jews of Mizpah (vv. 4–10).

Johanan seems to have been away from Mizpah, but news of Ishmael's crime soon reached him, and he started in pursuit. He overtook the fugitives at Gibeon, only three or four miles from Mizpah on the eastern road, and recovered the captives, though Ishmael and eight of his attendants escaped to Ammon. Johanan and his companions now felt that they were in danger of an attack by a Chaldean army. It is true that they had had no hand in the murder of the governor, but they were afraid that Nebuchadrezzar or any force he might send against them would fail to make distinctions, and would exact indiscriminate vengeance on any whom they might find. They made up their minds, therefore, to escape to Egypt, and travelled some distance southwards. There for a time they remained (vv. 11–18).

Ch. **42–43**[7] describes the circumstances of the flight to Egypt. It is clear that Johanan and his friends had no intention of abandoning the national religion, and in their perplexity they determined to consult Jahveh through Jeremiah. We may suppose that the fall of Jerusalem, which Jeremiah had so long foretold, had given him fresh prestige, and now, as never before, men were ready to see in him the true prophet. It is to be noted, however, that on one point the people's minds were already made up : they intended to escape to Egypt, and were only concerned as to the best way of getting there.

Ancient figure of Ishtar, the Babylonian ' Queen of Heaven '.
Photograph by Les Archives Photographiques d'Art et d'Histoire

At the same time they solemnly swore to do whatever Jahveh bade them (vv. 1–6).

Unlike the ' false prophets ' of his own and earlier days, Jeremiah could not control the divine inspiration, and ten anxious days elapsed before he was in a position to report an answer to their question. And the answer was very far from being what they wished or expected. Jeremiah told them that their only safety lay in staying where they were. The King of Babylon would do them no harm, but if they insisted on going to Egypt, calamity would follow them there. Jeremiah seems to have clung to the soil of Canaan as the proper place for Jahveh's people, and indeed the only place where a new Israel could arise. And his heart was set on that new Israel. Therefore it was essential that there should be left behind some nucleus about which a true reformed Israel could gather (vv. 7–22).

Jeremiah's message, however, seemed to his auditors to be the height of folly. It could not, they thought, have come from Jahveh, and they charged Baruch with having maliciously instigated Jeremiah to give this reply, believing that it could only bring on them the ruin that they feared. They therefore collected every Israelite, male and female, whom they could find, and made their way southwards, crossing the frontier near Tahpanhes. This has been identified with the place called Daphnae by Herodotus, and the modern Tel Defenneh, on the Pelusiac branch of the Nile. It seems to have been the most north-easterly of the fortified cities of Egypt, and was naturally the first important place at which the refugees arrived (43^{1-7}).

In 43^{8-13} we have the account of a symbolic action performed by Jeremiah at Tahpanhes, together with the oracle which accompanied it. This is, as it were, a continuation of the warning he had given before the actual flight. Large stones were hidden under the threshold of the royal palace at Tahpanhes (probably a building used by the Pharaohs as a temporary lodging on their return from campaigns or journeys in Asia), and Jeremiah announced that over those stones Nebuchadrezzar would some day set up his throne. Thus the very fate that the Jews had dreaded would pursue them, and would overtake them on the land to which they had fled for refuge. As a matter of fact, it was not till 568 that Nebuchadrezzar invaded Egypt, but his ultimate conquest of the country had become a certainty on the day of Carchemish.

Ch. 44 tells the story of Jeremiah's protest against the apostasy of the Jews in Egypt, and of its results. His address opens with a brief summary of the dealings of Jahveh and His people, extending down to v. 6. Then he deals with the matter immediately in hand. It has not been enough for Judah to arouse the anger of her God by the worship of other deities in her own land, she has so far failed to learn her lesson that she is falling into apostasy also in Egypt (vv. 7–14).

The particular form which this apostasy took was the worship of the Queen of Heaven (v. 17). This was a cult spread over the whole of Western Asia, though the great goddess was known by different names. She is the 'mother goddess' of Asia Minor (the 'Diana of the Ephesians' of whom we hear in Acts 19), the Ishtar of the Babylonians and the Astarte of the Phoenicians. Her worship had already been denounced by Jeremiah in Jerusalem (7^{17-19}), but it was resumed in Egypt, probably under the influence of the cult of Isis. It was essentially a women's worship, and the men were only concerned indirectly. We have a striking illustration of the inferior position of womanhood, even in Israel, in the fact that a woman was not sufficiently a free agent to be able to make a vow. She might utter the necessary words, but they were not held to be binding unless her husband or some other man under whose tutelage she lived had heard and assented. The assent might be given silently; it was enough that the man did not annul the vow. These Jewish women had vowed to engage in the worship of the Queen of Heaven, and their words had been heard without protest by their men. Therefore the vows were binding and must be performed, and the men were implicated equally with the women. The law of the vow is to be found in Num. 30^{4ff}. The reason given by the women for their apostasy is that calamity had fallen upon them only after they had abandoned the cult in question. As long as the goddess had been duly worshipped in Jerusalem, the country had been prosperous, but with the reforms that had swept it away, a period of disaster had set in, ending in the fall of the city and the desolation of the land (vv. 15–19).

Jeremiah replies that they have drawn the wrong inference from the facts. It is in reality the foreign worship that has so angered Jahveh that He has brought destruction on the people (vv. 20–23). At the same time, the vow has been made, and if they feel it to be irrevocable it is irrevocable—they must go their own way (vv. 24–25). But Jahveh too has His honour, and His word also must stand. If the last remnants of Judah will have their own way, they must recognize that their association with Him is at an end. They shall no more swear by His name. The old covenant formula had been 'I will become their God and they shall become my people'. On their side this agreement has been finally broken ; they have refused to be the people of Jahveh, and there can be only one result. The national religion had begun in the days when they had come out of Egypt ; for them it ended when they returned thither ; Jahveh was no more their God. Yet, even at this moment, when all that Jeremiah really cared for perished in a spiritual catastrophe more terrible to him than even the destruction of Jerusalem, his faith and his magnificent optimism rose to their greatest heights. Jahveh was not dependent on Israel. She might refuse to have more to do with Him ; that was her loss. He would continue to work His will and to execute His purposes for mankind. 'They shall know whose word shall stand, mine or theirs.' Soon the Egyptian king's fate would testify to the truth of Jahveh (vv. 26–30).

To Jeremiah this was the real end of the nation. He had looked on the remnant left in the land as the seed from which the new people should spring, and had expected that in them, purified by their sufferings, the will of Jahveh would at last be realized. Instead of remaining to build up a fresh community, they had betaken them to Egypt, and there they had finally severed the bond that had linked them through the centuries to their God. We have no record of the prophet's death, though tradition says that he was stoned by the Jews in Egypt. But a record even of martyrdom could only have been an anticlimax ; to him the final sentence which he had been compelled to pronounce was more terrible than any death. With the decisive breach between the people whom he loved and the God whom he served, his life ended in failure and despair.

We have no certain knowledge of the later history of the fugitives in Egypt, though it seems unlikely that the Jewish community which played so important a part in Alexandria in the era of the Ptolemies and under the Roman Empire was descended from them. The Egyptian Jews of the Greek and Roman periods were most probably taken from Palestine and perhaps from Babylon by Alexander and his immediate successors. But within recent years there has been recovered a number of papyrus documents from Assouan, far up the Nile. These belonged to a community of Jews who served as a Persian garrison there during the fifth century, and in one of them it is claimed that they were there before the accession of Cambyses (528 B.C.). It is possible that these Jews were the descendants of those who had fled to Egypt with Johanan fifty or sixty years before. If so, then it is clear that to a large extent they had failed to learn the lesson that Jeremiah and his predecessors had tried to teach. It is true that they still worshipped Jahveh, and had a Temple erected to Him, but alongside of Him they had also two goddesses, possibly of Egyptian origin. They were unpopular with the Egyptians, and were probably wiped out in an Egyptian insurrection against the Persian power early in the fourth century.

But the life of Israel did not perish with them. It continued to live in Babylon amongst the exiles, and it was from this community that the Jewish state eventually made its new beginning. Those who returned in the fifth century (and there seems to have been a series of migrations of Jews from Mesopotamia to Palestine) had learnt the lessons of the prophets, and from them there sprang the three great monotheistic religions of the world, the later Judaism, Christianity, and Islam. Jeremiah's work was not in vain, his message lives on, and he remains one of the greatest figures in the long train of the spiritual history of mankind.

ADDITIONAL NOTES

I. THE TEXT OF THE OLD TESTAMENT

THE various books of the Old Testament were written in
Hebrew, except for portions of the Books of Daniel and
Ezra, which were written in Aramaic. The actual material
used was probably papyrus, at least when the books came to
take their present form, though archaeologists are of opinion
that in earlier days portions of them may have been written
on clay tablets in the form and script familiar to us from
Babylon. In considering the textual criticism of the Old
Testament, however, we may neglect this point, as it belongs
to a much earlier stage of development than that which we
have to consider. As we know from Jer. 36 rolls either of
leather or (more probably) of papyrus were in use for the literary
compositions, whatever medium may have been employed for
legal and official documents.

For centuries after the completion of the books they must
have been copied by hand, and this is a process which always
leaves open ample room for error. Not only would mistakes be
made, but from time to time the scribe would believe that he
could improve on what he had before him, and deliberately alter
it. One important source of additions to the text is to be found
in the fact that often marginal notes would be made on the edge
of a document, illustrating or explaining the words of the text.
A copyist frequently assumed that such notes were words that
had been accidentally omitted, and, desiring to give the complete
text, would insert them in the body of the copy he was making.
Such an inserted note is called a *gloss*. At other times words
might be accidentally left out or misread or, being illegible through
some accident, would have their place taken by a guess on the
part of the scribe. The belief in the sanctity of the text was of
slow growth, though when once that was established it served as
a very strong preservative. It was not till after the destruction
of the second Temple in A. D. 70 that really careful precautions
were taken to preserve the *ipsissima verba* of the sacred writers,
but then, so skilful and scientific were the Rabbinic scribes who
gave themselves to this task, that probably no body of ancient
scholars has ever done more faithful or effective work. It is
a noticeable fact that while we can trace very wide divergences
in tradition in earlier times, from the Christian era onwards the
variations in textual tradition are comparatively slight. By about

the beginning of the sixth century practically all Hebrew MSS. of the Old Testament (and we have none earlier than the ninth century) were in agreement. This is the text of the Massora or tradition, and is that represented in our printed Hebrew Bibles. It is indicated by the symbol MT. In recent years MSS. have come to light which show that there was some slight variation within the Massora itself, but these differences are insignificant when compared with others that will have to be noted.

The text, then, represented by the Hebrew Bible as we know it to-day, is the result of the labours of the Rabbinic scholars of the early Christian centuries, and represents the text that was handed down in Palestine and, perhaps, in Babylon. In the Dispersion, at least in those periods of it which accompanied and followed the conquests of Alexander, the scattering Jews took with them as much of the Bible as they had. At first, this was probably only the Law. As time passed these copies too would be themselves copied and re-copied. Naturally this might, and indeed would, give rise to changes in the text, though these would not be the same as those which were taking place at the same time in Palestine. Finally, it became necessary to translate the books into Greek, partly for the sake of Jewish families who were forgetting their Hebrew, and partly for propaganda purposes, for the Jews of the Dispersion seem to have had a genuine missionary spirit. This Greek translation, made in Egypt, is commonly known as the Septuagint (LXX), because of the tradition which states that it was carried out by seventy of the elders of Israel. At first it was only the Pentateuch that was thus rendered into Greek, but other books followed. The Greek Old Testament, then, by the beginning of the Christian era included all the books which exist to-day in the Hebrew Bible, with the addition of a number of others, either written originally in Greek or compiled too late for inclusion in the Palestinian Canon. These are the books now comprised in the Apocrypha.

Other versions were made later. The Old Testament was translated into Syriac apparently in the first century A.D. The first Latin version was made from the LXX and is a most useful witness to the text of that version itself, but being a secondary[1] version is of comparatively little value for the direct elucidation of the problems of the Hebrew text. But at the beginning of the fifth century Jerome made a translation direct from the Hebrew

---

[1] A 'secondary' version is one which is made from a translation, as distinguished from a 'primary' version, which is made from a text in the original language.

text current in his day. This is substantially that which is still found in our Latin Bibles, and is known as the Vulgate.

As has been already remarked, our Hebrew texts show only the slightest variations, and carry us back only to a text of about A.D. 500 or 600. A fair number of divergent readings are found in both the Syriac and the Vulgate, but again the differences are insignificant beside those exhibited by a comparison of the MT with the LXX. It is clear that in many books the divergence between the Palestinian and the Egyptian texts must have been very great indeed. It is particularly noticeable in the Books of Samuel, Jeremiah, and Ezekiel.

The problem of textual criticism is, then, to ascertain as nearly as possible the text of the book at the time when it reached substantially its present form. The main authorities on which we may work are the MT and the LXX, though the two later versions may give some assistance. We are not justified in saying without further study that the MT is to be preferred to the LXX in all cases, or vice versa, though we may expect that they will show different kinds of error. A Palestinian text, handed down in a land where the language was still fairly familiar, might be expected to contain additions, intentional or accidental. On the other hand, where the language was not so freely understood, it is more likely that words would be misread, and the *a priori* probability in these cases lies with the MT. Of course, it has to be remembered that we are using a version— we have no Hebrew representative of the Egyptian text [1]—and that this fact calls for special care. We have to translate its words back into Hebrew (or Aramaic, as the case may be) in order to find out what the original *Hebrew* variant was. Sometimes we find that a word in the Greek means something totally different from that which we find in the MT, whilst it is easy to see that it is a misunderstanding of the present Hebrew text. This is particularly likely to happen in cases where the difference depends on the vowels, because the Hebrew language was always written without any vowels in ancient times, and the vowel signs attached to the consonants as we write the language to-day were only invented gradually in the first centuries of the Christian era. Thus certain forms of the words for 'shepherd', 'evil', 'friend', might be written with identically the same consonants. The vowels adopted by the Rabbis might give one meaning to the word whilst those assumed by the LXX might give another. But both would testify to the same Hebrew consonantal text.

[1] Unless the so-called Nash Papyrus be a fragment of an old Egyptian text.

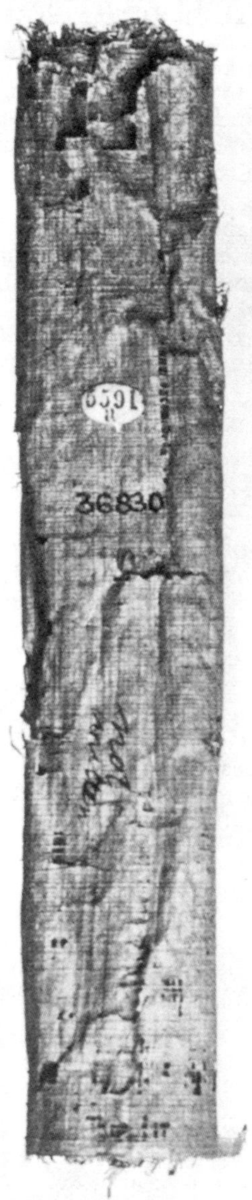

Papyrus Roll
British Museum

Another difficulty is to be sure that the alteration is not due to changes in the Greek text itself, made long after the translation. Thus if we find the MT saying 'out of *the land of* Moab' while the Greek text has ἐν τῆς Μωαβιτίδος, we cannot assume that the Egyptian text omitted the words 'the land of', because τῆς may quite well be a Greek copyist's mistake for γῆς (ΤΗΣ→ΓΗΣ), and in this case very probably the two texts were really the same.

The subject is an interesting one, with many ramifications, but enough has probably been said to enable the reader to appreciate alike the difficulties which attend the textual criticism of the Old Testament, and the kind of material on which the critic has to work.

II. THE CHRONOLOGY OF THE PERIOD

The precise dating of events in the history of Israel is a matter of practical impossibility. The system adopted by the compiler of the Books of Kings has already been mentioned. A convenient starting-point for discussion is the date of the accessions of Jehu and Athaliah, which coincided. It is further stated that the invasion of Palestine by Shalmaneser V, which culminated in the fall of Samaria, began in the sixth year of Hoshea of Israel (=the third year of Hezekiah of Judah) and the city was taken three years later. These two may be taken as fixed points for the time being. Omitting the synchronistic notes, we find in the Books of Kings the following figures for each king's reign:

ISRAEL			JUDAH	
Jehu	28 years		Athaliah	7 years
Jehoahaz	17		Joash	40
Jehoash	16		Amaziah	29
Jeroboam	41		Azariah	52
Zechariah		6 months	Jotham	16
Shallum		1 month	Ahaz	16
Menahem	10		Hezekiah (down to	6
Pekahiah	2		fall of Samaria)	
Pekah	20			
Hoshea	9			
Total	143 years, 7 months		Total	166

That is to say that there is a discrepancy of twenty-three years between the two lists. A certain amount of this might be saved by assuming that the sixteen years of Jotham's reign include the period for which he was regent during his father's illness, but at the most, even supposing that his death immediately followed that of Azariah, only sixteen years can be saved, and there is still a discrepancy of seven.   It is clear that there has been some error in the transmission of the figures, either in the completed Books of Kings or (more probably) in the records which were at the disposal of the compiler.

Further difficulties arise when we compare the Biblical figures with the chronology of Babylon.   Documents which have come to light during the last two or three generations show that for centuries the official scribes of Babylonia kept their formal records strictly accurate.   As in ancient Rome every year was known by the names of the consuls, and in Athens by the name of one of the archons, so in Babylon each year was known by the name of a special official.   A number of copies of lists of these officials—' Eponym ' lists, as they are called—have been found and their agreement is such as to make the record certain. Under each name the most important events of the year are mentioned, and this enables us, with the aid of astronomy, to be certain in our Babylonian dates.   Several times there are references in the Assyrian and Babylonian royal annals to contact between Babylon and Assyria on the one hand and Israel and Judah on the other, which enable us at least to see what kings were on the throne in certain years.   It is interesting to note that the references are often to events not recorded in the Biblical record.   The following is a list of the most important :

> 853 Shalmaneser III invades western Asia, and at Ḳarḳar meets a Syrian coalition including the forces of Israel and Damascus, the former under Ahab.
> 841 Jehu pays tribute to Shalmaneser III.
> 738 Menahem pays tribute to Tiglath-pileser III.
> 732 Tiglath-pileser captures Samaria, kills Pekah and places Hoshea on the throne.
> 724 Shalmaneser V attacks Samaria, which is captured by his successor Sargon II in 721.
> 701 Sennacherib invades Judah and besieges Jerusalem.
> 677 Manasseh, amongst other Syrian princes, does homage to Esarhaddon.
> 612 Fall of Nineveh.
> 605 Battle of Carchemish (cf. Jer. 46[2]) in the fourth year of Jehoiakim.

Curiously enough, no Babylonian account of the fall of Jerusalem has yet been found.   The achievements which Nebuchadrezzar thought most worth recording seem to have been his buildings, and even the newly discovered Babylonian Chronicle does not carry the story beyond the accession of that king.

But we have here a certain amount of very important material, which helps us to see still further how unreliable are the figures which have come down to us in the Books of Kings. Take for example the first two references. Between the battle of Ḳarḳar in the reign of Ahab and the payment of tribute of Jehu we have a space of only twelve years. Yet between these two kings in the Jewish record there are two sovereigns whose united reigns yield fourteen years. There is no reason to doubt the accuracy of the Biblical record of Ahab's death (apart from the figures), which tells us that he fell in battle against the forces of Damascus at Ramoth Gilead. It is hardly likely that in one and the same year he was fighting a desperate battle as an ally of Damascus and also fighting against her. It would seem that 853 is the earliest date that we can possibly assign to his death. On the other hand, it is quite possible and even probable that it was at the beginning of his reign that Jehu paid tribute to Shalmaneser, in order that he might secure his support in case of need. We may thus date the beginning of the reign of Jehu in 842. A more serious discrepancy occurs later. Tiglath-pileser claims to have killed Pekah in 732, only four years after he received the tribute of Menahem. Yet even supposing that this tribute was paid at the end of the reign of Menahem (and, as in the case of Jehu, it is much more likely to have been near the beginning), the Biblical figures give twenty-two years to the reigns of Pekahiah and Pekah. It is therefore usual for modern historians of Israel to assume that the figure of twenty years of Pekah's reign is an error for two years. Even this assumes that Menahem died almost immediately after the payment of tribute. Perhaps the two years of Pekahiah's reign were not full years (this explanation may help in other cases, though it will not solve all difficulties), or it is possible that the original time allowed him was only two months. Again, it is far more likely that the fact is as stated in 2 Ki. 15[19], namely, that the tribute of 1,000 talents of silver paid by Menahem was a bribe to secure his own position. This would rather point to an event occurring near the beginning of the reign, which was therefore short. If this can be accepted, no further change in the figures is needed, and we have at present no reason to reject the traditional Biblical figures in the case of any of the kings from Jehu to Menahem. The dates will then be:

Jehu	842-814	28 years	
Jehoahaz	814-797	17	
Jehoash	797-781	16	
Jeroboam II	781-740	41	
Zechariah	740		6 months
Shallum	740		1 month
Menahem	740-737	3	
Pekahiah	737-736	2	
Pekah	736-732	4	
Hoshea	732-723	9	

According to the Assyrian account of the final war with Samaria, Hoshea was apparently taken and killed before the siege began. Otherwise it will be necessary to allow eleven years for his reign, since the date of the actual fall of the city is 721. In that year Shalmaneser died and was succeeded by Sargon, who completed the conquest of northern Israel.

In the case of the kings of Judah after the fall of Samaria, the Book of Kings gives the following figures:

Hezekiah	23 years (after the fall of Samaria)	
Manasseh	55	
Amon	2	
Josiah	31	
Jehoahaz		3 months
Jehoiakim	11	
Jehoiachin		3 months
Zedekiah	11	
Total	133 years, 6 months	

The period covered is from 721 to 685, i. e. 136 years. If it be possible to assume that the capture of Samaria is wrongly placed in the sixth year of Hezekiah, and that it really took place in the third year, these figures will be seen to correspond almost exactly with those derived from the Assyrian and Babylonian records.

In the case of the period preceding 721 this can hardly be said, and the question is somewhat more difficult. The Assyrian figures give 120 years, i. e. 841-721, whilst from the beginning of the reign of Athaliah to the third year of Hezekiah in the Book of Kings covers 163 years. There is a further complication in the reference to the dating of the invasion of Judah by Sennacherib. This took place in 701, which is stated to have been the fourteenth year of Hezekiah (2 Ki. 18[13]). If this figure is correct, then Hezekiah must have come to the throne in 715, and the fall of Samaria, instead of occurring in his third (or sixth) year, must have taken place seven years before his accession. We may assume that the compiler of the Book of Kings was relying on records which lay before him, and the synchronisms, which seem to be due to him rather than to his sources, show that a large proportion of the errors, if such there be, must be assigned to a misreading of, or mistakes in, his sources. In our Hebrew texts of the Bible numbers are always indicated in words, and the different figures are not easily confused. But it is not unlikely that in the older official records —perhaps in the earliest copies of the Hebrew text also— numbers were given in separate signs, as they are in the Jewish Aramaic papyri of the fifth century recently discovered near Assouan. In the case of these documents the forms for 10 and 20 are somewhat similar, and a carelessly written 20 may be— and has actually been by some readers—mistaken for a 10. The actual signs in these papyri are ר = 10, ך = 20. We have no evidence to prove that the same signs were used by the Palestinian Jews in the eighth century, but at the same time the facts suggest some such method of recording numbers, and the original figure in 2 Ki. 18[13] may possibly have been 24 and not 14. Additional probability is lent to this conjecture by the fact that it agrees better with the record of the events. It is much more probable that there was a mistake in a figure than that the historian should have dated the fall of Samaria in the wrong Judahite reign.[1]

We may now go further back to the reigns of Azariah and Jotham. As already suggested, it is extremely probable that these two reigns are to be regarded as overlapping to an extent which cannot be exactly estimated, but may be presumed to have covered the greater part of the later reign, say thirteen or fourteen years. This still leaves a space of about thirty years unaccounted for, and this must be due to an error elsewhere. It is usual to suggest that the reign of Joash may have occupied thirty years instead of the forty assigned to it by existing Hebrew texts. If numerals similar to those of the Aramaic papyri already mentioned were used, this again would be a fairly easy confusion. 40 was written as two twenties (ךך), 30 as a twenty followed by a ten (רך), so that the mistake would consist in reading the ten as a twenty, just the opposite of the error suggested in considering the figure mentioned in 2 Ki. 18[13] above. A similar

---

[1] It should be noted, however, that there is a very strong body of opinion in favour of dating Hezekiah's accession in 715, lengthening the reign of Ahaz, and reducing that of Manasseh. It is barely possible that Hezekiah was associated with Ahaz for a time, and that events are sometimes dated from the joint reign and sometimes from the death of Ahaz.

mistake may have made either the reigns of Amaziah and Azariah each ten years longer than they really were. This is more probable than that the reign of the former is twenty years too long, since the narrative assumes that Amaziah was contemporary with Jehoash of Israel, and the statement in 2 Ki. 14[17] that Amaziah outlived Jehoash by fifteen years may well be a deduction by the compiler on the figures which he read in his documents. Also it is clear that Amaziah had a long reign, which should not be too much reduced. Admitting these readjustments we have a scheme somewhat like the following :

Athaliah	842–835	7 years
Joash	835–805	30
Amaziah	805–786	19
Azariah	786–744	42 (in seclusion 757–744)
Jotham	757–741	16 (regent during the first 13)
Ahaz	741–725 (or 741–715) [1]	16 (or 26)
Hezekiah	725–696 (or 715–686) [1]	29
Manasseh	696–641 (or 686–641) [1]	55 (or 45)
Amon	641–639	2
Josiah	639–608	31
Jehoahaz	608–607	3 months
Jehoiakim	607–596	11
Jehoiachin	596	3 months
Zedekiah	596–585	11

It must of course be remembered that the above reconstructions are largely conjectural. We know that the figures in the Book of Kings cannot all be right, and we can see that some such scheme will satisfy the demands of the ascertained facts, and is designed to offer as little interference as possible with the Biblical figures, but it does not follow that this is the only possible reconstruction, and fresh archaeological discoveries may at any time compel us to revise our views. It will be noticed that as the story approaches the Exile, during which it may be suspected that the work of the compiler was done, the need for modification of the Biblical figures disappears.

It only remains to add that the LXX version gives no help in this matter. There are a few variations in the figures as compared with the Hebrew text, but they are demonstrably due to corruptions which have crept in during the course of the transmission of the Greek text.

---

[1] See note on previous page.

III. THE PROPHETS

The prophets whose names are borne by certain of the books of the Old Testament were far from being the first to whom the title applied, and the prophetic order had a long history behind it before the days of Amos. Down to the time of the establishment of the monarchy there were in Israel two classes of men whose peculiar characteristics were subsequently combined. These were the seer and the prophet. Both classes were men of peculiar and abnormal powers and behaviour. The seer, as his name implies, was a man gifted with the power of second sight, able to enter a world different from that which ordinary men inhabit, and to become conscious of sights and sounds which are beyond the range of others. Such a one was Samuel, as depicted in the earliest narrative of the foundation of the kingdom of Israel (1 Sam. 9). In this passage he seems to be definitely contrasted with the prophet, who is a person of a very different kind. His characteristic is that he is subject to sudden fits of a wild frenzy, in which he does things that he could not or would not do in ordinary circumstances. He may be able to some extent to induce these fits by means of music, drugs, or other methods, or they may be entirely out of his own control. Such men tended to live together, and to go about the country in companies, for the 'ecstasy', as the peculiar condition is commonly called, was to some extent contagious, and was more likely to affect a large company than a lonely individual.

Whilst there were thus very wide differences between the seer and the early prophet, they had this in common : both were believed to owe their peculiar powers, actions, and experiences to direct contact with their God. The phenomena were by no means confined to Israel, and by the beginning of the Christian era are found in the greater part of the world. Everywhere, and under every form of religion where they appeared, the prophets were held to be men temporarily or permanently possessed with a spirit other than their own, that is to say, the spirit of a divine being. Virgil's description of the Sybil in *Aeneid* vi furnishes a good illustration of the typical prophet and the ordinary appearance of the ecstasy in the ancient world, though the passage itself is centuries later than the time of Samuel.

In Israel, apparently early in the period of the monarchy, these two types of men coalesced. At all events we find in our canonical prophets men who seem to have the psychological characteristics of the seer, while they are called by the name of 'prophet'. A note in 1 Sam. 9[9] tells us, in fact, that 'seer' was the old name for 'prophet'; and both terms are applied to Amos. There has been, therefore, especially in recent years, a good deal of discussion as to the extent to which the canonical prophets, from Amos onwards, resembled the earlier type depicted for us in 1 Sam. 9. It is generally admitted that ecstatic experiences and conduct played some part in the life of all who bore the name of prophet, and that at least the initial call to their ministry came in this way. Even this view, however, is by no means universally held, and at present comparatively few British Old Testament students are prepared to agree that everything the canonical prophets said was communicated to them through the medium of ecstatic vision and hearing. It is, nevertheless, to this view that most of the *direct* evidence points, scanty as it is, in the judgement of the present writer.

From this point of view the story of each prophetic utterance may be reconstructed along some such lines as the following. The prophet was a man who had thought and meditated long and seriously upon God and man and their relations with one another. At length the ecstasy falls upon him. Convulsions seize him, or his muscles may stiffen into complete rigidity. He becomes insensible to pain, foam drips from his lips, his gaze is fixed and wild, and inarticulate sounds are uttered by him. The bystanders, if there are any, recognize that this is the effect produced by the Spirit, and that for the time the man is under the complete control of his God. Meanwhile he himself is conscious of another world as well as the normal; he hears voices, amongst which he recognizes one as being that of his God, he sees forms and is conscious of doing acts and of having acts performed on him which are entirely outside the ordinary experience of men. Features of the usual world still remain present to his senses, and the two may be inextricably blended together. Both are equally real to him, but the significant elements in the inner experience are those of the abnormal. A good example of the content of such an experience is furnished by the great vision recounted in Is. 6, though the external features of the ecstasy are not there mentioned.

Presently the tumult of body and soul would subside, and on the return to normal consciousness the prophet would be in a position to tell others what he himself had seen and heard. For it seems to have been characteristic of the ecstasy in Israel that it left men with clear memory of what had passed. As a rule it may be taken for granted that there was little or nothing that was not in harmony with the prophet's own thinking and outlook. But the form which the truth took and the occasion on which it was to be uttered seem to have been conditioned by these abnormal experiences. If it were simply words that he had heard they would be repeated in poetic form, for so they would be more striking and win a deeper hold on the minds of those who heard them. If the greater impression had been made by what he had seen, he might tell the story in prose, though even then such words as had been heard would tend to a certain rhythm which approximated to poetic form. Occasionally (as, for instance, in Jer. 4^{23-26}—a vision of chaos) even a vision in the course of which no words were heard might be described in a short poem. The result is that, with the exception of the Books of Ezekiel, Haggai, and Zechariah, most of the prophetic literature, or at any rate most of the oracles contained in it, has come down to us in the form of poetry.

It must be remembered that the canonical prophets were far from being the only persons who were subject to such experiences as these. Long before their time, and long afterwards, not only in Israel but throughout a large part of the Mediterranean world, similar manifestations were to be found. There is evidence to show that prophets were numerous in Israel all through the period of the monarchy, and a denunciation of their methods and character is a frequent feature of the message of the canonical prophets. As far as we can tell the 'false' prophet was indistinguishable from the 'true' to the eyes of his contemporaries. It was in the content of their message that they differed. There may have been other thoughtful, serious, and honest men who had reached the same conclusions and shared the same views as Amos, Isaiah, and Jeremiah. But in this small group of men there appeared a combination of the necessary qualities. They had sought and found the truth for their own day, as other prophets had not done, and they had the seal and guarantee of the prophetic afflatus to assure them that their message was of God. It was only such men who could be used as the medium of divine truth in that age and to that people. And while the external phenomena continued, with the passing of the need for certain teaching, prophecy ceased to be the channel of divine communication. It is as though God had temporarily and for a particular purpose taken up and employed a tool which was there already and continued to exist long after it was laid aside by Him, in order to bring home to Israel truths which she could have accepted under no other conditions.

IV. THE PROPHETIC BOOKS

That section of the Old Testament which contains the prophetic literature consists of fifteen books. Three of these (Isaiah, Jeremiah, and Ezekiel) are long enough to maintain a complete independence; the other twelve (Daniel is not included amongst the prophets in the Hebrew Bible) were in ancient times included in a single volume. Within the scope of this literature the material is very varied, even within the limits of individual books. But in general three types of writing may be distinguished:

A. Poetry. Sometimes there are short poems or hymns which can hardly be classed as normal prophetic utterances, and occasionally there are artistically constructed poems, sometimes of considerable length, but the greater part of this poetic material consists of short utterances, seldom extending beyond a dozen lines, and mostly confined to a single theme. This is often expressed with extraordinary beauty, and nearly always with force and vigour. Through these impassioned and inspired utterances the prophet's message, whether received through ecstasy or not, was from time to time transmitted to his contemporaries and neighbours. These we call ' oracles '.

B. Prose narratives *about* the prophets. These are not confined to the prophetic literature proper, though many of the prophetic books contain them. Some are found, for instance, in the Books of Kings, and in one case, that of Isaiah, a biographical passage of some length is found both in 2 Kings and in that of the prophet Isaiah. These seem to have been attempts made by some contemporary and follower of the prophet to record events and circumstances in the life of the prophet, and they seldom contain any extended report of the actual messages delivered.

C. Prose passages in which the prophet himself speaks in the first person. These are frequently narratives describing visions, but practically all contain not merely the experiences of the prophet, but also a message for the people. They are comparable in this respect to the oracular matter, but differ from it in being obviously works of art as distinct from the free lyrical outpouring of spirit which characterizes passages of the first class.

These types of passages are irregularly distributed throughout the prophets. Some, especially amongst the smaller books, contain nothing but poetry, though even there the more artificial type of poem is sometimes found, as in Nahum and Habakkuk. One book—that of Jonah—contains no oracular matter at all, and, apart from the probably later psalm, no poetry. It thus belongs almost entirely to type B. Ezekiel, Haggai, and Zechariah 1-8 are to be assigned entirely to type C, except some rather long poems in Ezekiel, which can hardly be included under the head of oracular utterances. But others, especially the longer books, contain all three. In Isaiah, for instance, chs. 1–5 are clearly oracular, ch. 6 belongs to type C, whilst chs. 36–39 must be classed under B. In Jeremiah all three are to be found, and in fairly equal proportions. Hosea is mainly oracular, but ch. 1 belongs to type B and ch. 3 to type C. All three appear in Amos. The other books—Joel, Obadiah, Micah, Nahum, Habakkuk, Zephaniah, and Malachi are oracular throughout.

Amongst them all, those which show the most consistent development and the most careful logical structure are Ezekiel, Haggai, and Zechariah 1-8. The suggestion naturally is that these books were actually written and reduced to the present form (or approximately to their present form) by the prophets whose name they bear. This makes it likely that C passages in other books also are due to the literary activity of the prophets themselves, being either written or dictated by them. It is clear that B passages are not likely to have been produced in this way; they suggest at once the pen of a nameless historian. And it may be doubted whether the oracular poems and fragments—and there is direct evidence to show that much of this matter was fragmentary—were actually written down or even dictated by the prophets themselves. It seems more likely that they were retained in the memories of those who heard them, handed on from mouth to mouth, and finally written down independently by people who valued and wished to preserve them. From time to time men would desire to make collections of these oracles, and those of which the authorship was known would be gathered into little booklets. To these might be added others whose origin was less certain or altogether forgotten. Often such collections were concerned with definite subjects; the Book of Obadiah, for instance, is a collection of oracles directed against Edom, some of which appear again in a similar col-

lection now included in the Book of Jeremiah. Occasionally
an oracle would maintain an independent as well as an incorporated existence, and a different oracle-collector would place it
in a different group and under a different name. Thus one of
the most valued of Old Testament oracles found its way both
into the collection which bears the name of Isaiah (2^{2-4}) and to
a group attached to the Book of Micah (4^{1-4}). The ways and
methods of these collectors are very interesting, and have as
yet been very imperfectly studied. Eventually more ambitious
compilers would find a number of these collections, and would
combine them with documents of the B and C class, thus producing books of the form in which we have them to-day.

A word should be said about the interpretation of prophecy.
The old Jewish method, taken over by the early Christian
Church, which treated prophecy as a detailed history of future
events, can no longer be maintained. Instead we have learnt
to see in prophecy the statement of eternal truths in language
and form suited to immediate occasions. The prophets spoke
to their own day, and strove to apply to their own times universal
principles. Yet there is necessarily an element of prediction in
their work. If the principles are eternal and the truths universal,
then they will produce certain effects wherever the necessary
conditions are found. An astronomer who knows the laws of
material nature can predict an eclipse with accuracy ; a prophet
who understands the laws of God's dealings with humanity can
with equal accuracy foretell the outcome of any given course of
action and the issue of any given conduct. An interpretation
for modern use must determine what the essential principles
and laws are, then isolate them from the local and temporal
context, and finally apply them once again to the new conditions and the changed circumstances which the modern world
presents.

V. DEUTERONOMY AND THE DEUTERONOMISTS

The narrative of 2 Ki. 22 and 23 is one of the most important
we have for the history of the religion of Israel. It records the
discovery of a law-book, and a consequent reform of the whole
cultus, first in Jerusalem and then throughout Judah and as far
north as Bethel. Details may be gathered from a study of the
passage itself.

It is only natural that an attempt should be made to discover how large a part, if any, of our present Pentateuch is to be identified with the book thus discovered. The outstanding features of the reform are (i) the purification of worship and all that was associated with worship, (ii) the centralization of sacrifice in Jerusalem. The sweeping away of the local altars, the 'high places', had been attempted by Hezekiah, but there is no mention or suggestion of a written law lying behind this movement, and it seems to have been abortive. But the law-book found by Hilkiah was one which contained stringent regulations on this point. The portion of the Law in which this rule is most explicitly laid down is Deuteronomy 12, and there are other details in that book which suggest a readjustment of the social and religious life of Israel to meet the situation presupposed in the change from a localized to a centralized system of worship. Hence it has been generally held during the last century and a half that the book discovered by Hilkiah was Deuteronomy or a part of it.

Opinions differ as to the form which Deuteronomy had when it thus produced a revolution in the religious life of Judah. As it stands at present, the book is in the main a legal code, dealing with a large number of subjects, mostly questions of civil law. This code is found in chs. 12–26, 28, and is preceded by an introduction and followed by an appendix which includes two ancient poems, the Song of Moses (ch. 32) and the Blessing of Moses (ch. 33). These in themselves have little or nothing to do with the code, and this fact suggests that, however early their origin may be, they were only appended to Deuteronomy some time after the first appearance of the book. Can the same thing be said of chs. 1–11 ? This, again, falls into two parts, (i) chs. 1–4, which are in the main an historical retrospect, forming a summary of the history as it is found in Exodus and Numbers mainly if not entirely in that element in these two books which is commonly supposed to have its origin in pre-exilic northern Israel, (ii) chs. 5–11, in the main an exhortation to obedience, reinforced by historical reference to the behaviour of Israel in the desert. Again the references are to events more fully described in Exodus and Numbers, though there are one or two discrepancies which it is difficult, if not impossible, to harmonize. The natural suggestion is that, inasmuch as ch. 12 begins with a formal introduction to the Law which follows, the preceding sections are introductions prefixed at later periods. This reduces the amount which we are compelled to assign to the law-book of Hilkiah to the actual code, and this in turn will be found to reproduce, in an expanded and sometimes modified form, the

greater part of the civil and ritual law comprised in the so-called
' Book of the Covenant', Ex. 20-23, with, of course, the addition
of the special laws which are associated with the Reform.

A comparison of the two codes, that of Ex. 20-23 and that of
Dt. 12-26, shows a marked difference in outlook. The latter are
distinguished by their humanitarian tone, and especially by their
consideration for the poorer and more defenceless classes. The
slave, the resident alien and the widow are frequently cited as
people to whom special attention must be paid, and laws which
might act rigorously upon them are modified and softened. There
is further a deeper spiritual appeal, and it is clear that the Law
of Deuteronomy has the spirit of something more than Law. In
other words, it would seem that it is an attempt to interpret the
rules which govern an organized society in accordance with the
principles of ' righteousness' and ' mercy' as those qualities were
understood and expounded by such men as Amos and Hosea.
Thus, Deuteronomy is an attempt to translate the spiritual and
moral principles on which the eighth-century prophets had
insisted into the actual social and political life of Israel.

Further study of the literature of the Old Testament shows
that the activity of the type of man who produced this book was
not confined to the Law alone. It is clear that either before or
after the discovery of Deuteronomy (and probably after rather
than before) there was a whole school of writers whose unity is
displayed not merely by the moral and spiritual outlook which
they have in common but also by their very literary style. It
seems that they took the old narratives of Israel's history (apart
from these which are found in the Pentateuch itself) and edited
them, that is re-wrote them with additions and modifications,
from time to time passing judgements on the various characters
which were in accord with their principles rather than with
those of the period they were describing. The books of Joshua,
Judges (this, perhaps, more than any other), Samuel, and Kings
have clearly been either revised or compiled by some such
Deuteronomic literary school, and there are more than traces of
their activity in some of the prophetic writings, notably in the
Book of Jeremiah, who may himself in turn have come largely
under their influence. All this points to the accuracy of the
dating of the main portion of the Book of Deuteronomy at the
period immediately preceding the Reform of Josiah.

In recent years, however, doubt has been cast on the whole
theory, and it has been supposed that the Book of Deuteronomy,
even in its earliest form, belongs to the exilic or post-exilic age.
This is not the place to enter into a discussion of the critical

question[1] but it may be said at once that it will involve a complete denial of the historicity of the narrative of 2 Kings 22 and 23. If, as the theory supposes, Deuteronomy was the law promulgated by Ezra, and compiled in the generations which immediately preceded his work at Jerusalem, rather than that which underlay the activities of Josiah, it will be necessary to re-write the story of the reign of Josiah, and the existing narrative must be explained as an attempt by the later Deuteronomic school to claim the authority of a really good king for their principles. In itself the theory cannot be said to be impossible, but there are and will remain many who prefer a view which accepts the substantial accuracy of the narrative of Kings.

Undoubtedly one of the strong features of the case for the later date of Deuteronomy is to be found in the complaint of Jeremiah, 'How do ye say, We are wise, and the law of the Lord is with us? But, behold, the false pen of the scribes hath wrought falsely' (8^8). The whole attitude, indeed, of the prophet towards the Law is a subject of much discussion. In ch. 11 we have an account of a command given to him to accept a 'covenant', which most expositors regard as a direct reference to Deuteronomy. If this be accepted as genuine it implies that at one time Jeremiah was an enthusiastic adherent of the new Law. How is this to be reconciled with the passage already quoted from 8^8? Some scholars would go so far as to deny outright any connexion between Jeremiah the Prophet and ch. 11 of the book that bears his name, and ascribe the latter to the literary activity of later Deuteronomistic scribes. An alternative view is to suppose that some years of experience, both of the Law and of its working, had convinced the Prophet that it was being altered and modified to suit the convenience of the Jerusalem priesthood. In particular he had come to believe that no sacrifice at all was really valid. Deuteronomy had tended to give a smaller place to the 'peace-offering' (the communion sacrifice in which the greater part of the victim was eaten by the worshipper), and Jeremiah would reduce to the same level the 'burnt-offering' in which the offerer himself had no share at all (Jer. 7^{21} ff.). This last passage has largely influenced some of those who would assign a later date to Deuteronomy. To complete the Drama of the Covenant, as Jeremiah saw it, it is necessary to take into account the great passage in Jer. 31^{31} ff.,[2] in

---

[1] The position may best be studied by English students in Canon R. H. Kennett's little book, *Deuteronomy and the Decalogue.*

[2] This is another passage whose Jeremianic authorship is sometimes questioned, but see L. E. Binns, *Jeremiah* (Westminster Commentaries), pp. 241 ff.

which the doctrine of a New Covenant is laid down. Deuteronomy had failed, and failed because it was only a 'scrap of paper'. A valid covenant must be written on men's hearts; that is the spiritual principle which underlies all true religion.

This leads us up to what is, after all, the real importance of Deuteronomy in the history of the Jewish faith. It was the first time that a book was accepted as the divine method of communication to man. Here men could appeal to the written word, and find it in the authentic message of God. They need no longer be dependent on the utterances of inspired men, who might mingle their own words with the revealed truth; they could refer to a definite and final standard. For centuries, indeed, the spoken word continued to have its place in religious experience, and was accepted as from God. But the new influence had been introduced, and in the gradual extinction of the flame of prophetic inspiration its power grew greater, until in the end it prevailed and the words of the Prophets—or such of their words as survived—were added to the Law. With the discovery of Deuteronomy, though it may be far from being the oldest portion of our Old Testament literature, begins in reality the history of the Bible as an inspired and authoritative revelation.

VI. ESCHATOLOGY

It is natural to speculate both on the way in which the present world order began and on the way in which it will end. The first speculation yields a cosmogony, the second an eschatology. It not infrequently happens that the two are closely connected in thought, and the same powers and agencies which brought the world into being and gave it its present shape are thought of as those who will ultimately throw it back into the primitive stuff from which it first emerged. The more highly civilized a people is, the more complicated become both its cosmogony and its eschatology, and practically all the great historic religions of the world offer a somewhat extensive theory of the end of things.

It may be said that as a rule an eschatology, unless associated with some form of pessimistic philosophy, does not contemplate the extinction of the human race, or at least of the particular people amongst whom it is current. A more normal form is that of a strongly nationalistic outlook, according to which the end of the existing order of things means the triumph of that people over their enemies and their establishment in a unique position amongst their neighbours, if any of the latter survive. Thus in the case of a national or tribal religion, just as the cosmogony commonly represented the tribal or national deity as the creator of the whole universe, so the eschatology represents him as conquering and destroying all that is injurious or distasteful to his own people.

An interest in eschatology seems always (not unnaturally) to be heightened in times of calamity and distress. Conditions reach a point at which it seems that no regular or normal process and no existing agency can work an improvement. The only hope lies in the sudden and violent interference of the ruling god, and the final catastrophic reversal of the whole situation. It is thus to some extent characteristic of the imagination rather than of the intellect. Maturer consideration of the facts of the past as well as of the present may lead to a modified judgement on the hopelessness of the case, while a deeper faith in the Creator will tend to the assurance that He will not lightly admit His failure by the utter destruction of His own work.

Such a height, however, was beyond Israel in the eighth century B.C. It is clear from references in the Book of Amos that there was in and probably before his time an eschatology current in Israel. Men in times of distress looked for a Day of Jahveh, a day in which He should be triumphant and all the enemies of Israel should fall before Him. Unfortunately we have no details of the popular belief, and we are therefore unable to make even a guess at its origin. It has been plausibly urged in recent years that it came originally from Babylon, and that it was a part of that large heritage of thought which Israel unconsciously received from Mesopotamia through the medium of Canaanite civilization and culture. This, however, must remain to some extent conjecture, though it must be admitted that there are elements in the later Israelite and Jewish eschatology which certainly recall the well-known Babylonian or Sumerian cosmogonies.

With Amos and his successors a new feature appears. Jahveh is no longer coming into the world to avenge and exalt His own people. He is coming, as Amos agrees with his contemporaries, but it is to vindicate the moral principles of which he was *par excellence* the champion, and to vindicate them as thoroughly and as drastically on the sinners of His own people as on the foreigner and the enemy. His appearance will be heralded by extraordinary events. Descriptions of these are not frequent, and, as a matter of fact, we have no extensive treatment of the subject before the time of Zephaniah, though in several of the prophetic visions before his days there is a genuine eschatological element. Certainly the chaos vision in Jer. 4^{23-26} seems to be purely eschatological. The accompaniments of the Day and its premonitions are of two kinds. In the first place they consist of events which, though not frequent, are natural, though the occasion may be abnormal. Storm, plague, locusts would be included here, and even at times the coming of a human enemy might herald the end. All these things are natural, and their peculiarity is not inherent in their character but lies in their extraordinary intensity or magnitude. Thus the visions of Amos all have an eschatological tone, but most of them involve natural events.

On the other hand, nearly all forms of eschatology known to us include to a greater or less extent features which are entirely outside the normal experience of man, not merely in degree but in kind. This appears, for instance, in the last vision of Amos, where he sees Jahveh Himself standing by the altar and hears Him give orders for the utter destruction of the Bethel temple by miraculous means. Such conceptions of the manifestation of divine power are characteristic of the later developments of eschatology rather than of the earlier, and belong properly to that type of literature which we call Apocalypse. They are, nevertheless, to be found in the earliest and simplest forms known to us, even amongst prophets of such intellectual balance as Amos.

We may, then, distinguish between two main forms of eschatology. The first is the old pre-prophetic popular type, an Eschatology of Bliss. In its earlier details it is practically unknown to us, though from such later passages as Is. 24–27 (probably the latest element in the whole Book of Isaiah) we can see what may have been traditional features. The other is the Eschatology of Doom, which probably originated with the great prophets of the eighth century, and endured only as long as prophecy remained a vital and efficient force in the spiritual life of Israel. It is the natural product of the combination of the older eschatology and of the moral principles of the Prophets, and as the ethical standard of these old preachers of righteousness permeated the nation, the distinction tended to disappear. Israel was forced by her knowledge of the world round about her to recognize that she alone professed a faith in which goodness was associated with the will of God, and readily came to believe that only through her triumph and the overthrow of the rest of the world could the essential principles of Jahveh find expression in earthly life. At the same time the normal methods of Divine activity sank gradually into the background, and their place was taken by the miraculous. The sense of the nearness of the Living God to human affairs began to fade with the decline of prophecy, but the belief in His power and will to interfere remained. Thus Apocalypse, that form of literature which we most commonly associate with eschatology, came to be the characteristic form of religious expression in Israel from the second century B.C. onwards till the final destruction of the second Temple in A.D. 70. There are traces of apocalyptic elements even in the eighth-century Prophets, and there are prophetic elements in the latest Apocalypse. Different as it is from the ancestor, apocalyptic Eschatology is the legitimate descendant of Old Testament Prophecy.

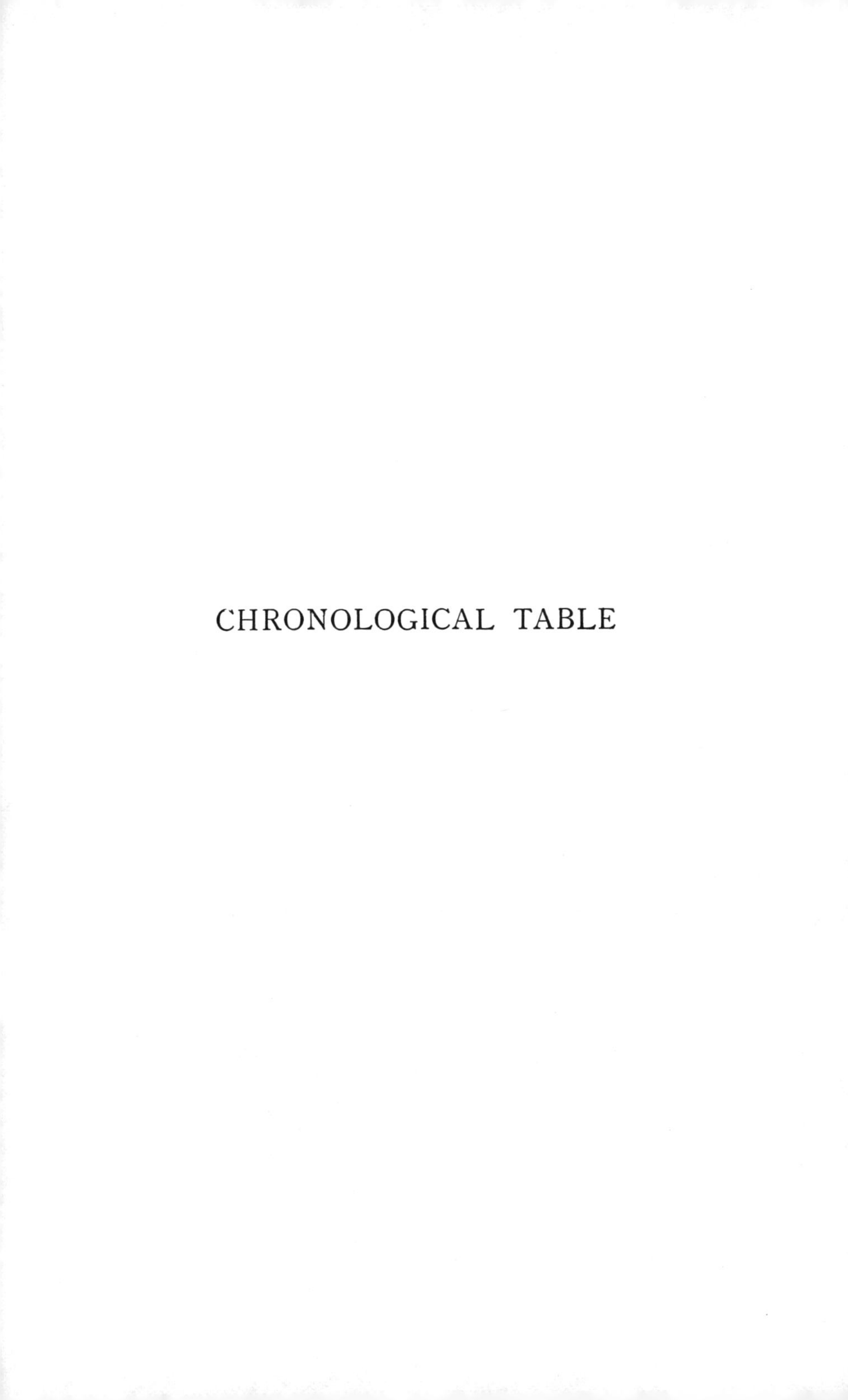

CHRONOLOGICAL TABLE

THE OLD TESTAMENT
CHRONOLOGICALLY ARRANGED
by EVELYN W. HIPPISLEY, S.Th.

*Licensed Teacher in Theology, Tutor to Women Theological
Students, King's College, London.*

N.B.—The dates of the Kings of Israel and Judah are taken from
the article 'Chronology of the Old Testament' in the *Encyclo-
paedia Biblica*; and the articles in Peake's commentary and in
Hastings' *Dictionary of the Bible* on the separate books have
been consulted. Other books which have been used are the
International Critical Commentary, the *Westminster Commentaries*, the *Expositors' Bible*, the *Century Bible*, Dr. Driver's
Introduction to the Literature of the Old Testament, Dr. Oesterley's
Books of the Apocrypha, and Dr. Charles' *Apocrypha and Pseud-
epigrapha.*

Principal Foreign Power = the principal foreign power with which
Israel was in contact at the time.

Inscriptions = inscriptions, chiefly on Babylonian and Assyrian
monuments which refer to events in the history of Israel. These
are mostly translated in the Appendix to Dr. Foakes-Jackson's
Biblical History of the Hebrews. The Code of Hammurabi,
Selections from the Tell el-Amarna letters, and the Babylonian
Flood Stories are published by S.P.C.K. (1s., 4d., and 6d. each).

The Book of Genesis, divided into sources by Dr. T. H. Robinson,
is published by the National Adult School Union (1s.).

Book.	Contents.	Origin.
The Hexateuch	Genesis to Joshua—contains four strands of narrative: (i) Jahvistic, Judaean in origin, *circ.* 850 B.C.; (ii) Elohistic, Ephraimitic in origin, *circ.* 750 B.C., both written from a prophetic standpoint; (JE combined *circ.* 650 B.C.). (iii) D Deuteronomic revision, 7th century B.C.; (JED combined early in Exile). (iv) P Priestly author and editor, 5th century B.C.; (JEDP combined and re-edited before 3rd century B.C.).	

N.B.—*No analysis of sources is given, but large portions belonging to the Priestly writer are indicated, as it is important to recognize the later standpoint.*

Book.	Contents.	Origin.
Genesis	i–xi. Prehistoric Narratives. xii–xlix. Stories of the Patriarchs.	JEP.
Exodus	The Exodus and Wanderings.	JEP (xxv–xxxi, xxxv–xl P).
Numbers	The Story of Wanderings.	JEDP (i–x. 28, xvii–xix, xxvi–xxxi, xxxiii–xxxvi P).
Joshua	The Conquest of Canaan.	JEDP (xv–xix P).
Judges	The Conquest of Canaan and Settlement of Tribes.	Compiled from old material (perhaps JE) by a Deuteronomic editor, 6th century B.C.
1 and 2 Samuel	History of Establishment of Monarchy, and Early Kings.	Two strands of narrative of 9th and 8th centuries B.C. woven together by a Deuteronomic editor, 6th century B.C.
1 and 2 Kings	History of Kings of Israel and Judah from Solomon to Fall of Jerusalem.	Compiled from Court and Temple records and biographies of prophets by a Deuteronomic editor, and re-edited during the Exile.

Important Events.	Date B. C.	Principal Foreign Power.	Inscriptions.
		First Babylonian Empire, 2050–732 B.C.	
Hammurabi's Code of Laws, based on an older Sumerian Code.	*circ.* 1950		Code of Hammurabi.
			Tell el - Amarna Letters (1450–1370).
			Stele of Raamses (Rameses) II (1300–1234) found at Beth-shan, showing that Semites had built city of Raamses.
	circ. 1230	Egypt.	Stele of Merneptah (1234–1225 B.C.).
Crossing of Jordan.	*circ.* 1196		
Philistines settling in Canaan, *circ.* 1200 B.C.			
SAUL	1025		
DAVID	1000		
SOLOMON	970		
Division of Kingdom.	933		
Kings of Judah. *Kings of Israel.*			
REHOBOAM JEROBOAM	933		
ABIJAM	916		
ASA	914		
NADAB	912		
BAASHA	911		

Book.	Contents.	Origin.
Amos	Warning to Israel by a Judaean.	Prophecies delivered in the reign of Jeroboam II (2 Kings xiv. 23–9), 760–746 B.C.
Hosea	Warning to Israel by an Israelite.	Prophecies delivered in reign of Jeroboam II, and later (2 Kings xiv. 23–xv), 746–734 B.C.
Micah	Denunciations of Israel and Judah by a Man of the People.	Chapters i–iii—prophecies delivered in reigns of Jotham, Ahaz, and Hezekiah (2 Kings xv. 32. xvi, xviii–xx)—739–693 B.C. Chapters iv–vi anonymous prophecies, added later.
Isaiah i–xxxix	The Statesman - Prophet's Warnings to Jerusalem.	Prophecies delivered in reigns of Uzziah, Jotham, Ahaz, and Hezekiah (2 Kings xix. 20, xx), 739–701 B.C. (omit xiii–xiv. 23, xxi, xxiv–xxvii, xxxiv, xxxv, and possibly other passages which are post-exilic).

Important Events.		Date B.C.	Principal Foreign Power.	Inscriptions.
Kings of Judah.	*Kings of Israel.*			
	ELAH	888		
	ZIMRI	887		
	OMRI	887		
	AHAB	876		
JEHOSHAPHAT		873	Assyria	
Battle of Karkar		853	(Shalmaneser	Moabite Stone.
	AHAZIAH	853	III. 859).	Karkar Inscription.
	JORAM	853		
Completion of Jahvistic narrative.		850		
JEHORAM		849		
AHAZIAH		842		
ATHALIAH	JEHU	841		
Jehu pays tribute to Shalmaneser.		841		Black Obelisk of
JOASH		835		Shalmaneser.
	JEHOAHAZ	814		
	JOASH	797		
*AMAZIAH		795		
AZARIAH or UZZIAH		789		
	JEROBOAM II.	782		
JOTHAM (regent)				
Compilation of Elohistic narrative		750		Tiglath-Pileser III
	ZECHARIAH	743		reduces Hamath.
	SHALLUM	743		
	MENAHEM	743		
JOTHAM		739		
Menahem pays tribute to Tiglath-Pileser III.		738		Tribute of Menahem.
	PEKAHIAH	736		
AHAZ	PEKAH	735		
Ahaz pays tribute to Tiglath-Pileser III.		734		
	HOSHEA	730		Hoshea placed on throne by Tiglath-Pileser III.

* The Biblical Chronology here obviously needs reconstruction. The dates given here are those of Marti in *Encycl. Biblica* ; cf. Steuernagel, *Einleitung*, and Box, *Isaiah*.

Book.	Contents.	Origin.
Jeremiah	Warnings and Pleadings to Jerusalem.	Prophecies uttered in reigns of Josiah, Jehoiakim, Jehoiachin, and Zedekiah (2 Kings xxii–xxv). Earlier prophecies written down by Baruch; later prophecies, especially xlvi–li, added by a compiler during or after the Exile—626–500 B.C.
Zephaniah	Doom of Wicked Nations.	Prophecy uttered *circ.* 626 B.C., when the Scythians were threatening Jerusalem, and edited in post-exilic times.
Deuteronomy	The Law-Book (with additions) found in the Temple, on which Josiah based his reform.	A revision of the earlier laws, compiled *circ.* 640 B.C.
Nahum	Doom of Nineveh.	Chapters ii and iii written *circ.* 612 B.C.; chapter i a post-exilic acrostic poem.
Habakkuk	Moral Problem raised by God's use of Chaldaeans.	Chapters i and ii written *circ.* 600–550 B.C., when Chaldaea, i.e. New Babylon, was becoming powerful; chapter iii a lyric ode of post-exilic date.
Ezekiel i–xxxii	Prophecies of Doom, and Denunciations of Jerusalem and foreign nations.	Written in Babylon before the Fall of Jerusalem by an exile banished in 596 B.C.
Ezekiel xxxiii–xxxix	Picture of the Restitution of Israel.	Written in Babylon after the Fall of Jerusalem—584–572 B.C.

Important Events.	Date B. C.	Principal Foreign Power.	Inscriptions.
Kings of Judah. *Kings of Israel.* Fall of Samaria	721		Capture of Samaria by Sargon II.
End of Kingdom of Israel			
*Hezekiah	720 ? 715 ?		Siloam Inscription. Invasion of Sennacherib.
Invasion of Sennacherib	700		
Manasseh	692		
Amon	638		
Josiah	637		
	625	New Babylonian Empire founded by Nabopolassar.	
Finding of Law-Book (2 Kings xxii)	621		
Reform of Josiah	621		
Fall of Nineveh	612		
Battle of Megiddo	608		
Jehoahaz	608		
Jehoiakim	607		
Battle of Carchemish	605	Nebuchadrezzar King of Babylon 604–561.	
Jehoiachin	597		
First deportation to Babylon	596		
Zedekiah	596		
Fall of Jerusalem	586		
Exile.			

* See Dr. Robinson's note, p. 232.   If the view is accepted that Hezekiah was associated with Ahaz for a time, this would dispose of part of the discrepancy.

Book.	Contents.	Origin.
Ezekiel xl–xlviii	A Vision of the Ideal Theocracy.	Written after 572 B.C.
Lamentations	A Book of Dirges.	These poems, arranged as acrostics (except ch. v), are of exilic date.
Isaiah xl–lv	The Promise of Return.	Prophecies delivered by an unknown author at the close of the Exile, probably between 549 and 538 B.C. The Servant-Songs are possibly later.
Obadiah	Doom of Edom.	Verses 1–14 belong to an exilic prophecy; the rest is probably post-exilic.
Leviticus xvii–xxvi	The Law of Holiness.	Old Laws of Priestly character grouped together towards the close of the Exile.
Haggai *Zechariah* i–viii	Call to rebuild the Temple.	Prophecies delivered 520 B.C. (Ezra v, vi). Prophecies delivered 520, 518 B.C.
Isaiah lvi–lxvi	The Restored Community: its Faults and its Blessings.	Prophecies delivered by an unknown author in Palestine *circ.* 450 B.C.
Malachi	Rebuke of the Moral and Religious Condition of the Jews.	Probably delivered *circ.* 450 B.C.
Ruth	A Pastoral Idyll.	Probably used as a Tract for the Times about Foreign Marriages in Nehemiah's day.
Job	A Wisdom-Book, treating of the Problem of the Innocent Sufferer.	Probably based on an older story by a post-exilic author.
Leviticus	The Priestly Code of Laws.	Compiled during the Exile, and possibly published by Ezra.
Joel	The Day of the Lord.	The date is probably early in the fourth century B.C.

Important Events.	Date B.C.	Principal Foreign Power.	Inscriptions.
Cyrus overthrows the Medes.	549	Persian Empire.	
Capture of Babylon by Cyrus.	538		
Edict of Cyrus.	538		
The Return.			
Return of Zerubbabel and Joshua (Ezra i, ii).	537		
Building of Temple.	520–516		
Dedication of Second Temple (Ezra vi. 16).	516		
		Artaxerxes I.	
Return of Nehemiah (Neh. ii).	445		
Nehemiah's second visit (Neh. xiii. 7).	433		
		Artaxerxes II.	
Ezra's Return.	? 397		
		Artaxerxes III (Ochus).	
Jaddua, High Priest (Neh. xii. 11).	351		
Samaritan Schism	335		

Book.	Contents.	Origin.
Zechariah ix–xiv	An Apocalyptic Vision.	The work of a post-exilic prophet or prophets, *circ.* 320 B.C. or later.
Jonah	An Evangelical Allegory.	Written *circ.* 300 B.C., and probably based on an old tradition.
1 and 2 Chronicles	History re-edited from an ecclesiastical standpoint.	Compiled, with additions, from previously existing sources by a Temple Levite, *circ.* 300–250 B.C.
Ezra *Nehemiah*	Narrative of the Return and Rebuilding of the Temple.	Compiled by the Chronicler, *circ.* 300 B.C., from City and Temple records, Aramaic documents, and memoirs.
Proverbs	One of the Wisdom-Books of the Hebrews, containing Moral Maxims.	Several collections of Proverbs of various dates combined by an editor, *circ.* 250 B.C.
Song of Songs	A Marriage Drama, showing the triumph of faithful love.	Probably written in Jerusalem during the Greek period.
Esther	A Didactic Romance.	Written, perhaps on an historical basis, *circ.* third century B.C., to defend the keeping of the Feast of Purim.
Ecclesiastes	A Wisdom-Book, containing the Meditations of an Unsatisfied Man.	Written *circ.* 200 B.C.
Psalms	The Hymns Ancient and Modern of the Second Temple.	Five books of gradual growth, containing 'Praise-Songs' dating probably from the time of David to the second century B.C.
Daniel	An Apocalypse of Encouragement.	Probably founded on an older story, and written *circ.* 168 B.C. to encourage the Maccabaean party.

Important Events.	Date B.C.	Principal Foreign Power.	Inscriptions.
Alexander the Great becomes ruler of the world.	331	Macedonian Empire.	
Conquest of Palestine by Alexander.	331		
Death of Alexander and division of his Empire.	323		
		Ptolemaic and Seleucid Empires.	
Palestine under the Ptolemies of Egypt.	311		
Antiochus III conquers Palestine.	198		
Persecution of Jews by Antiochus IV (Epiphanes).	169		
Maccabaean Revolt against Antiochus Epiphanes.	167		

A list, chronologicai as far as possible, is appended of the principal
in the Alexandrian Canon (the Septuagint), but not in the
were never included in either Canon, but are important as greatly

Book.		Contents.	Origin.
APOCRYPHA.	APOCALYPTIC.		
Ecclesiasticus (Wisdom of Jesus,' son of Sirach.)		A Wisdom-Book. containing counsels for daily life.	Written in Hebrew, probably *circ.* 180 B.C., and translated into Greek by the author's grandson, *circ.* 130 B.C.
Tobit		An Idyll of Home-Life.	Written probably in Aramaic, *circ.* 190–175 B.C.
	Book of Enoch	A series of Apocalyptic Visions.	Written in Palestine by several Hebrew authors belonging to the party of the Ḥasidim, between 170 and 64 B.C.
Prayer of Azariah			An addition to the Greek text of Daniel, probably written in Hebrew, *circ.* 170 B.C.
Song of the Three Children.		The Thanksgiving of the Three for Deliverance (*Benedicite*).	Dating from the Maccabaean triumph, *circ.* 165 B.C.
1 Esdras		History of the Jews from the reign of Josiah to the Proclamation of the Law (639–? 400 B.C.).	Written probably at Alexandria between 170 and 100 B.C.
Rest of Esther		Contains additional details as to Esther, probably imaginary.	A Greek interpolation in the Hebrew text, *circ.* 150 to 100 B.C.
Judith		A story of the Deliverance of Israel from Assyria by a Jewess.	Written *circ.* 150 B.C. and edited *circ.* 60 B.C.
Baruch		A work in four divisions, containing prayers of Exiles and messages to Exiles.	Written by three authors, probably between 2nd century B.C. and 2nd century A.D.
	Testaments of the XII Patriarchs.	The Dying Commands of Jacob's Twelve Sons.	Written, probably in Hebrew, by Ḥasidim, *circ.* 130–10 B.C. (contains later Christian interpolations).
2 Maccabees		History from the reign of Seleucus IV to the death of Nicator (176–161 B.C.). (Parallel with part of 1 Maccabees, but not so trustworthy.)	Probably abridged *circ.* 40 A.D. from a larger work by an Alexandrian Jew, written *circ.* 120 B.C.

Apocryphal and Apocalyptic Books. The *Apocrypha* were included
Palestinian Canon (Massoretic Text). The *Apocalyptic* writings
influencing New Testament thought and phraseology.

Important Events.	Date B. C.	Principal Foreign Power.	Inscriptions.
		Seleucid Empire.	
Maccabaean Revolt.	167		
Re-dedication of Temple.	165		
Death of Judas Maccabaeus.	160		
Jonathan, High-Priest.	160		
Simon, High-Priest, and Ethnarch.	142		
Independence of the Jews.	142		
John Hyrcanus.	135		
Rise of Pharisees and Sadducees.			
JOHN HYRCANUS, King of Judaea (Hasmonean Dynasty).	107		

Book.		Contents.	Origin.
APOCRYPHA.	APOCALYTIC.		
1 Maccabees		History of the Jews from the accession of Antiochus Epiphanes to the death of Simon (175–135 B.C.).	Compiled from existing sources in Hebrew by a devout Jew, between 100 and 90 B.C.
Story of Susanna		A Story in praise of the wisdom of Daniel.	Probably written to support new laws as to witnesses, *circ.* 100 B.C. An addition to the Greek text of Daniel.
Story of Bel and the Dragon			Perhaps written originally in Aramaic ; an addition to the Greek text of Daniel, *circ.* 100 B.C.
Wisdom of Solomon		A Wisdom-Book inculcating the beauty of Divine Wisdom.	Written by an orthodox Alexandrian Jew, *circ.* 100–50 B.C.
Prayer of Manasses.		A Jewish Penitential Psalm.	Perhaps written in Greek —date uncertain.
	Psalms of Solomon or *Psalms of the Pharisees.*	Eighteen Psalms, containing important Messianic teaching.	Written in Hebrew by a Pharisee, 70–40 B.C., probably for use in synagogues.
	Book of Jubilees	The narrative of Genesis, rewritten from a later standpoint.	Written in Hebrew by a Palestinian Jew, *circ.* 40–10 B.C. or later.
	Secrets of Enoch	An Account of the Creation.	Written in Greek by an orthodox Alexandrian Jew between 30 B.C. and 50 A.D.
2 Esdras		An Apocalypse, containing Visions of Ezra at Babylon.	A Jewish work, probably belonging to 1st century A.D., with later Christian interpolations.

Important Events.	Date B.C.	Principal Foreign Power.	Inscriptions.
ARISTOBULUS I.	105		
ALEXANDER JANNAEUS.	104		
ALEXANDRA.	78		
HYRCANUS II and ARISTOBULUS II dispute the throne. Rise of the House of Antipater.	69	Roman Empire.	
Pompey enters Syria and conquers Jerusalem.	65		
Judaea divided into five districts.	57		
Antipater becomes Procurator of Judaea.	47		
HEROD, King of Judaea.	37		
Herod marries Mariamne, the last of the Hasmoneans.	35		
Herod's Temple begun.	20		
Death of Herod.	4		